kou ʼ   ord.

Renegade states

One of the flashpoints of international relations is the tortuous relationship between established 'status quo' powers and revolutionary states such as China, North Korea, Iran, Nicaragua and Iraq.

This textbook bridges the gap between analyses of revolutions, which tend to concentrate on their domestic causes, and the study of the impact of 'renegade' states on the international system. It sees revolutionary states as a central dynamic of modern international society, rather than as aberrations damaging an otherwise stable international body politic. The authors provide a series of historical and contemporary case studies, and theoretical analyses. They contribute significantly to a debate on the nature of international politics that has foundered into complacency and self-congratulation about the 'end of history'.

To John, Jane and Marja

Renegade states

The evolution of revolutionary foreign policy

edited by
Stephen Chan and Andrew J. Williams

Manchester University Press
Manchester and New York

Distributed exclusively in the USA and Canada by St. Martin's Press

Published by Manchester University Press
Oxford Road, Manchester M13 9NR, UK
and Room 400, 175 Fifth Avenue,
New York, NY 10010, USA

Distributed exclusively in the USA and Canada
by St. Martin's Press, Inc.,
175 Fifth Avenue, New York, NY 10010, USA

British Library Cataloguing-in-Publication Data
A catalogue record for this book is available from the British Library

Library of Congress Cataloging-in-Publication Data
Renegade states : the evolution of revolutionary foreign policy /
  edited by Stephen Chan and Andrew J. Williams.
      p. cm.
    Includes index.
    ISBN 0-7190-3169-9 (hbk.). — ISBN 0-7190-3170-2 (pbk.)
    1. Civil war. 2. Revolutions. 3. International relations.
  I. Chan. Stephen. II. Williams, Andrew J., 1951-   .
  JX4541.R46 1995
  322.4'2—dc20   94–12636

ISBN 0 7190 3169 9 *hardback*
ISBN 0 7190 3170 2 *paperback*

Typeset in Hong Kong
by Graphicraft Typesetters Ltd, Hong Kong

Printed in Great Britain by
Biddles Ltd, Guildford and King's Lynn

7716965

Contents

Acknowledgements

Many people have helped in the writing of this book, both by commenting on individual chapters and by giving general encouragement. We would like in particular to thank all the members of the Centre for Conflict Analysis, and especially Michael Banks, John Groom, Mark Hoffmann, Viv Jabri and Keith Webb. Many undergraduate and graduate students at the University of Kent at Canterbury have over the years provided feedback and entertainment during the long march of the manuscript, especially in Andrew Williams' course on 'Revolutions and the International System' and Andrew Williams' and Stephen Chan's course on 'Foreign Policy Analysis'. Special thanks must also be extended to other individuals who have discussed chapters or ideas with us, especially Osmo Apunen, David Armstrong, Chaloka Beyani, Chris Brown, Lloyd Chingambo, Fred Halliday, James Mayall, Hasu Patel, André du Pisani, James Piscatori, Jack Spence and Halat Talman.

Celia Ashcroft and Richard Purslow at Manchester University Press have as usual been pillars of encouragement, patience and good sense. Marja Kokkonen, Jane, Nicholas and Rebecca Williams will be glad that we have finished and can now write them the novel we have been promising for years.

Part I
Theoretical issues

1 *Andrew Williams and Stephen Chan*

Introduction

Rationale

There have been few attempts to link the growing but dispersed theory about both revolution and international relations (IR) in a coherent way with the historical, journalistic and contemporary literature that exists on major revolutionary phenomena in a 'case study' format. The attempts that have been made, notably by Peter Calvert,[1] have only been partially successful and have now in any case been overtaken by events, especially the end of the Cold War. Equally some useful primers for the political theorist[2] exist. But the student must plough through a vast quantity of material that will not necessarily make the links useful to a scholar of IR in general and foreign policy in particular. The best recent book in this field is David Armstrong's *Revolution and World Order*, especially thanks to his use of the notion of 'international society'.[3] This book is made up of a series of case studies of many historical and more recent revolutions, with a consideration of the theoretical literature in IR and beyond it that we believe might prove valuable for drawing more general conclusions about the behaviour of 'renegade states'.

A first observation has to be that the literature on revolution and that on international relations has, until recently, been seen as existing in discrete 'boxes', one dealing with domestic problems, a second with the international. However, a second observation must be that many of the concerns of the IR scholar are addressed in much of the literature on revolutions. The notion of power, of state formation, of the 'legitimacy' of regimes, of morality, as well as broad epistemological and philosophical questions like 'what is a revolution?' (as opposed to, say, a 'revolt') and 'how can we attain even a minimum of objectivity about such phenomena?' are all there. There is also the ontological problem of how a revolution 'feels' to those who participate in it. How do *they* relate themselves to different historical traditions, for example those of 1776, 1789 or 1917? Or are they actually creators of 'new' traditions? These are of course also problems of a far wider centrality for the thinking person and ones that predate by a long way the slow emergence of the discipline of IR.

Fred Halliday none the less was able to make the reasonable claim at the March 1989 meeting of BISA[4] and in a later article that revolutions had been largely left out of the study of IR, or at best given a 'marginal existence'. He enumerated the ways in which the main 'paradigm' of IR, realism, has managed to sidestep the revolution by stressing that even revolutionary states become 'normal' after a time. Although he rather spoils his argument by going on to enumerate many works within the realist tradition that *have* taken revolutions seriously as a central part of their analysis, the assertion that there has been a deal of 'mutual neglect' between IR and the study of revolutions is undeniable.

The more general questions that need to be addressed in this book are:

1. What links exist between the study of revolutions in broad social science literature and the sub-field of international relations? In particular, what can the literature on specific revolutionary states provide us with in our analysis of the foreign policy of these states and hence of *status quo* states' policy options towards them?

2. Is there something *distinctive* about revolutionary states, both in their make-up and in their practice? Does this lead to a breakdown of the processes of normal diplomacy and the norms of 'civilised' international behaviour?

3. Given the common claim that revolutionary states are more 'ideological' in both their theory and practice, what use can be made by the analyst of their foreign policy or the political theory generated either by them or by their detractors? What, for example, can the importance be of Voltaire for the French Revolution or for Burke against it? Or of the Ayatollah Khomeini for the Iranian Revolution or Mao Tse Tung for the Chinese? Equally . . .

4. What broad normative questions do revolutionary states pose for the student of international relations? For example, can we draw conclusions about the nature of 'justice', of 'human rights', and about the debate between those who advocate 'cultural relativism' or 'cosmopolitanism'. Should we accept that violence is an acceptable part of revolutionary struggle and, if so, which victims should we tolerate?

None of these questions has simple solutions, and we cannot provide definitive answers. But they guide the writing of this book and the case studies that make it up. They also show that our blithe use of the first person plural in the paragraphs above could change depending on who is reading this book. We are not entirely sure where we stand on revolutionary struggle because we feel differently about different revolutions. John Dunn's dictum that 'a value free analysis of revolutions is logically impossible' is one with which we agree. What we are sure about is that the response of the 'West' to most revolutions, including those of the West, has left 'us' in the West largely bereft of an understanding of the deep-seated passion that leads to their outbreak and therefore bereft of coherent and sensible responses to them. If this book has a single purpose it is to shed some light on how this might be changed. In particular we believe that there is a need for a more humanistic response to the revolutionary state, and less crowing about the 'end of history'. It is perfectly possible to agree that the end of communism was a victory against obscurantism and injustice, while accepting that we are not ourselves immune from the ills of modernity. We do not, in other words, 'win' when a revolution like that of 1789 or 1917 is defeated; we should use such events for an auto-critique, not a victory parade. The victorious West does not seem to have yet fully appreciated that we need to make far more effort to express solidarity with such areas as Eastern Europe or Africa, not merely get rid of regimes in those regions for a narrow *raison d'état*.

In addition we feel that the study of the foreign policy of revolutionary states shows that it is necessary to try and move the language and the practice of 'foreign policy analysis' (FPA) away from the very 'Allison-centric' approach that has dominated up till now.[5] FPA has concentrated almost exclusively on 'Western' states and has in consequence assumed certain practices as normal behaviour (such as complex decision making). True, FPA has now moved more in the direction of saying that one must look for the appropriate 'unit' of decision before attempting analysis, namely the 'predominant leader' (either 'more principled' or 'more pragmatic'), or the 'group' or 'multiple autonomous actors'.[6] But, what does this do except to describe, and then inductively, what are diverse and only explainable as discrete phenomena, using mainly, if not exclusively, 'Western' data? FPA has in addition posited a supplementary frame of reference (often collectively called 'perception') that also assumes a 'Western' point of departure ('role theory' is one example of this), but one that has been found largely wanting even in this narrow context.[7]

The widespread claim that FPA is largely 'Americanology' has more than the ring of truth to it.

Most importantly, FPA largely deals with the notion of the 'state' as a given, when it might be argued that (a) states vary enormously in their impact on given populations and that (b) the state is not a universal category, but a catch-all phrase. Often the revolutionary 'state' refuses to accept being defined as such, or is only ambiguously susceptible of being so described.[8] Hence we also hope to start a discussion about the different levels of analysis we should be examining to understand the behaviour of revolutionary states, and even more widely of many of the new states that exist in our present international system. There is indeed a tendency to dismiss many new states as 'quasi-states', at least partly because they do not fulfil our narrow definitions of 'stateness'.[9]

Existing theories of revolution – some problems

The expression 'revolution' has been overused to the point of becoming almost meaningless. Where now can we draw the boundaries between rebellion, revolt, revolution and lesser forms of change? There has never been so much publicised 'revolt' or 'revolution' as in the last twenty years, but how many of these should concern the student of international relations? Paul Rich addresses this and other questions in Chapter 2, but some preliminary comments are in order here.

Domestic and foreign
Most writers on revolutions have tended to concentrate on the domestic causes and effects of these events.[10] The only ones who have consciously eschewed this path are those who see revolutions as 'the motors of history', loosely defined to include 'world society' theorists, Marxists and systems theorists. Their views take in a wider, even 'universalist' context, whether it be of international capitalist crisis, or of cyclical change of some other kind. Many of them, and especially the Marxists, tend to see the world in terms of progress towards some generally definable goal, of 'socialism' or some other come-uppance for the present rulers of the international system (Galtung, Wallerstein, Baran, Sweezy all come in this category). They have been lent succour in this by the revolutionaries themselves who often speak of their revolution as wreaking massive damage on the existing power-structure and stressing the 'irreversible' nature of their achievements. This is patently an exaggerated and often demonstrably ridiculous position to hold.

Goldstone usefully summarised the different schools of revolutionary theory as three 'generations': the first being the 'natural histories' of Brinton *et al.* in the 1930s which dominated until the arrival of the general theories of 'political violence' in the 1960s and early 1970s (Huntington, Gurr and Tilly being the best examples), which in turn was modified by the 'structural' theorists of the late 1970s and 1980s (of which Theda Skocpol is the best example).[11] While the first group tried to draw general lessons about the courses of particularly the 'great' revolutions, the second concentrated on the causes and major indicators of change, especially 'modernisation' and 'mobilisation'. The most recent generation has reintroduced the historians' sense of greatly differing structure in different states. It has also most importantly stressed the immense differences that exist in the *international system* into which revolutionary states are born at different times. The structuralists naturally tend to stress the interests of the Marxist-economic disparities, capitalism and its various 'stages'. They also take from the previous generation an interest in elite quarrels and the importance of peasants. While they are clearly not 'unreconstructed Stalinists' their conclusions are essentially a restatement of much other structuralist writing.[12]

As with all Marxists there are some important gaps in their analysis, the main one being the neglect of non-economic factors. Is it really the case that elites and populations *only* revolt because of economic complaints? A subsidiary problem is that they usually explicitly downplay the importance of ideology, which is seen as a post-revolutionary product, not an intrinsically important input or factor during the revolution. Perhaps a third problem is that there is a major assumption that revolutions are major break-points of a state or people's history, not in many ways a symbol of a long process of cultural maturation into a 'nation'.

The 'Great' revolutions (by which we mean France 1789, Russia 1917 and China 1949) have quite clearly changed much for the inhabitants of their countries and for the international system, but many of their achievements can be said to have been laid down by their *anciens régimes* or to have been massively reversed by subsequent reflection. For example, de Tocqueville's writing on the French Revolution and more recent writings such as Schama on the same event do not shirk the massive elements of change wrought by 1789, nor the massive symbolic importance entailed, but they do stress the revolution as a confirmation of changes already taking place. In particular they both stress the developing ideas of 'nation', 'people' and 'citizen'. It could be countered that these are merely symbolic representations of world economic roles in a new capitalist age.

But even if this is true, it was the French Revolution that redrew these definitions of state and citizen, not the 'international economic system' that created these entities. The action of human agency has to be placed more firmly at the centre of the debate about revolutions and this implies looking at human motives in a far broader sense than 'man as an economic animal'.[13] It also probably requires the use of cultural anthropology as much as conventional political or IR routes of enquiry.

Normative considerations
This leads us directly to another key *leitmotiv* of much writing on revolutions. As Cohan has pointed out, a key school of thought on revolutions, what he calls 'theorists of mass society', have tended to look on all revolutions of a 'popular' kind, and especially the French, Russian and Chinese revolutions as morally reprehensible, leading to the extinguishing of individual freedoms, totalitarianism (Arendt is a key writer here) and 'terror'.[14] The 'democratic' revolutions of Britain and the United States are often explicitly used by this large body of writers to counter the revolutions based on 'popular sovereignty', so hated by Burke and others since 1789. The international consequences of this dislike have been enormous, not just from the viewpoint of the philosopher, but also from that of all members of the democratic states. Most of the wars or of the 'cold' wars of the last two hundred years have been fought out over the slogans of the two great European revolutionary 'families'.

For example, any summary of the debate on the French Revolution since Burke will reflect the widespread distaste felt by commentators since Burke about the results of 1789. Schama's *Citizens* is a great book precisely because it does not dodge moral issues, but indeed places them on centre stage. There are few civilised individuals who can blot out visions of bloated corpses and dangling, but not yet dead, opponents of the regime, when thinking about Khomeini's Iran, or the Gulag when thinking about Lenin's Russia. But can this give the comfortable feeling that we are somehow superior to these revolutionary states and that revolution is a plague, a contamination that we must both avoid catching and if possible extirpate? The result can arguably be that we support equally horrendous opponents of these states, even if on a temporary and pragmatic basis.

Here the normative and critical debate now permeating IR has great uses. Although it would be impossible to sum it up easily in a few sentences, these theorists seem to be urging a greater self-criticism of our own motives in the 'West' and a greater sympathy for the different cultures where all revolutions since 1917 have taken place. The argument about this sympathy being based on a 'cosmopolitan' culture has been countered by others who assert a need to conserve difference, both to avoid cultural imperialism of a new kind and to reflect the way the world really *is*.[15] Nardin in particular stresses the need to realise that association, in international as well as domestic society, is dependent on the acceptance of norms and rules of behaviour that allow 'practical' association, without implying agreement on 'purpose'. This view seems reinforced by writers such as James Der Derian, who point to the Western value-system inherent in international political discourse.[16] Richard Rorty asks for an appreciation of the different needs of other cultures (and others in our own culture) struggling for a new awareness.[17] What we draw from all this is that we need to use different 'tools' (linguistic, philosophical and practical) when approaching different problems and an end to seeing historicist views of society in necessary contradiction to those of individual development as a welcome and long overdue alternative to the sterile debate over whether society's claims should come before or after those of the individual.

The problem is that this is far easier said than done. There have been many occasions in the last two hundred years when citizens of Britain or America have sympathised with the revolutionary struggle in France, Russia, China, Iran or wherever. Have they not by doing so suspended their moral disgust at the results of such struggles in favour of the process, appreciated the omelette without worrying too much about the fate of the eggs? There are many writers in many languages who have sneered at liberal sentimentalists who would never have accepted behaviour that was all right in the Kremlin but not in the streets of London. But this point, valid as it is, must not cover up the fact that the Western tradition of searching for peace through reason has failed to deliver the goods for vast numbers of the world's oppressed, and that they have turned to revolution to try and better their lot, whether or not they have succeeded in doing so. Der Derian's observation that there is a 'crisis of modernity' in IR could be extended to Western thought as a whole. Hence the rebirth of Nietzsche in new clothes by critical theorists. The man who declared that 'God is Dead' is being used to say that the great God Progress is also dead, in whose name much of Western intellectual arrogance and action was exercised.

This does not, however, mean that critical theory is by any means yet accessible to the ordinary scholar of IR. We still have to look for insights into older established branches of our literature for more banal but practical insights. In particular, theories of causality and social change cannot be ignored, nor in a more instrumentalist mode can theories of 'coercive diplomacy' or intervention. And we also have a marvellous work of a structural sort in Theda Skocpol's *States and Social Revolutions*. Even though the criticisms of structuralists made above stand, by bringing the state back to centre stage and showing the links between domestic and international contexts, she has made it much easier for the student of IR to fit the study of revolution into the existing realist 'paradigm' of inter-state relations. Thus the geopolitical impact of the First World War could take its place with Russian class-struggle and the decadence of Tsarism and so could the international effects on the system of the time. Her other great contribution has been to restress the contingency of revolution on the international system of the day, both as *cause* and as *effect*.

One way to start developing the debate is to look anew at the widely accepted notion of 'international society' so well expressed by Hedley Bull and David Armstrong.[18] The notion of rules, values and interests being common to such an international society of course dates back to Christendom's quarrels with the 'Turk' or 'Tartar' but has seen many other incarnations. We are currently deciding whether the Russians might be 'civilised' after all, by which we mean 'European'. But as Gong has pointed out, the Russians are only one of a long and unending stream of peoples and states that we have deigned to consider as useful members of our 'society'.[19] Most of these will of necessity stay on the periphery of our consideration because they are irredeemably different from us. They are tolerated in the United Nations, allowed to submit their needs and fealty in the corridors of our power but never accepted. In truth the whole 'South' is beyond the pale of our 'International Society'. They know it, we know it, but we are all surprised when, one after the other, they revolt against our hegemony (an overworked word, but a serviceable one).

The distinctiveness of the actions of a revolutionary state?

What do they want from us?

The IR scholar must therefore take a new look at both the underlying (and largely occult) assumptions of his 'paradigms' but also at the opera-tional areas that naturally derive from this re-examination. The study of the foreign policy of revolutionary states is a greatly neglected area, as is indeed that of non-Western states in general. In taking up this theme Halliday pointed out that ideology plays a role in *all* states' foreign policy. His major blow is aimed at the 'Liberal' interpreters of revolution who 'argue that if only revolutionary states were treated better, they would not seek to "export" revolution.' On the contrary, says Halliday:

> all revolutionary states, almost without exception, *have* sought to promote revolution in other states . . . they make the altering of social and political relations in other states a major part of their foreign policy and regard themselves as having not just a right, but an obligation, to conduct their foreign policies on this basis. Much of the literature, realist and transnational, understates this.[20]

Therefore he asserts that until the internal social and economic systems in the 'revolutionary' and *'status quo'* states homogenise, there can be no peace between the two. The implication is that the international system really is a Hobbesian or perhaps Darwinian survival of the fittest, that *'status quo'* states should do nothing to calm revolutionary fires, by aid or trade for example, and that they must assume that the revolutionary state will work for their downfall. The problem with this is that, if we do assume that states, once 'revolutionary', cannot change their spots, eventually all states will be at war with each other in reality or metaphorically.

One debate that sheds further light on the problems raised by Halliday is clearly that over 'neo-realism'. Ashley's taunt that this new orthodoxy being taught to American undergraduates tries (wrongly) to reduce the world to competing economic structures that can be analysed and even predicted empirically has much merit.[21] Far too little is known about the non-Western parts of our 'global world system' to make empirical judgements about future developments. There may well be parts of the world where we can talk about 'the end of history'as does the American 'new' right (Francis Fukuyama being one famous example),[22] but we feel there is a need to do far more in-depth examination of future world trends, as so often illustrated by revolutionary movements, before we talk of enduring world structures. There is a real danger that we will be trapped by the 'neo-realists' or indeed the 'structuralists', into believing that we have reached the final phase of our development. Such pride can herald a rude fall and awakening, as after 1789 and 1917.

A more likely eventual development, even in a system dominated by the 'West', is of a plurality of systems where the only choice is between permanent confrontation and agreement to differ. In this there will be competition, usually ideological but sometimes violent, between differing values and policy aims, but no necessary 'homogenisation' of the system as a whole. To assume that capitalism is the same in its many different manifestations is to believe that modernisation is always achieved in the same way, or that a liberal democracy is the inevitable end. Ernest Gellner has for example pointed out that Islam, with its de-emphasis of the mythical (as compared with Christianity) might well lead to an alternative path for Iran and other states that will produce just as much economic success as now enjoyed by the West, but with radically different institutions. In a post-modernist mode, Kristeva insists that the only universality is the universal appreciation and recognition of a global multitude of differences.

That said, there is considerable interest to be derived from reading versions of the 'triumph of the West' hypothesis. The current developments in Eastern Europe, freeing itself from an imposed political and economic framework, lend credence to the idea that Western capitalism will conquer there. It will, because the cultural bedrock is essentially that of the West. However, the same cannot be said with anything like certainty of China or any of the other new states being dealt with in this book.

This must of necessity have an impact on the foreign policy of these revolutionary states. They do not like our rationales of power, and they do not respect our rules and practices. They fear 'contamination' by us. But here confusion can creep in, because many of the 'revolutionary' states of the past are now the *'status quo'* of today, with the best possible example being the United States of America. Armstrong points out that practically until 1900 Americans were warning against diplomatic 'contamination' of the US by Europeans in not too dissimilar terms to those used by the Chinese or Libyans in the more extreme moments of their revolutions.[23] The problem is that definitions of 'us' and 'them' change with the international system itself. Perhaps a state must have its revolution in order 'to come of age', much as a teenager must revolt against his/her parents in order to become an adult. It may be, but it is beyond the scope of this book to prove it, that a revolution is for a state the functional equivalent of the process of individuation for the human being.

What do we want from 'them'?
As a corollary to asking what are the goals of the revolutionary state, we must ask what it is we wish them to conform to and how they should do it. The idea that diplomacy as a means to global levels of civilisation was a neutral tool usable by all is increasingly being questioned, most notably by James Der Derian. He points out that the diplomat evolved in a very Western frame of reference. It might also be reiterated that the state the diplomat represents is a form that is far from being a universal category of political organisation.[24]

However, we have to ask what alternative there is to the normative demand for 'practical association', which denies a cosmopolitan global system? Can we find solace in those like James Piscatori who find basic support in the *practice*, if not the doctrine, of Islamic international relations for maintaining that Islamic 'states' have long adopted the diplomatic norms of 'international society' while attacking the West for its decadence, etc.[25] The Islamic Republic of Iran now conducts a reasonably 'normal' foreign policy through reasonably normal channels in spite of its leader issuing *Fatwahs* condemning writers in England to death in flagrant disregard of the norms of international society and certainly the usual practices of international law. Or does this just mean that new 'actors'' needs must be accommodated – laws on blasphemy included – within the existing norms?

Indeed, there is plenty of evidence that this has happened in the past, even in the 'West'. For example, one importance of the events of the French and Russian revolutions for the student of IR lies in the fact that both states had enormous influence before their respective upheavals, both have contributed immeasurably to a recognisable Western *Weltanschauung*, and both put themselves beyond the pale for a significant period after their revolutions. However, both are now seen as valued members of the *status quo* even though retaining great pride in their revolutionary achievements and indeed carrying that pride into their political interactions, both domestically and internationally. The student of these two revolutions must also note that the state structure in both countries had completely broken down *before* the most momentous events. The countries were also both 'backward' in the modern sense. As Huntington pointed out, all the 'Eastern' revolutions (by which he essentially means those since 1917) have had partly modernised and well-armed state structures for the revolutionaries to combat. One final commonality is of course that both France and Russia experienced essentially urban revolts, whereas the modern revolution is usually (though not always) a peasant revolt.[26] One enduring importance of 1789 for us is clearly the blow that it struck at the *ancien régime*. New notions of *nation* and *peoples* were incorporated into the international litany and have stayed there ever since, a clear link between the older 'great' revolutions and those since 1917 of the 'East'.

There are also many enduring features in the reaction of the *status quo* to revolutionary states, much as in 1789 and 1917. A recent example is that of British relations with Iran. At the very instant that many in the West assumed that the Iranian Revolution had been 'socialised', the

Ayatollah delivered a death sentence on Salman Rushdie for his *Satanic Verses*. It is significant that, although a number of writers of a 'liberal' persuasion did rally round Rushdie to defend freedom of speech, many (like Roald Dahl) attacked him for being gratuitously provocative and insulting to a religion (Islam) then clearly in a state of ferment. Some, like Brian Appleyard, went much further than condemning the *Fatwah*. He commented that: 'Islam, to the fundamentalists, acknowledges no national boundaries and accepts no benign ideal of peaceful coexistence'.[27]

Quite apart from the sweeping generalisation of this statement, the (un?) conscious use of a Soviet revolutionary term ('peaceful coexistence') to describe difficulties with a latter-day Robespierre-Lenin sums up the universality of dealing with revolutions that believe as implicitly in their own 'propaganda' as we believe in the self-evidential nature of our own tolerant liberalism. But are we not also guilty of double standards? Does not our own liberalism evaporate at the slightest challenge? And is it not rather ridiculous that the British literary left can produce such comments as Fay Weldon's, quoted by Appleyard, that '[what the Rushdie case proved was that] The American system was better . . . because at school all the children saluted one flag, worshipped one God and acknowledged one nation'? So much for the benefits of pluralism. The issues in this case are far from being easy to resolve, but the net result of the book has been a set-back for those who believed in the possibilities of a tolerant multi-culturalism.

Conclusions?

The revolutionary state rouses fierce passions and cannot be ignored, or bludgeoned to death (except *very* rarely), or traded into peaceful behaviour (except long-term) or appeased.

An alternative starting-point must be to look at the specificity of the cultural origins of the revolutions we now and will increasingly in the future have to study, especially those outside Europe. We must also question our own cultural motives in attacking revolutionary states. Do we not have an implicit model of 'civilisation' that we impose on others but to which we are largely unwilling to impose on ourselves, such is our self-righteousness and persuasion of our own superiority, economic, moral or organisational? The revolutionary spirit has been aroused time after time in the recent past by the same forces that prompted revolutions in France, America and Russia. They were certainly economic, obviously in response to foreign domination however variously perceived, but principally

were expressed in a clear demand for liberty so that a new and revolutionary people could be considered as the *equal* of any *'status quo'* people in
cultural as well as political terms.

Clearly we therefore need to shift our analysis of revolutionary states
away from the classical areas examined by the student of IR. Foreign
policy analysis, the preoccupations of 'realism', 'structuralism' and even
more 'neo-realism', will not suffice. Equally to claim the existence of a
cosmopolitan and all-embracing 'international society' is misleading, if
seductive given our desire to believe in a better, more peaceful world
order. Revolutionary states exist to contest this 'order'. We have to pursue the far more difficult task of normative analysis and even cultural anthropology, through the study of literature and popular culture. We have
more than anything else, as analysts, to try and develop some sympathy
for our objects of study. Stephen Chan will enlarge on this point in the
conclusion to this book, but we would make the point that if we do not
adopt such a strategy we will be caught out time and time again in the
next 100 years as revolutions break out in places that are just as unlikely
as Versailles in 1789, the Winter Palace in 1917 or Teheran in 1979.

Format of the book

This is a collaborative venture by several people with very different
approaches to international relations but with similar concerns about the
future. As a consequence, there are some differences of a presentational
kind, as for example in the approach to which literature we separately
consider useful. The editors have edited with a light hand, because we
want to encourage a debate, not present readers with another set of
'certainties'. We are now moving into an exciting moment in world history where many certainties will probably disappear. To use the by now
rather hackneyed Chinese parallel, there will be both crisis and opportunity. The successful peoples of the planet will be those who can grasp this
double nettle. We have a vested interest in ensuring that we are among
the successful.

Notes

1 The writings of Peter Calvert have performed an immense ground-clearing
service in this area, an achievement that we fully acknowledge and thank him for.
Among his key writings in the area are: *A Study of Revolution*, Oxford, Clarendon
Press, 1970; *Revolution and International Politics*, London, Pinter, 1984; *The
Foreign Policy of New States*, Brighton, Wheatsheaf, 1988.

2   John Dunn, *Modern Revolutions*, Cambridge, Cambridge University Press, 2nd ed., 1989. A much more detailed list of the main literature on revolutions and international relations can be found in Chapter 2.

3   David Armstrong, *Revolution and World Order: The Revolutionary State in International Society*, Oxford, Clarendon Press, 1993.

4   Fred Halliday, 'Revolutions and International Relations: Some Theoretical Issues', paper presented to BISA/ISA, March 1989. Revised as ' "The Sixth Great Power": On the Study of Revolution and International Relations', *Review of International Studies*, vol. 16, no. 3, July 1990, pp. 207–21.

5   Graham Allison, *Essence of Decision*, Boston, Little Brown, 1971. For a thorough recent critique of decision making theory in FPA see Michael Clarke and Brian White (eds), *Understanding Foreign Policy: The Foreign Policy Systems Approach*, Aldershot, Edward Elgar, 1989 and Deborah Gerner, 'Foreign Policy Analysis: Exhilarating Eclecticism, Intriguing Enigmas', *International Studies Notes*, Fall 1991/Winter 1992, pp. 4–19.

6   See, for example: Margaret F. Hermann, Charles F. Hermann and Joe Hagan, 'How Decision Units Shape Foreign Policy: Development of a Model', paper presented to the International Society of Political Psychology, Helsinki, July 1991.

7   For a good example of this literature, see: Martha Cottam, *Foreign Policy Decision Making: The Influence of Cognition*, Boulder, Westview, 1986.

8   See, for example, James Piscatori, *Islam in a World of Nation States*, Cambridge, Cambridge University Press, 1986.

9   See especially Robert H. Jackson, *Quasi-states: Sovereignty, International Relations and the Third World*, Cambridge, Cambridge University Press, 1990.

10   See Chapter 2 for many more details on this literature.

11   Jack Goldstone, *Revolutions: Theoretical, Comparative and Historical Studies*, New York, Harcourt Brace Jovanovitch, 1986. For details of other writers mentioned, see Chapter 2, pp. 30–3.

12   Goldstone, *Revolutions*, pp. 10–11.

13   This is in no way to belittle the importance of 'little' revolutions, the vast majority in the twentieth century.

14   A. S. Cohan, *Theories of Revolution: An Introduction*, London, Nelson, 1975.

15   See Charles Beitz, *Philosophy and International Relations*, Princeton, Princeton University Press, 1979; John Rawls, *A Theory of Justice*, Oxford, Oxford University Press, 1971 and Mark Hoffman, 'Cosmopolitanism and Normative International Theory', *Paradigms*, vol. 2, no. 1, 1988 for a summary of the 'cosmopolitan' position. The counterargument to this has been made by Terry Nardin, *Law, Morality and the Relations of States*, Princeton, Princeton University Press, 1983, and Chris Brown, 'Not My Department: Normative Theory and International Relations', *Paradigms*, vol. 1, no. 2, 1987. Brown has also given us an overview of the normative debate in IR in his *International Relations Theory: New Normative Approaches*, Hemel Hempstead, Harvester Wheatsheaf, 1992.

16 James Der Derian, 'Mediating Estrangement: A Theory for Diplomacy', *Review of International Studies*, vol. 13, April 1987, pp. 91–110; *On Diplomacy*, Oxford, Blackwell, 1987; and *Antidiplomacy*, Oxford, Blackwell, 1992.

17 Richard Rorty, *Contingency, Irony and Solidarity*, Cambridge, Cambridge University Press, 1989.

18 Hedley Bull, *The Anarchical Society*, London, Macmillan, 1977 and *Intervention in World Politics*, Oxford, Clarendon Press, 1984. Armstrong, *Revolution and World Order*, also uses the concept.

19 Gerrit Gong, *The Standard of 'Civilisation' in International Society*, Oxford, Oxford University Press, 1984.

20 Halliday, 'Revolutions and International Relations', 16.

21 Richard Ashley, 'The Poverty of Neorealism', in Robert Keohane (ed.), *Neorealism and its Critics*, New York, Columbia University Press, 1986.

22 Francis Fukuyama, *The End of History and the Last Man*, New York, The Free Press, 1992.

23 Armstrong, *Revolution and World Order*, 252.

24 Der Derian, *On Diplomacy*.

25 Piscatori, *Islam in a World of Nation States*.

26 Cf. discussion in Goldstone, *Revolutions*.

27 Appleyard in the *Sunday Times*, 3 December 1989. See also Geoffrey Wheatcroft, 'Five Years on Death Row', *The Guardian*, 11 February 1994.

2 *Paul Rich*

Theories of revolution in international relations

The study of revolutions has been a rather neglected terrain by scholars of international relations. The conservative state-centric paradigm which has dominated the subject since the Second World War has tended to inhibit enquiry into the global implications of revolutionary changes within nation states. Such a paradigm tends to confine the political significance of revolutions to the particular states where they occurred and to render them of secondary importance to the generally orderly manner in which international society is seen to have evolved, particularly since 1945.[1]

Thus, when revolutions have been considered from an international perspective they have often been viewed as of relatively minor long-term significance. A good example of this is Peter Calvert's study *Revolution and International Politics*, which sees revolutions in narrow terms of struggles for political power to the exclusion of any wider impact they may have on the functioning of the international system.[2] The theoretical debate on the nature of revolutionary change has thus tended to be preoccupied with the comparative study of the internal dynamics of individual revolutionary movements within nation states. The research in this field since the 1960s has been voluminous and has explored revolutionary changes in pre-industrial societies such as France, China and Russia as well as more recent phases of revolutionary change in urbanising societies such as Iran. Only recently have historians and social scientists begun to approach the question of explaining revolutionary change at the international as well as the nation state and local levels.

This chapter, therefore, has four central objectives. Firstly, it will examine the intellectual genealogy of the historical sociology of revolutions and survey what can be described, using Jack Goldstone's categories, as three central 'generations' of research into revolutionary change.[3] Secondly, it will outline the recent emergence of a fourth 'generation' of analysts of revolution who are more concerned than previous generations with the political and international dimensions of revolutionary change. Thirdly, the chapter will outline developing theoretical approaches to revolution in terms of the evolution of the states system since the end of the European Middle Ages. Finally, the chapter will suggest that this conventional state-centred approach to revolutions is now being superseded by the emergence of a more globally-based civil society which is increasingly blurring the divisions between international and national forms of conflict and revolution.

The historical sociology of revolutions

Since the 1930s the study of revolutions has had a particular fascination for historians and social scientists in both Europe and North America. The fact that most of this work occurred outside the arena of IR meant that it tended to develop in a comparative rather than international perspective. The development of IR as an academic discipline in the period before the Second World War was dominated, particularly in the United States, by a belief in progress and this tended to preclude any serious attention to forces conducive to the revolutionary breakdown of states.[4] IR at this time was mainly concerned with themes such as the study of diplomacy, the fostering of an international public opinion in favour of peace and statecraft and the study of *Realpolitik*. Only the small group of Marxists in IR had any real interest in the study of revolution, but they tended to see it as part of an inevitable global process of history in which the capitalist system would be superseded by the emergence of a victorious world proletariat.[5]

The first generation that studied revolution between 1900 and 1940 tended to use quite simplistic descriptive categories, though one of the most notable of them, Crane Brinton, developed in his study *The Anatomy of Revolution* (1938) a historical model – heavily based on the experience of the French Revolution – to describe four uniform phases through which a revolution passes: from the overthrow of the government, rule of the moderates, accession of the extremists and a reign of terror leading to an eventual Thermidorian reaction.[6]

This phase of study of revolution failed to develop any particularly rigorous analytical categories to explain revolutionary change and was not averse to employing quite vague psychological theories based on Gustav Le Bons's idea of the 'mob psychology' of revolutionary crowds or Pitrim Sorokin's notion that societies repressed 'basic instinctual needs'.[7]

It was this collective psychological dimension which was of particular interest to the second generation of analysts of revolution who emerged in the period after the Second World War. Scholars such as James C. Davies, Ted Gurr and the Feierabends tried to explain revolutions in terms of psychological theories of 'frustration-aggression' or 'deprivation' relative to some specific set of social goals.[8] The work of Davies was particularly notable for the famous J-curve theory of revolution in which the theories of Marx (on growing immiseration leading to revolution) and de Tocqueville (where it is the lifting of oppression that causes revolutions) were apparently reconciled. Davies argued that revolutions were most likely to occur when a period of economic and social development was followed by a sharp reversal leading to an intolerable gap between what people want and what they can actually get.[9] The problem with the thesis, as with the frustration-aggression theory generally, is that it fails to explain why revolutionary behaviour in some societies only takes the form of relatively minor disturbances and in others full-scale revolutionary overthrow of the state.[10]

Moreover, the psychological theory of revolution assumed that societies were most prone to revolutionary change when they underwent a process of social and economic 'modernisation'. This was supposed to undermine peoples' traditional allegiances and make them more susceptible to revolutionary appeals than more cohesive and stable 'traditional' societies. This theory, however, became undermined by evidence from continents like Latin America which revealed no close correlation between modernisation and revolution. In some instances, countries such as Argentina and Uruguay were more 'advanced' in terms of indices of modernisation than states such as Cuba and Nicaragua and yet remained examples of revolutionary failure. This clearly suggested that more detailed historically-based analyses were needed of the different societies in question.[11]

The same sort of problem emerged with the structural functional theory of revolution contained in Chalmers Johnson's well-known book *Revolutionary Change*. The text exemplified the domination of Parsonian functionalism in American post-war sociology as well as its intrinsically insular quality. Johnson remained concerned with the sources of revolutionary instability in individual societies to the complete exclusion of any international or global variables. His functionalism led him to look for those values that sustain social cohesion in societies and it was only when these and 'non-revolutionary' methods of social change broke down that revolutions emerged. In particular, Johnson saw three main necessary conditions for revolutions to occur: the disequilibrium of the social system, the 'deflation' of power in a similar way to the deflation of money and the abdication or reactionary resistance to change by ruling elites.[12] The approach was ahistoric and critics have objected that Johnson's conception of the yardstick of a society in equilibrium by which to evaluate revolutionary change is a utopian and nonsensical one.[13]

For the purposes of international relations theory, though, *Revolutionary Change* is chiefly of interest in terms of the centrality of the nation state in its analysis. This is taken as more or less a primordial given and even supranational bodies like the European Common Market are seen as politically unfeasible. Johnson saw revolutions occurring strictly within nation states and was generally uninterested in wider trends that might enhance revolutionary movements beyond basic indicators such as 'unchecked population growth' and 'extremely rapid yet socially unsupervised rates of scientific and technological innovation'.[14]

This approach was symptomatic of a more general disdain the second generation had for historical theories of revolutionary change. The postwar years were notable for the rise of behaviourism in the social sciences and the belief that it is possible to develop value-free laws of human behaviour. The historical trajectories of individual revolutions seemed rather unnecessary impediments in this quest for laws of revolution and historians as a consequence tended to be rather marginal onlookers; this did not stop some of them, though, such as Lawrence Stone, from complaining about the 'verbal juggling in an esoteric language' of the social scientists 'performed around the totem pole of an abstract model, surrounded as far as the eye can see by the arid wastes of terminological definitions and mathematical formulae'.[15]

The social science study of revolution in fact is quite closely connected to non-revolutionary processes of social change. Analysts of revolution are concerned with more general issues of modernisation and development/underdevelopment within societies. Revolutionary ideology, too, in the form of theories such as those of Mao Tse Tung or Che Guevara exhibits strong similarities to more general theories of warfare dealing with guerrilla insurgency and 'internal war'.[16]

Social scientists of the second generation failed though to develop a particularly convincing predictive theory of revolution and appeared to be running out of steam by the 1970s.[17] Some critics pointed to the impossibility of developing an ahistorical theory of revolution when the term itself is one with a conceptual history.[18] It appeared in fact that the main form of progress would occur through the comparative historical study of different revolutions. In the course of the following decade a third generation of analysts of revolution began to emerge based on the work of scholars centred at the University of California such as Theda Skocpol, Ellen Kay Trimberger and Jack A. Goldstone. This school has developed a more structurally-based historical sociology of revolutionary movements, which are seen in relationship to ruling elites and the apparatus of the nation state.

Skocpol has been particularly important in her classic study *States and Social Revolutions* for focusing on the role of the state interacting with class relations in what she has termed 'agrarian-bureaucratic' societies such as Russia, France and China. Revolutions occurred in these societies because they were marked by particular structural characteristics such as the independence of peasant communities from close landlord supervision and a degree of landlord class leverage against the state bureaucracy. If these features combined with growing pressure on the ruling regime to mobilise resources to meet external threats from foreign powers (as in the case of Tsarist Russia during the First World War and China during the war against Japan in the 1930s and early 1940s) then there was an enhanced likelihood of revolutionary breakdown.[19]

For all its strengths in terms of a structural approach to understanding social revolutions, *States and Social Revolutions* remained weak in terms of its understanding of urban revolutionary movements. It came at the end of a decade of reappraisal of the revolutionary potential of peasant movements in Africa and Asia and rather overlooked the potential of urban based groups to foment revolutionary change.[20] Skocpol's interpretation of revolutionary breakdown failed to provide in fact a satisfactory explanation for urban revolutionary insurrection of the kind that led Fidel Castro to seize power in Cuba in 1959 or the Khomeini regime in Iran in 1979.[21] Her structuralist approach also led her to underplay the role of revolutionary ideology which has been crucial both for revolutionaries and counter-revolutionaries alike. There is a learning process involved in the development of revolutionary movements which by the twentieth century have increasingly acquired a global dimension. Just as revolutionaries try to emulate previous revolutions so ruling regimes learn to try and protect themselves from potential revolutionary challenges: in 1871 the French government of Theirs was determined to prevent the Paris Commune being a replica of previous nineteenth-century revolutions and successfully crushed it with huge loss of life. There have been numerous examples of the same phenomenon in the twentieth century such as pre-emptive coups in Indonesia in 1965 and Chile in 1973.[22]

This feedback process has made revolutions increasingly difficult to achieve in modern societies where it is essential for revolutionaries to win over substantial sections of the urban population as well as those of the rural peasantry. Even then they have to take on the full apparatus of regimes that have received support and military assistance from external powers. Thus, the small number of revolutionary successes in international politics since 1945 in states such as China, Cuba, Nicaragua and Iran has to be set alongside the larger number of 'counter insurgency states' that have been armed and fortified by rival superpowers to prevent revolution breaking out. In the case of South America, for example, the military coup in Brazil in 1964 ushered in a new type of bureaucratic authoritarian regime different in kind to the old style *caudillo* in the region. This was emulated over the next decade in other states such as Uruguay and Chile in 1973 and Argentina in 1976 leading to a counter-revolutionary cycle that produced a closer relationship with foreign capital at the same time as the organised labour movement was crushed.[23]

The increasingly important role of states in suppressing urban revolutionary movements in the twentieth century has led Skocpol into responding to her critics by arguing that in the modern system only two types of state are really vulnerable to revolutionary overthrow: Sultanistic regimes like those of the Shah of Iran or the Somoza regime in Nicaragua based on an absolutist rentier state and direct systems of colonial rule like the French in Algeria.[24] Both are relatively rare and the implication of this line of argument is that revolutions are a decreasingly important feature of the international political system. We will return to this issue at the end of the chapter.

In response to the perceived weaknesses of Skocpol's theory, Jack A. Goldstone has developed a more wide-ranging theory in order to account for revolutionary outbreaks based upon the three variables of fiscal distress, elite alienation and a high degree of mass political mobilisation. It is the conjuncture of these three factors which he sees as vital for revolutionary crises to develop, though the forces that cause them to emerge are varied. Attempts by a regime to resolve them may also prove to be counter-productive. Economic growth may expand a regime's resources but if it fuels inflation then it may lead to social instability. If it is accompanied by increased corruption (as in Nicaragua under the Somoza regime in the 1970s) then it may also alienate business elites. Likewise, a regime may seek to secure a safer international environment by winning over other states as allies, but this may also lead it to take actions that will intensify domestic opposition.[25]

Both Skocpol's and Goldstone's framework provide valuable insights into the circumstances of state breakdown. Revolution emerges as one extreme variant of social development and economic change which may or may not be contained with existing state structures.[26] However, its structural emphasis leads analysts away from developing a specifically causal theory of revolution that can also operate at the political level. To this extent, it fails to address the basic historical distinction between long-range preconditions – which Skocpol and Goldstone term 'structural factors' – from immediate precipitators of revolutionary outbreak.[27]

Political and international dimensions of revolutions

Revolutions need in fact to be understood in the context of the outbreak of war and collective violence. They are the product of the breakdown of diplomatic channels between social groups competing for access to power, influence and economic resources. It is thus important for analysts to have a theoretical framework that can also explain the outbreak of revolutions at the political level. Revolutions are not volcanic outbreaks that simply erupt for they occur in a specific set of political circumstances; in many cases they do not even mark a profound break with the political past for when mass mobilisation occurs it follows along channels that have been already developed.[28]

Some analysts such as Samuel Huntington and Charles Tilly have been arguing for the centrality of a political perspective on revolutions since at least the early 1970s.[29] In contrast to the school of historical sociology, the political science interpretation of revolution is as concerned with the immediate precipitators of a revolutionary upsurge as the longer-term structural preconditions. It focuses on the nature of the bargaining and diplomatic relationships between the ruling regime and those outgroups which manifest the potential for revolutionary mobilisation. The structural conditions are important to the extent that they 'distribute social power chances' of the groups involved in a particular society.[30] This still leaves open the question of how far outgroups see it as in their interest to organise revolutionary mobilisation. Ideological revolutionaries will have a commitment to revolutionary change no matter what the political circumstances. They may, as in the case of Ireland from the end of the nineteenth century, be championing a cause in a society becoming increasingly stable and resistant to such appeals.[31] Likewise (as in the case of early nineteenth-century England), a revolutionary leadership may be badly organised, dominated by a ruling class paternalist ideology and have only a weak sense of ideological direction in a society exhibiting potentially revolutionary characteristics.

One possibility is that radical revolutionaries with mass support may be pre-empted by a bureaucratic-authoritarian state engineering its own 'revolution from above', such as the Meiji Restoration in Japan in 1868 or Turkey under Kemal Ataturk, involving a modernisation of social structures and the opening up of avenues of social mobility as a way of containing unrest. This model of revolution depends upon a fairly autonomous class of state bureaucrats which is largely free of pressures from external class forces and has a high degree of moral cohesion. It is increasingly less likely to be pursued in the contemporary international system as growing economic interdependence has eroded such bureaucratic classes in surviving 'traditional' societies, though the model provides a kind of ideal type for elite-led attempts at industrialisation in developing states.[32]

Another form of political revolution that is likely to become increasingly prevalent in the contemporary international system is the model of the 'moral revolution' of the kind that overthrew the communist regimes in Eastern Europe in 1989–90. These resulted from the ideological and moral breakdown of the model of democratic centralism imposed on Eastern European states in the post-war era. One of the major driving forces was generational change as a younger generation emerged that had been brought up after the Second World War and the Stalinist terror of 1945–56. It rejected the basic tenets of Stalinism and initiated a 'moral revolution' that was based on core values such as dignity, justice and truth rather than societal blueprints. Though there may yet be exceptions in states such as Rumania, the model tends to be rooted in moderate elite change and is geared to securing governments that respect an international discourse on human rights and democratisation.[33]

Revolutions and the states system

The emergence of the fourth generation of analysts of revolution has provided considerable potential for seeing revolutions in terms of the evolution of the states system. As Charles Tilly has pointed out, when looked at over the last one thousand years, revolutions can be seen as an intrinsic part of the development of war, the nation state and international relations generally. While societies were governed by more patrimonial and feudalistic structures before the advent of the mature nation state, war and revolution tended to collapse into each other. As states started to become consolidated in Europe by the sixteenth century, however, a more formal distinction began to emerge between war and peace while revolution too began to acquire its own meaning distinct from struggles between rival groups of dynastic power holders.[34]

The potential for revolution really emerges with the nationalisation of state control and the consolidation of power at the centre of the emerging nation state in the seventeenth and eighteenth centuries following the Peace of Westphalia in 1648. This system, as Martin Wight pointed out, was one of the loosest forms of political associations known to man and its mechanisms for collective defence were highly imperfect, tending in fact to 'exist in the realm of aspiration rather than operation'.[35]

The system has proved increasingly incapable in fact of resisting the emergence of nation states forged under the aegis of dominant ethnic and tribal factions, whose cultural symbols such as flags and national anthems become in turn those of the new nation state.[36] As the state concentrates power at the centre so groups and classes marginalised at the periphery provide the social base for a possible revolutionary movement. This nationalising process leads to a considerable heightening of coercive power by the central state as national armies and navies are formed and uniform taxation introduced. Informal mechanisms of political influence through systems of local patronage are either abolished or severely restricted and rule is more directly exerted by the central state itself.

This process of state centralisation was carried to new heights in the era of European absolutism in the seventeenth and eighteenth centuries and reached perhaps its logical conclusion with the well-known phrase of Louis XIV of France, 'l'état c'est moi'. This really represented an aspiration rather than a fact since the central state in France became increasingly weak as absolute monarchy rested on a fixed system of privileges that could not be changed without bringing the whole edifice down.[37] International conflict frequently demonstrated the close link between war and revolution as defeat in a war undermined the sovereign claims of the central state and provided a fillip to the alternative claims of a revolutionary movement in the domestic periphery.

The effect of such a revolutionary transformation has often been the longer-term strengthening of the state through the mass mobilisation of the population under its control. As Skocpol has shown in the case of the French, Russian and Chinese revolutions, the social revolutions that overthrew these relatively weak, semi-bureaucratic and centralised states replaced them with regimes with far greater ability to control and organise its population and discipline them into mass armies.[38]

In this respect there is an important relationship between social revolution and war in the functioning of the international system. This is a dimension that has been neglected by students of IR, who have tended to focus upon the origins of war to the exclusion of its potential effect in fomenting revolutionary change, or of revolutionary change in turn leading to the outbreak of war. This neglect is really rather inexcusable given that many revolutionary states see the exporting of their revolution as crucial to the stabilisation of the revolution in their own society.[39] From the French Revolution onwards, protecting the state system against revolutionary challenge became one of the cardinal objectives of governments even if in the long run collaborative efforts such as the European Concert organised by Talleyrand, Metternich, Castlereagh and the Prussian representatives after the Treaty of Vienna ultimately failed to prevent the emergence of *popular* states.[40] Quarantining and containment of revolutionary states became a major strategy that the dominant powers of the international system employed to ensure its stability right through the Cold War to the attempts to contain the impact of revolutionary Iran in the Middle East after 1979.

At one level, of course, revolution can be distinguished from war by virtue of the fact that it represents the transformation of a governing elite and the dominant values of a political system rather than its military disruption through armed conflict between nation states. Revolution is, as Isaac Kramnick has written, 'an illegal change in what are considered the fundamental principles of legality' and is thus far more wide-reaching that the simple change of personnel within a ruling elite by a putsch or *coup d'état*.[41]

However, revolution is clearly, like war, an important dynamic in the evolution of the states system, though its exact nature and role is still imperfectly understood. Knowledge and understanding of revolutionary processes may help to transform the nature of revolution in contemporary societies. Absolutist and agrarian-bureaucratic societies such as pre-revolutionary France, Russia and China no longer exist. Modernising and developing societies in the twentieth century have been increasingly governed by elites who have consciously acted to pre-empt revolutionary breakdown.

By the time of the Cold War many of these elites were able to look for aid and assistance from one of the superpowers in a situation of global power rivalry. The basic currency of revolutionary politics became 'national liberation', though this often meant appealing to a rival superpower to sustain the goals of the new revolutionary regime. If this was not immediately forthcoming then the prospects of the revolution might be doomed as the dominant superpower intervened in its sphere of influence to pre-empt a revolution from taking place, as in the case of the Soviet invasions of Hungary in 1956 or Czechoslovakia in 1968 or, in the case of the West, United States assistance to the Magsaysay regime in the Philippines in the 1950s against communist insurgents.

This superpower rivalry led to the development of certain common ground rules that gave their behaviour a certain level of predictability, though on occasion there could still be surprises such as the Soviet intervention into Angola in 1975–76 to sustain the Marxist MPLA regime in Luanda. Both superpowers were willing to resort to intervention to contain revolutionary upsurges, though it would be an exaggeration to claim that they succeeded in the process in subjecting revolutions to bureaucratic control.[42] The evidence from case studies such as the US destabilisation of the Arbenz regime in Guatemala (which was hardly revolutionary) suggest that decision makers were often poorly informed and acted on the basis of extremely slender intelligence information. Moreover such intervention often ends up making the situation worse as it reinforces patrimonial regimes which fail to implement liberal reforms. When these are insisted upon, as in demands by the Carter administration that the Shah's regime in Iran implement a human rights programme, they further undermine the regime and help precipitate a revolution they were intended to prevent.[43]

With the end of the Cold War, the era of rival superpower intervention to sustain or undermine revolutionary movements has, for the moment, come to an end. The upsurge of revolutions in Eastern Europe suggested that the post-Cold War era might be a revolutionary one, reminiscent of 1848 in Europe. Such predictions may well be premature, however, as the upsurge of ethnic nationalism suggests that the international appeals of revolutionary movements based on a discourse of human rights may well be blunted by a more insular series of ethnic nationalisms that reproduce an older pattern of inter-state warfare reminiscent of the era before the nuclear balance of terror. It is therefore unclear what the future role of revolution, if any, will be in the international system, and it is to this last issue that we now turn.

Revolutions and the global civil society

With the end of the Cold War, it may be possible to start reassessing the global impact of revolutions in a new way. The phenomenon of revolution has had its own history since it was first formally thrust into national and international politics with the French Revolution in 1789. The longer-term meaning and significance of revolutions in global politics cannot be captured from a series of case studies, which has often been the preferred method in the social sciences.[44] The saliency of revolution has in fact waxed and waned in international politics and needs to be seen in the context of other processes such as European imperial expansion in the nineteenth century which did much to neutralise the impact of the French Revolution. Likewise the Cold War also tended to freeze political and ideological rivalries and blunted the edge of many revolutionary movements, particularly in developing states.

The collapse of communism has led to a resurgence of neo-liberalism and powerful bodies like the World Bank and IMF, but it is not yet clear what role these will play in the history of global revolution. Many developing states in Latin America and Asia have developed a strong enough set of structures to be able to cope in some degree with structural adjustment programmes. However, others in Africa remain weak and 'juridical' as opposed to the 'empirical' states whose durability has been subject to the ultimate test of war.[45] Structural adjustment threatens to unravel the bureaucratic apparatus of the post-colonial state completely and has been seen by some analysts to pose a long-term law and order problem. In the absence of a compelling revolutionary idea and a cohesive evolutionary party, though, the threat of revolution in the developing world remains remote.

It is by no means clear that the global system faces a complete 'end of history' and effective termination of the revolutionary ideological process that began in 1789.[46] However, for the foreseeable future the idea of revolution has been demobilised outside the world of radical Islam as the phase of Third World 'national liberation' has more or less run its course. The revolutionary idea has thus begun to fragment into a series of eclectic ethnic, environmental and even animal liberation groupings some of which have violent or terrorist wings but do not in themselves contain a coherent programme for the revolutionary transformation of an entire society.

This decline of revolutionism can be related to the emergence of an as yet primitive global 'civil society' which like civil societies at the nation state level contains institutions and mechanisms for the resolution of disputes and the enforcement of certain common standards of law and human rights. This civil society may not be strong enough to prevent the emergence of newer forms of revolutionary movements in dispossessed and marginalised societies; much will depend upon the capacity of bodies like the United Nations to develop a peace enforcing as well as peace-keeping role. If it falls too much under the control of a small concert of great powers then it is possible that, as in Europe in 1848, there will be new revolutionary challenges to this global Holy Alliance. The pattern of twentieth-century politics hardly suggests that the revolutionary idea can be considered dead.

Notes

1   Alan James, 'Law and Order in International Society', in Alan James (ed.), *The Bases of International Order: Essays in Honour of C. A. W. Manning*, London, Oxford University Press, 1973, pp. 60–84. Though Martin Wight has calculated that between the years 1492 and 1914, 256 years were ones of 'international revolution' and 212 'unrevolutionary': Martin Wight, *Power Politics*, Harmondsworth, Penguin Books, 1979, p. 92, n. 17.

2   Peter Calvert, *Revolution and International Politics*, London, Frances Pinter, 1984, p. 198.

3   Jack A. Goldstone, 'Theories of Revolution: the Third Generation', *World Politics*, XXXII, 3 (April 1980), pp. 425–53; 'The Comparative and Historical Study of Revolutions', *Ann. Rev. Sociol* (1982), pp. 187–207.

4   Hedley Bull, 'The Theory of International Politics, 1919–1969', in Brian Porter (ed.), *Aberystwyth Papers 1919–1956*, Oxford, Oxford University Press, 1972, pp. 31–55; Clarke A. Chambers, 'The Belief in Progress in Twentieth century America', *Journal of the History of Ideas*, XIX (April 1958), pp. 197–224.

5   William C. Olson and A. J. R. Groom, *International Relations Then and Now*, London, HarperCollins Academic, 1991, p. 38; Vendulka Kubalkova and Albert Cruickshank, *Marxism and International Relations*, Oxford, Oxford University Press, 1989.

6   Crane Brinton, *The Anatomy of Revolution*, Englewood Cliffs (NJ), Prentice Hall, 1938.

7   Goldstone, 'Theories of Revolution', p. 427.

8   James C. Davies, 'Toward a Theory of Revolution', *American Sociological Review*, XXVII (February 1962), pp. 5–19; Ted Gurr, *Why Men Rebel*, Princeton, Princeton University Press, 1970; Ivo K. Feierabend with Rosalind L. Feierabend and Betty A. Nesvold, 'The Comparative Study of Revolution and Violence', *Comparative Politics*, 5, 3 (April 1973), pp. 393–424.

9   Davies, 'Toward a Theory of Revolution'.

10   Stan Taylor, *Social Science & Revolutions*, New York, St Martin's Press, 1984, p. 65.

11   Robert H. Dix, 'Why Revolutions Succeed and Fail', *Policy*, XVI, 3 (Spring

1984), pp. 423–46; Charles Tilly, 'Does Modernisation Breed Revolution?', *Comparative Politics*, 5, 3 (April 1973), pp. 425–47.

12   Chalmers Johnson, *Revolutionary Change*, Boston, Little Brown and Co, 1970.

13   Taylor, *Social Science & Revolutions*, p. 17.

14   Johnson, *Revolutionary Change*, pp. 170–2.

15   Lawrence Stone, 'Theories of Revolution', *World Politics*, XVIII, 2 (January 1966), p. 175.

16   Sheldon S. Wolin, 'The Politics of the Study of Revolution', *Comparative Politics*, 5, 3 (April 1973), pp. 343–58.

17   Michael Freeden, 'Review Article: Theories of Revolution', *British Journal of Political Science*, 2, pp. 339–59.

18   James Farr, 'Historical Concepts in Political Science: The Case of "Revolution" ', *American Journal of Political Science*, 26, 4 (November 1982), pp. 688–708.

19   Theda Skocpol, *States and Social Revolutions: A Comparative Analysis of France, Russia and China*, Cambridge, Cambridge University Press, 1979; 'Social Revolutions and Mass Military Mobilisation', *World Politics*, XL, 2 (January 1988), pp. 147–68;

20   John S. Saul, 'African Peasants and Revolution', *Review of African Political Economy*, 1 (1974), pp. 41–68; Claude E. Welch, Jr, 'Obstacles to "Peasant War" in Africa', *African Studies Review*, 20 (1977), pp. 121–30.

21   Josef Gugler, 'The Urban Character of Contemporary Revolutions', *Studies in Comparative International Development*, V, 17 (Summer 1982), pp. 60–73. See also Michael Tien-Lung Liu, 'States and Urban Revolutions: Explaining the Revolutionary Outcomes in Iran and Poland', *Theory and Society*, 17 (1988), pp. 179–209; Farideh Farhi, 'State Disintegration and Urban-Based Revolutionary Crisis', *Comparative Political Studies*, 21, 2 (July 1988), pp. 231–56.

22   William H. Sewell, Jr, 'Ideologies and Social Revolutions: Reflections on the French Case', *Journal of Modern History*, 57, 1 (March 1985), pp. 57–85.

23   Ronaldo Munck, 'The "Modern" Military Dictatorship in Latin America: The Case of Argentina', *Latin American Perspectives*, 12, 4 (Fall 1985), pp. 41–74; Michael Lowy and Eder Sader, 'The Militarisation of the State in Latin America', *Ibid*, 12, 4 (Fall 1985), pp. 7–40.

24   Theda Skocpol, 'Rentier State and Shi'a Islam in the Iranian Revolution', *Theory and Society*, 11 (1982), pp. 265–83; Jeff Goodwin and Theda Skocpol, 'Explaining Revolutions in the Contemporary Third World', *Politics and Society*, 17, 4 (1989), pp. 489–509.

25   Jack A. Goldstone, 'An Analytical Framework', in Jack A. Goldstone *et al.* (eds), *Revolutions of the Twentieth Century*, Boulder, Westview Press, 1991, pp. 37–51.

26   'The process of revolution is simply a marginal instance of the range of

processes of political change', Carl J. Friedrich, *The Pathology of Politics*, New York, Harper and Row, 1972, p. 55.

27 Perez Zagorin, 'Theories of Revolution in Contemporary Historiography', *Political Science Quarterly*, 88, 1 (March 1973), p. 44.

28 Rod Aya, 'Theories of Revolution Reconsidered', *Theory and Society*, 8 (1979), pp. 39–99.

29 Charles Tilly, 'Does Modernisation Breed Revolution?', *Comparative Politics*, 5, 3 (April 1973), pp. 425–47; Samuel Huntington, *Political Order in Changing Societies*, New Haven, Yale University Press, 1968.

30 Aya, 'Theories of Revolution Reconsidered', p. 77.

31 'The cultural revolution of Victorian Ireland prefigured much of what is happening in the underdeveloped world of the late twentieth century, where the efforts of peoples to cope with the invading culture and power of the West often bear an uncanny resemblance to the almost desperate attempts of the Victorian Catholic Irish to come to terms with the overwhelming culture and power of imperial England', Tom Garvin, *Nationalist Revolutionaries in Ireland, 1858–1928*, Oxford, Clarendon Press, 1987, p. 3.

32 Ellen Kay Trimberger, 'A Theory of Elite Revolutions', *Studies in Comparative International Development*, 2 (7) (Fall 1972), pp. 191–207; *Revolution From Above*, New Brunswick (NJ), Transaction Books, 1978.

33 John Higley and Jan Pakulski, 'Revolution and Elite Transformation in Eastern Europe', *Australian Journal of Political Science*, 27 (1992), pp. 104–19.

34 Charles Tilly, 'Changing Forms of Revolution', in E. E. Rice (ed.), *Revolution and Counter Revolution*, Oxford, Basic Blackwell, 1991, pp. 1–25.

35 Martin Wight, *Systems of States*, Leicester, Leicester University Press, 1977, p. 149.

36 Anthony D. Smith, *The Ethnic Origin of Nations*, Oxford, Basil Blackwell, 1986.

37 Sewell, 'Ideologies and Social Revolutions', p. 64.

38 Skocpol, *States and Social Revolutions*; 'Social Revolutions and Mass Military Mobilization'.

39 Fred Halliday, 'State and Society in International Relations', in Michael Banks and Martin Shaw (eds), *State and Society in International Relations*, New York, Harvester Wheatsheaf, 1991, p. 204.

40 Kalevi J. Holsti, *Peace and War: Armed Conflicts and International Order 1648–1989*, Cambridge, Cambridge University Press, 1991, p. 139.

41 Isaac Kramnick, 'Reflections on Revolution: Definition and Explanation in Recent Scholarship', *History and Theory*, XI (1972), p. 32.

42 Jonathan R. Adelman, 'Introduction', in Jonathan R. Adelman (ed.), *Superpowers and Revolution*, New York, Praeger, 1986, pp. 10–12.

43 Jack A. Goldstone, 'Revolutions and Superpowers', in Adelman, *Superpowers and Revolution*, pp. 38–48.

44 See in particular Elbaki Hermassi, 'Towards a Comparative Study of

Revolutions', *Comparative Studies in Society and History*, 18, 2 (1976), pp. 211–35; John M. Gates, 'Toward a History of Revolution', *Comparative Studies in Society and History*, 28 (1986), pp. 535–51.

45 The terms come from Robert H. Jackson and Carl G. Rosberg, 'Why Africa's Weak States Persist: The Empirical and Juridical in Statehood', *World Politics*, XXXVI (October 1982), pp. 1–24.

46 Francis Fukuyama, *The End of History and the Last Man*, Harmondsworth, Penguin Books, 1992.

Part II
Historical antecedents

3 *Andrew Williams*

The French Revolution

Revolutions figure little in world history before 1789. Since then it seems that world history has consisted of little else.

Geoffey Best, *The Permanent Revolution: The French Revolution and its Legacy, 1789–1989*, 1988, p. 1

Why study the 'Great' revolutions?

Chapters 1 and 2 of this volume aim to show why the study of revolution is so important to the scholar of international relations (IR). This chapter will show why the study of the 'Great' revolutions of the early modern era, particularly the French Revolution of 1789, is crucial both to an understanding of IR in the broad sense and to a comprehension of the coming phase of tension between what are referred to as 'North' and 'South'. Those who believe that we have arrived at the 'End of History' predicted by Hegel in the early nineteenth century[1] would do well to look at the beginning of that same period more closely. The Hegelian dialectic that sees the emergence of the modern Western nation state as the key exemplar for the planet carries within itself the risk for those same nations of a continuing dialectical challenge to their leadership of the international community. It will be argued here that an understanding of the importance of the French Revolution of 1789 is particularly crucial, or as James Mayall has put it that 'the Revolution set in train developments which were to transform international society into the form that we now take for granted'.[2] More widely, it is acknowledged here, with Fred Halliday and Barrington Moore[3] that *all* transition from traditional to modern society is violent, whether it is 'revolutionary', as in France and Russia, or non 'revolutionary' (like in America and Britain). Some form of violent change is the *sine qua non* for the emergence of statehood, not an abberation. But in this chapter and the one on Russia that interesting debate will make way for a concentration on two case studies of seminal importance.

What this chapter, and its sequel, will *not* do is to recite 'what happened', or, at least centrally, 'what caused it', both enduring obsessions of generations of historians and social scientists. There are many excellent books that will do this.[4] The purpose of this chapter is to suggest how this revolution helped to create 'ideal types' of political organisation, including varying models of democracy, governance and political culture, that are at the heart of the present organisation of our current international society,[5] one that dominates the current international system through the various practices and institutions of Western statecraft. The 'Great' revolutions can be seen as midwives to two Western 'camps' that have emerged from and continued to shape the same political and social traditions, those of modernity. The victory of liberal democracy, epitomised by 1688 and 1776, over that of democratic centralism, epitomised by 1789 and 1917, is thus largely a Western affair, part of a historical 'conversation', and not to be confused with a total 'victory', as suggested by Fukuyama and others in the triumphalism of the post-Cold War period. As such the 'lessons' that they have taught are seminal for a further critique of the rules of international society in a search for logical challenges to its dominance of the *status quo* powers of the 'West' by any who would challenge that dominance, the revolutionary states and peoples of the present and future.

The French Revolution as basic model

The importance of the 'Great' revolutions has been challenged by none in the West. The main debate has been about which of these revolutions were truly 'seminal', and which had the greatest positive normative impact. Hence Barrington Moore's *Origins of Dictatorship and Democracy* was only challenged by Theda Skocpol on the grounds that Moore had wrongly identified the English and American revolutions as 'revolutions', in the sense that Skocpol only accepted as revolutions ones which have radically and fundamentally changed state and society.[6] Her work, important as it is, makes the mistake of amputating one side of the body of the revolutionary Leviathan that has formed the West, so that Locke, Cromwell, Jefferson and Madison are dropped as only bourgeois subversives, while Robespierre, Marx and Lenin stay in as true revolutionaries. Armstrong has persuasively argued that whereas the American and (by retrospective logic) the English revolution were the creators of the model of the state and *people*, the French revolution (and by forward logic the Russian revolution) created the model of the state and *nation*. The true dialectic lies in them being two heads of the same beast, a beast that we must accept as the founding father of the West's political, cultural and anthropological project. But the main definition of a revolution as a fundamental change in state and societal relationships within a political entity sees its origins in the examination of 1789.

For the student of IR, a factor of key importance has clearly been that all subsequent revolutions have been compared, implicitly and explicitly, with 1789. Crane Brinton's *Anatomy of Revolution*, rightly identified by Paul Rich in Chapter 2 as one of the key 'first generation' analyses of revolution (although it could be argued that Carlyle and a host of others did so in the nineteenth century) is a good example of the identification of 'stages' of a revolution, with Brinton using the analogy of an illness, from which the patient, the state, happily always recovers, even if marked forever by the experience.[7] This process is one for the analyst of *periodisation*, without which no revolution can make sense for the IR scholar. The key questions thrown up by periodisation are (a) how does the revolution affect the target state and society itself and the international system of the day, but also (b) how does the system 'socialise' the revolution. At what point does a revolutionary state become 'normal' again, and for what reasons? Does it create its own sub-system, can it maintain such a sub-system faced with the inevitable backlash as it tries for export-led growth? Asking these questions about the Russian revolution has become a commonplace, but they first became relevant in 1789. Halliday's parallel but slightly more functional 'historical generalisations' also only make sense after 1789: What are the international (as distinct to domestic) factors that cause revolutions? How do revolutionary states conduct their foreign policy? How do other states respond? How does the international system then constrain the state's post-revolutionary development? Some of these questions will be attempted in this chapter, and they guide the overall reasoning to a significant degree.

Homo occidentalis?

Peter Calvert's identification of the four 'aspects' of revolution: as 'a *process*' culminating in revolutionary change; as an '*event*'; as a '*programme* . . . *after*' [the event] and as '*political myth*' is a basic but very serviceable framework within which to explain the enduring significance of the 'Great' revolutions.[8] This chapter cannot go into all these categories, but the last one is that which has most enduring significance for the student of IR, because myth is the most readily exported commodity, whereas events, processes and programmes are inevitably contingent on local conditions. Churchill recognised this when he ranted about the 'plague bacillus of Bolshevism', a direct, indeed lineal descendant of 1789 (and of which more in the next chapter). It is now widely acknowledged that there was as much *continuity* as change in the events around 1688, 1776 and 1789.[9] These events can be seen as the founding myths of the West. American Presidents often embellish their authority by reference to the Founding Fathers (and President Reagan even extended the compliment to the Nicaraguan Contras!). The evocation of 1789 is widespread in the French press, with a recent example being the reminder of the *Grande Peur* of 1788 with French farmers' resistance to reform of the Common Agricultural Policy in the summer of 1992. The atmosphere of the British Parliament is redolent of the symbolism of the Civil War, the left in particular anxious to establish itself as the natural inheritor of Cromwellian authority.

The actual unravelling of the 'event' and the 'process' that led up to it has dominated the undergraduate literature on revolution. But increasingly the student of 1789 will be directed vigorously in the direction of the French Revolution as the creator of a political myth. The classic book by D. M. G. Sutherland, *France, 1789–1815: Revolution and Counterrevolution*, is prefaced (by Douglas Johnson) with '[wh]ether the French Revolution was model for all revolutions or not, whether it is a myth or not, whether it is a jumble of unpredictable events or not, it is an inescapable subject . . . It is always there. It is always with us.' The two hundredth anniversary of the French Revolution reinforced this tendency, reminding us how much of an 'industry' the revolution has become, dominating the political culture of France and of Europe.[10] There have been few over the last two hundred years who did not identify themselves by their relationship with the great revolutionary groups – Jacobin, Girondin or Royalist (for which read Socialist/Communist, Liberal and Conservative). The latest milestones on the phenomenon now go much further along this road, and like Simon Schama recognise that a new kind of political actor was created by 1789 – the 'citizen'. Even if arguably he was only a newer model of the one created by 1688 and 1776, and has seen a number of incarnations since, it is in the French Revolution that we see the emergence of a Hegelian 'homo occidentalis'. Even those like François Furet, who would like to declare the Revolution 'over' cannot get away from its continuing fascination.[11]

Political theory

Although the ideas of the French Revolution have had the most obvious impact on revolutionary thought, the contribution of *English* revolutionary ideas cannot be overlooked, both on the events of 1789 and beyond. Although there are those who deny the importance of the 'English' or 'Puritan' Revolution (as does Skocpol who feels that it did not change both state and society), or dismiss it as a tiff within the English ruling class, there was clearly an influence expressed by those who followed the example of 1688 to change their own states and/or societies.[12] The impact of the Glorious Revolution is most clearly seen in the works of John Locke, especially in his *Second Treatise on Civil Government* of 1690, which summed up many of the achievements of the period 1641–88. Key among these was that the monarch had a 'contract' with the people that could be broken by that people under certain circumstances, and that the foundations for political liberty had to be the basis for all political and indeed societal progress. The American colonists used Locke to justify their own demands for liberty,[13] securing the agreement of key English thinkers like Edmund Burke, Thomas Wilkes and Charles James Fox, which has led many commentators to see 1776 as the logical extension of 1688.[14] But Locke, as Golo Mann has pointed out 'spoke for the old oligarchy and the new English upper middle classes.'[15]

It is therefore Jean-Jacques Rousseau who is most usually seen as the key exponent of a different kind of contract between rulers and ruled, even if often linked with Locke, as by John Rawls,[16] to demonstrate the links between contract and justice. If revolution has any overarching aim it is to clarify such domestic relationships. However, whereas Locke put people and sovereign in *opposition*, a free citizenry only mildly restrained by the state, Rousseau tried to abolish the distinction between citizen and state. The people are for him *themselves* sovereign because they represent the 'General Will.'[17] Whereas with Locke there is a feeling that the individual must make his own destiny, in Rousseau the polity as a whole must strive to rethink itself in an ideal based on the principles of 'virtue'.[18] He issued in the 'age of the masses', masses who were feared by the descendants of Locke (like Edmund Burke, of whom more below).

Those who fear a messianic 'General Will' subsuming the individual under the weight of the state have many grounds for their fears. Hayek's entire economic and political philosophy is premised on this apprehension. The practice of the 'Terror' by the 'sea-green incorruptible', Robespierre, who saw himself as Rousseau's 'virtue' made flesh, and who created a secular religion to replace Christianity, has led many writers to fear any form of 'ideal' state, especially one led by visionaries. Joseph Talmon was not alone in saying that 'Rousseau was one of the most ill-adjusted and egocentric natures who have left a record of their predicament' and to have this inner turmoil made into political reality by Robespierre, Saint-Just and Babeuf.[19] Burke directly blamed Rousseau for the outbreak and the course of the French Revolution.[20] Ronald Paulson even sees a moral blame attaching to Rousseau in Burke's condemnation, with the *Nouvelle Heloise* being blamed for the Jacobins' sexual depravity and the 'brutal sensuality' of the Parisian mob.[21] The logical implication is that Burke would have blamed Rousseau for the Marquis de Sade if he had been aware of him. The charge of a perverted sensuality is of course also to be found in condemnations of the Russian Revolution, as with the furore over Alexandra Kollontai's views on sex being like 'drinking a glass of water.' The revolutionary sport of *épater le bourgeois*, so beloved of juveniles the world over, is understandable given the more extreme of the charges bought against Rousseau. Hypocrisy and righteous indignation are not the sole resort of the Jacobin.

The charge of being gripped by a messianic totalitarianism is of course not exclusively directed against revolutionaries of the left. Hannah Arendt and others have warned us against the tendency from wherever it may come.[22] The post-Second World war social scientists such as Chalmers Johnson[23] and what have been identified (somewhat confusingly for the IR student) as 'structuralists', all see the 'left' and the 'right' as threats to their ideal of liberal democracy, although since 1945 the right has been seen largely as a historical enemy of the West. These writers are central to a Lockean view of contract and liberty, children of 1688 and 1776, but meaningless unless seen as a contrast to the idealists of 1789 and, arguably, 1917. The Rousseauian ideal has more accurately been portrayed as that of one of 'popular sovereignty'. However far the reality of revolutionary France, in particular, falls short of that ideal, it none the less forms the basis for a widespread belief in the need to stress the collective as well as the Lockean individual will as the basis of Western democratic thought. Even where the opposition to popular sovereignty is strongest, as in the writings of Burke, it is the *tension* between the two emergent traditions that makes the debate interesting and significant, not merely the rejection of one in favour of the other.

The French Revolution must also be seen as a constant part of the political and social discourse of the West. Marx's role in affirming its importance is well appreciated, and he represents the strongest 'Jacobin' tendency, one that has a direct onward lineage to Lenin, Mao Tse Tung and Fidel Castro, to name but a few.[24] It was Marx who dominated the discussion from the Left, and received most of the attention until the end of the Stalin era, as for example in the writings of Edmund Wilson.[25] Marx saw the main importance of the French Revolution in its confirmation of the Liberal ideal, one which was to give birth to the greater ideal of the proletariat and Socialism. Liberalism, he recognised, drew from the French Revolution as a well-spring, but mainly he saw 1789 as the clarion call to the masses, the *locus classicus* of the 'political earthquake', as England was for him that of capitalist economics.[26] France was also to become a beacon for all other Marxist revolutionaries, and historians. Michelet, Jaurès, Mathiez, Lefèbvre, Souboul and Labrousse are the most obvious examples.[27] As Dunn says, the French Revolution was the basis of their deterministic view of political change: 'it became possible to think of violent revolutionary change as a motor for social transformations'. However, as Dunn goes on to say, this change was '. . . easy to start, but impossible to stop until they had reached their final destination . . . *Après nous le deluge . . .*'[28]

But of course not all have seen the revolution in a positive light. France has produced a host of conservative writers, often of a monarchist hue, including Joseph de Maistre (1753–1821).[29] The nineteenth century produced many more ardent right-wing rejections, with Charles Maurras and the other writers of the *Action Française* as their most extreme political offspring, but also including more incisive criticisms, such as that of Ernest Renan. The iconography of this school is most striking and even has its places of pilgrimage, such as the *Jardin de Picpus*, where a mass grave holds over a thousand victims of the guillotine, as well as many aristocrats and most notably the Marquis de Lafayette, although he did not himself end on the scaffold.[30]

The writer who has most dominated the French, as well as the international, imagination in recent years is, however, Alexis de Tocqueville. De Tocqueville is the hero of the liberal centre and has waned and waxed in direct correlation with this political current. If there is an 'ideological winner' of the French Revolutionary tradition, and possibly also the Cold War which has seen the (possibly final) rout of Western Jacobinism, he probably has the best claim upon the crown. Among the many who have made de Tocqueville their own two names stand out – Raymond Aron and François Furet. Aron's *Memoirs*[31] show how de Tocqueville influenced many key intellectual epochs of Aron's long career. De Tocqueville for Aron 'n'était pas un précurseur mais un pionnier de la pensée sociologique', one of the 'sept grands'.[32] Elsewhere Aron's praise was no less elegiac, portraying him as the essential definer of the links between the social and the political in the liberal democratic project, the very basis of liberty.[33] Furet's equally passionate embrace of de Tocqueville is also founded on his belief that the great man was not a historian in the normal sense, but a prophet of a new kind of society. Thus de Tocqueville's French Revolution is not that of Michelet, the great historian of the left, who Furet portrays as a 'sublime visiteur des cimitières.'[34] Nor is he seen as having made the mistakes of Marx, who saw everything (according to Furet) in terms of economic or class analysis. Rather de Tocqueville defined for Furet the 'l'état d'esprit des Français, ce qu'on pourrait appeler le tempérament ou le caractère national'.[35]

It is in the United States of America where Aron, like de Tocqueville,[36] found his best developed model of such liberty, based not on some false Rousseauian ideal of 'virtue' and certainly rejecting the idea of liberty somehow residing in the 'people'. For Aron the individual is the main guarantor of liberty, a fact shown by the American and the French Revolutions. But the English tradition has an arguably better claim on the lineage of anti-Jacobin liberalism, through Edmund Burke. Both de Tocqueville and Burke saw the Terror as the essential tool of Jacobin power. 'Formal' liberty had no meaning when it constrained the individual, as was inevitable in the democratic centralist society Robespierre was trying to create.

Burke was the first great denunciator of the political programme of Jacobinism (before it even really fully took power, since his famous work came out in 1792). It was also Burke that gave the Revolution its *international* importance and has sparked heated debate throughout the world ever since. But he was also quintessentially *English*: 'Burke's intention was to impress everyone with the idea that there was only one proper discourse on revolution, the one elaborated in Britain . . .'[37] Burke's intention was not to deny the need for democracy, it was just that he could not accept that the French Revolution would bring it about. He rejected Rousseau's belief in the 'state of nature' for the needs of a contract between state and people *à la britannique* of what Trevor-Roper calls the 'pragmatic' English revolution and was particularly scornful of contemporary 'fellow travellers' of 1789, like Tom Paine.[38] Others have blamed the French Revolution for every aspect of totalitarian political action ever since (most famously Talmon),[39] but Burke is still the mainspring of this feeling. His ideas were also widely influential on the early nineteenth-century German philosophers, even by those who greeted the Revolution as the beginning of a new rational age, like Kant and Hegel, but later came to see mainly its dark side, while admiring its power and recognising that it had changed Europe for ever. The Revolution must therefore be seen as the main inspiration for the most productive period of German philosophical thought.[40]

So for all these thinkers the Revolution was not only seen as ushering in an age of reason but, since it clearly did not in many ways, also as unlocking a Pandora's Box of future problems. Hence there are two lasting generalisable phenomena that are intimately but often confusingly linked to the French Revolution and that have had a lasting impact on Western political thought. These are of course those of the 'Enlightenment', which inspired it and many revolutions since, and what may be seen as a kind of naturally created antibody, 'romanticism', which largely rejects the former's espousal of the ideals of 'progress' and 'social engineering'. Possibly one would not have existed without the other or had any meaning in isolation. The Enlightenment was obviously a precursory movement and was greeted by many as seeing its culmination in 1789, whereas the French Revolution and the birth of romanticism as a cultural movement were virtually contemporaneous, for as Schenk suggests 'these two events shared one essential characteristic: namely, the eruption of the irrational.' Schenk will not go so far as to suggest a causal connection, although he says the Revolution 'helped to launch the Romantic Movement'.[41] Nowadays disillusion with 'progress' is widespread, largely if not entirely due to the totalitarian excesses of this century, but romanticism has flourished ever since its inception. The French Revolution was the first instance of Yeats' 'terrible beauty', the fanaticism that fascinates as it repels. The Romantics can be seen as the cultural counterpart to Burkean political commentary, and are an enduring well-spring for Western distrust of 'reason' as a way to 'progress'. To go further than this and claim, as some have (Popper and Talmon being good examples)[42] that the French Revolution was one of the well-springs of political irrationalism, the inspiration for Bolshevism, and the extreme nationalisms of the last two hundred years is (possibly) to go too far.

Many writers have also observed that the French Revolution was the standard bearer of a new *universalism*, a claim made much less strongly in the American and English cases, even if arguably also true of both.[43] This has seen particular significance in the discussion of human rights, with the French Revolution's 'Declaration of the Rights of Man' the main text that has inspired United Nations' declarations in the field. The classic battle between 'collective' and 'individual' rights that has been so much a feature of modern discussions about human rights[44] can be said to derive from the debate between the paramountcy of Lockean, liberal, views of civil and political rights versus Rousseau's espousal of the 'collective will' that sees such stark expression in the French and Russian revolutions.

Statecraft and diplomatic practice

In considering the impact of 1789 on the international system and foreign policy practice, the way in which the Revolution has impacted on statecraft and on diplomacy in particular is clearly of vital importance. Some recent explanations of the links between the theory of IR and its practice have yet to be accepted by those who study foreign policy and diplomacy in general, and even by those more specifically interested in the external actions of revolutionary states. As was suggested in Chapter 1, the best single contribution to a better understanding of the links that must be established has come from James Der Derian, especially in his *On Diplomacy*. There he suggests that we must look at the 'genealogy' of Western statecraft, especially in its diplomatic form, in order to understand how the West has created a diplomatic edifice both in its own image and in its own defence against those who are considered 'beyond the pale'. A similar idea has been put forward by Gerrit Gong in his *Standard of Civilisation*.[45]

Der Derian's particular contribution to the study of the French Revolution lies in his questioning the neutrality of the idea of diplomacy itself. The French revolutionaries appealed not to sovereigns by normal diplomatic channels, but rather indulged in 'neo-' or 'anti-diplomacy', directly to 'peoples', especially in the period from 1792 to 1800. By so doing they tried actually to *abolish* diplomacy by making it 'open'. The continuation of this ideal can be seen in later periods of modern history, especially in the diplomacy of the Bolsheviks (see Chapter 4). Der Derian believes that revolutionary states always revert to more 'normal' diplomacy, as under Napoleon and Stalin. However, France until 1815 and Soviet Russia can arguably be seen as never having abandoned entirely their neo-diplomatic methods, as will be seen below.

'Statesmanship and diplomacy occupied much more of Napoleon's time than strategy.'[46] Mowat's classic text on revolutionary diplomacy and Albert Sorel's even older classic[47] laid great stress on the continuities as well as the changes wrought in French foreign policy by the Revolution, as de Tocqueville did in his discussion of France as a whole. He also stresses that foreign affairs were what the French did *best* – French was the *lingua franca* of diplomatic practice, they wrote the best manuals of diplomatic practice (de Callières' *De la manière de négocier avec les princes* being the best example)[48] and they 'were acknowledged to be the best exponents of it.' Clearly the Revolution damaged the elaborate reputation built up, if only because many of the key diplomats, and indeed soldiers, fled abroad for their lives as *émigrés*. The Committee of Public Safety that emerged as the effective executive of the new republic in 1792 was initially less than respectful of diplomatic niceties, confiscating the Austrian Ambassador's belongings, but giving them back in June 1794 when the Austrians threatened to retaliate by not exchanging prisoners of war. The normalisation continued under Bonaparte[49] and by 1814 Napoleon's diplomatic service was the most extensive and sophisticated in the world, with thirty-nine missions in place from the United States of America to Asia (including Teheran).[50]

As to French revolutionary *actions*, they of course continued to be hostile to the states all around France, but this can be seen as largely a continuation of French expansionism since at least Louis XIII. But the *style* of the French armies' advance was quite different from that of the pre-revolutionary era. These troops were those of the *Levée en Masse*, led by young generals, imbued with revolutionary fire and, generally, greeted with open arms by a population that saw them as liberators from a long feudal night. Best quotes contemporary Clausewitz as saying '[s]uddenly war again became the business of the people . . . all of whom considered themselves citizens . . . the full weight of the nation was thrown into the balance.' The modern mass army may be said to have started in 1792 and been first blooded at the 'battle' of Valmy in September 1792. In reality this was only a skirmish, but it was the first where the propaganda and symbolic value was extracted to the full, most famously by Goethe.[51] If the French army of the revolution, like that later of Bolshevik Russia, still had great continuity of personnel (only 50,000 of the 228,000 strong army of 1793 were 'volunteers'), this was to prove the paradigm for all future revolutionary armies. What were in effect political commissars (the *représentants en mission*), an elite corps developed, one that was 'ideologically sound' – in Napoleon's army this was of course the Imperial Guard – and a mass of enthusiastic foot soldiers prepared to die for their country. Their behaviour was also often that of the mass army, but perhaps no worse than was usual at the time. The cost was commensurate with such an effort and France took many years to recover from the cost in men and *matériel*.[52]

The aims, and also the style of revolutionary diplomacy were tied in to the continued existence of the revolution as well as to the older aims of an expansionist France. As with Bolshevik (and indeed Imperial) Russia there was an attempt to put space between the republic and its enemies, or at least to strengthen its borders. The continuation of Louis XIV's Rhine policies was one of the aims consecrated in the new Republic's first major treaty, that of Basle in 1795. There was also a strong economic element, with incentives to increase French trade with Germany, dispensing with the 'middlemen of Switzerland.'[53] This aim was reinforced by other diplomatic/trade measures, such as the ban on all English imports of 31 October 1796.[54] All was seen through the prism of what Armstrong calls the 'revolutionary mind':

> At its worst, their [the revolutionaries'] distorted sense of reality helped to create illusory expectations, to nurture a sense of moral superiority and martial invincibility, and to feed xenophobic and paranoid suspicions and fears. The precise influence of such intangibles is impossible to quantify, but they undoubtedly contributed to the disruptive impact of the Revolution on international society.[55]

But the key new element was the *export* of revolution, after the battle of Jemappes (also in 1792), when the Convention promised its assistance to 'all wishing to recover their liberty'. Schama calls this the 'first manifesto of revolutionary war in European history', but he also reminds us that, as with Bolshevik Russia, a 'commitment to a proselytizing, ideological war . . . was almost always outweighed by much more pragmatically defined interests of [the French] state.'[56] 'Neo-diplomacy' was thus balanced by *Realpolitik*, so that it is often difficult to see where exporting the revolution stopped and enlarging France began. The same is also true of Bolshevik Russia. None the less the French Ministry of Foreign Affairs can be seen as a pioneer in the dissemination of that other enduring fear of the *status quo* states, propaganda, with an official newspaper, *Le Moniteur*, an active department to research the raw material (especially the Archives Division and its *bureau historique*), especially directed against the main enemy, England.[57] The success of this can be gauged by the ferocious counter-measures taken by Pitt against the so-called 'Corresponding Societies' in Britain.

The main architect of this stronger, enduring France was Charles Maurice de Talleyrand, the Litvinov of the French Republic, of the Empire that followed it (with a break between 1808 and 1814 when he was sent as legate to Switzerland after annoying the Emperor) and of the restored monarchy, one of the great diplomatic survival acts of all time. Schama sees him almost as a talisman of the whole process, from his meeting with Voltaire in 1778, through his becoming Foreign Minister of the Republic in 1798,[58] and his simultaneous seduction of the wife of the ex-Minister, Mme Charles Delacroix, making him father of Eugène Delacroix, painter of the famous 'Liberty Leading the People', to be found on every contemporary 100 French Franc note.[59] He was in many ways the architect of modern diplomacy, and put his mark most strongly on the Vienna settlement of 1814–15 and in the creation of modern Belgium in 1830. He was also not untypical as a diplomat of revolutionary France. Whitcomb has found that 31 of the 71 ministers or ambassadors were noble by birth, as Talleyrand was of course, a proportion that increased throughout the Empire to 60 per cent, with a corresponding decline of diplomats of bourgeois or lesser origin.[60] He also points out that the bureaucracy as a whole, including the ministry, was 'a champion of order, of rationality, of uniformity and centralization', and as such a main plank of Bonaparte's most enduring creation, a centralised state.[61] If Bonaparte had taken the advice of the bureaucrats more readily, perhaps the fate of the revolution and of France would have been different.

Crane Brinton identified Talleyrand as one of the great 'realists' of modern times, of the same school as Disraeli and Bismarck, ever adapting himself to change, and never hoping for 'improvement'. He was also paradoxically a great 'liberal' who tried to damp down the excesses of revolution, who could never have the charge of 'moral idealist' levelled against him, but who none the less managed to salvage a great deal from the mess left by such idealists after 1815.[62]

The impact on the international system (and 'society') of states

The creation of the idea of the 'nation', the 'people' and the 'citizen' have already been noted as enduring legacies of the French Revolution. So have the political and philosophical frameworks that have developed out of its phases. If we can assume the idea of a 'society of states' bound by rules of coexistence,[63] this last section aims to speculate as to what wider impact the French Revolution had on the creation and maintenance of such a society.

The main impact was in the political creation of the modern nation state and its corollary ideology of nationalism. In an inspired passage of *Franglais* Conor Cruise O'Brien has selected the expressions '*la grande nation, frontières naturelles, républiques soeurs* and *les patriotes*' as key neologisms concretised by 1789, even if some of them have older eighteenth-century origins, notably in the writings of Rousseau.[64] Without doing excessive damage to O'Brien's thesis, he suggests that the very *inter*nationalism of the key Enlightenment figures (most of whom were French) makes them the precursors of *la grande nation* because they were the ambassadors of *French* culture and also because they saw a strong need for a new kind of state, based on what came to be called 'popular sovereignty', where the people become synonymous with the state. O'Brien comments '[t]he words "National Assembly" are in fact a mandate for revolutionary change, with no limit set to that process.'[65] The export of these ideas, and particularly 'nationalism', was to become an essential part of their defence. This explains much of the revolutionary diplomatic practice outlined above, and also possibly the need for all subsequent revolutionary states to follow a similar path, given the hostility with which they usually perceive themselves to be greeted by the international society of their day.

Since 1789 the literature on nationalism has of course been vast and its reputation mixed. Nationalism served as the great liberalising and emancipating movement of the early nineteenth century throughout Europe, the *Volksgeist.*[66] It has been seen as the natural export of Napoleon's armies by many historians, an idea powerful primarily because it was (and is) couched in *universal* language.[67] It was the basis of Woodrow Wilson's 5 Points and 14 Principles, under the claim for 'self-determination', within *frontières naturelles*. It is now the primary demand of (post-1989) Eastern European and Third World peoples. Its most severe challenge has come from liberal and socialist internationalists,[68] but only when its full development came to fruition in Wilhelmine and later Nazi Germany did it earn the malevolent reputation that it now has for many European intellectuals.

But this extreme and its bitter condemnation has done little to undermine the idea of the nation state as the main, indeed the natural, unit of international society. Mayall's analysis of the process of the nationalist challenge to the international system and the eventual accommodation of that system shows that the ideal of *la grande nation* now has an almost universal echo, and that 'the major impact of nationalism has been to reinforce the tradition of hard line realism, and to weaken the version in which the ineradicable egotism of the separate state was at last softened by a residual solidarity amongst states.'[69]

The actions of the French (and possibly all) revolutionaries may therefore lead us to the conclusion that revolutions do nothing to weaken the institution of the state, but rather, by stripping away their inefficient *ancien régimes*, actually reinforce the state and make it into a more efficient engine of war, disruption and ultimately creativity, directed inevitably against the *status quo* of the day. It is therefore the revolution that allows a state to achieve, in the words of Charles Tilly, true 'stateness'.[70] The French Revolution may leave this as its main enduring legacy and guarantee that the international system and society will continue to be challenged by those peoples who believe the rules do not operate in their favour. However, we could also say that international society has actually been underpinned by the French Revolution. Armstrong quotes Sorel that 'the representation of Europe under the *ancien régime* as a regularly constituted community of states, in which each directed its conduct by principles respected by all . . . this Christian republic . . . [was] nothing more than an august abstraction.'[71] However, as Armstrong makes clear, Sorel's ideal international society was precisely an *ideal*, in perhaps the same way as Khomeini's 'Islamic' international society. The emergence of the French Republic certainly threatened, and was seen to threaten, the existing international society, that of the Westphalian monarchies, but ultimately it might be argued that it ended up reinforcing it. The French Revolution brought with it so many fundamental categories of present state action and concern (Conor Cruise O'Brien's list above) that what we must say is that the event changed for ever the nature of international society, but made it much stronger rather than destroying it. The nineteenth century, and how much more our own, belonged far more surely to the democracies than to the monarchies, and the revolutions that followed, whatever the upheaval they have caused, have in the end served that cause as well.

Conclusion

The literature on the French Revolution is vast, and this chapter has inevitably considered only a tithe of it. Very few events can have obsessed so many generations of historians and commentators as much as it has. It is the perfect example of the creativity of the destructive forces of revolutionary struggle and it is hardly surprising that so many should have been inspired or revolted by it. Many, like Wordsworth, Burke and Paine, started with enthusiasm and ended up disgusted, while others like Marx and Sorel felt it justified their views of man, politics and the ultimate necessity of political extremism. Many more, like Danton and Robespierre, were the victims of their own creation. It has formed the

backdrop to countless tales of literary and artistic prowess, from Dickens
to Shelley and beyond, a cautionary tale or a justification for the purifying
fire of revolutionary morality over corruption. The debates opened up by
Burke and Paine have had many echoes in virtually every revolutionary
situation since 1789.

The debate also continues as to whether the French revolution is
'over'. The question posed by Der Derian, Halliday and Armstrong
about the 'socialisation' of the revolution is a very difficult one to answer,
for the French Revolution changed the existing European order for
ever, even while being technically defeated in 1815. The world was
never 'restored',[72] but rather 'reimposed' temporarily before the winds
of nationalism and modernity, both products of 1789, finally blew it to
pieces in 1914 or, arguably, in 1848.[73] The Concert of Europe was initially an attempt to reimpose feudal monarchies, but it was progressively
transformed into one where the key actors were democracies, especially
Britain, to be succeeded by three New World Orders in the twentieth
century, all inspired by the ideals of 1776 (or 1688), as well as by those of
1789.

In the place where the revolution initially happened, the French propensity for major political upheaval (as in 1830, 1848, 1871 and 1968, to
name but the more obvious episodes) has led many writers to debate
whether the domestic results of the revolution have really ceased to
evolve. While there cannot seem to be any definitive decision possible on
this question, since the point is that the debate is seen as a continued
necessity, the French Revolution as an international phenomenon cannot
be denied.

We can now return to the questions that were asked at the beginning
of this chapter. On the effect of a revolution on the 'target' state and
society and the international system of the day and any subsequent
'socialisation', the French experience demonstrates that it would be foolish to talk in absolute terms of the 'failure' or 'achievement' of either the
revolution or its opposing forces. The revolution of 1789 was like a 'force
of nature' (to use a French expression). Neither France or those it affected could ever be 'normal' again because the context had been changed
for ever. In a sense the sub-questions that I have also tried to answer
here, about revolutionary foreign policy and the response of the '*status quo*'
states that are inevitably affected, are therefore secondary indeed, mere
formalisations or embellishments of much larger consequences. But they
are also the visible and most understandable manifestations of an ele-
mental process that would otherwise be impossible to grasp, the human
and individual face of international relations that it is a central task of this

book to show. The 'evolution' of the foreign relations of revolutionary or 'renegade' states got probably its biggest boost from the events of 1789 and this role as 'exemplar' is therefore crucial for an understanding of all other such states' behaviour ever since. *La révolution française ne terminera jamais . . .*

Notes

1 Francis Fukuyama, *The End of History and the Last Man*, Harmondsworth, Penguin Books, 1992.

2 James Mayall, *Nationalism and International Society*, Cambridge, Cambridge University Press, 1990, p. 297.

3 Barrington Moore, *Social Origins of Dictatorship and Democracy: Lord and Peasant in the Making of the Modern World*, London, Peregrine (Penguin), 1966 and Fred Halliday, ' "The Sixth Great Power": On the Study of Revolution and International Relations', *Review of International Studies*, Vol. 16, No. 3, July 1990, pp. 207–21.

4 See for example, D. M. G. Sutherland, *France, 1789–1815, Revolution and Counterrevolution*, London, Fontana, 1989; William Doyle, *Origins of the French Revolution*, Second ed., Oxford, Oxford University Press, 1980; J. M. Roberts, *The French Revolution*, Oxford, Oxford University Press, 1978; and William Fortescue, *Revolution and Counter-Revolution in France, 1815–1852*, Oxford, Basil Blackwell/Historical Association, 1988.

5 The use of this term is once again taken from the writings of Hedley Bull, *The Anarchical Society*, London, Macmillan, 1977 and David Armstrong, *Revolution and World Order: the Revolutionary State in International Society*, Oxford, Clarendon Press, 1993.

6 Theda Skocpol, *States and Social Revolutions*, Cambridge, Cambridge University Press, 1979.

7 Crane Brinton, The *Anatomy of Revolution*, Englewood Cliffs (NJ), Prentice Hall, 1938.

8 One of the problems with Calvert's *A Study of Revolution*, Oxford, Clarendon Press, 1970, lies in his refusal to take up his own gauntlet on the 'myth' aspect. He confines himself largely to the 'event' and presents us with an interesting work that is almost behaviouralist in its emphasis, a mistake which is nowhere near so evident in his *Revolutions and International Politics*, London, Pinter, 1984.

9 I am aware that in using these dates as a shorthand I will annoy those who have debated the exact date of the revolutions under consideration, but these symbols, like '1989', have the merit of being widely used and understood, even if they are anathema for the historically precise.

10 See for example: Pierre Lepape, 'L'héritage brûlant de la Révolution française', *Le Monde*, 29 January 1988.

11 Simon Schama, *Citizens: A Chronicle of the French Revolution*, London and New York, Viking, 1989 and François Furet, *Penser la Révolution Française*, Paris,

Gallimard, 1978 (translated into English as *Interpreting the French Revolution*, New York, Cambridge University Press, 1981).

12   For one magisterial denunciation of these views see Hugh Trevor-Roper, *From Counter-Reformation to Glorious Revolution*, London, Pimlico, 1993, especially Chapters 11 and 12.

13   Bernard Bailyn, *Ideological Origins of the American Revolution*, Cambridge (Mass.), Harvard University Press, 1967.

14   Edmund Burke (ed. P. Langford), *The Writing and Speeches of Edmund Burke: Volume 1: Party, Parliament and the American Crisis, 1766–1774*, Oxford, Clarendon Press, 1981; John Derry, *English Politics and the American Revolution*, London, J. M. Dent and Sons, 1976.

15   Golo Mann, *The History of Germany since 1789*, London, Pelican, 1974, p. 38.

16   John Rawls, *A Theory of Justice*, Oxford, Oxford University Press, 1971, p. 11.

17   Jean-Jacques Rousseau (ed. Lowell Blair), *The Essential Rousseau* (especially *The Social Contract*), New York, New American Library, 1974.

18   Carol Blum, *Rousseau and the Republic of Virtue*, Ithaca and London, Cornell University Press, 1986.

19   Jacob L. Talmon, *The Origins of Totalitarian Democracy*, London, Secker and Warburg, 1962, pp. 38–9 and *The Myth of the Nation and the Vision of Revolution*, London, Secker and Warburg, 1981.

20   Edmund Burke, *Reflexions on the French Revolution*, London, Penguin, 1970. Paul Johnson points out that many of Rousseau's contemporaries blamed him for the revolution, including Louis XVI and Napoleon. See Johnson, *Intellectuals*, London, Weidenfield and Nicholson, 1988, pp. 2–3.

21   Ronald Paulson, *Representations of Revolution (1789–1820)*, New Haven and London, Yale University Press, 1983, pp. 61–3.

22   Hannah Arendt, *The Origins of Totalitarianism*, New York, Harcourt Brace Jovanovich 1973 and *On Revolution*, Harmondsworth, Penguin, 1973.

23   Especially his *Revolution and the Social System*, Stanford, Hoover Institution, 1964.

24   For a comprehensive summary of Marx's views on the French Revolution see François Furet, *Marx et la révolution française*, Paris, Flammarion, 1986. For his wider views on international politics, see Miklos Molnar, *Marx, Engels et la politique internationale*, Paris, Gallimard, 1975.

25   Edmund Wilson, *To the Finland Station* (first published 1940), London, Fontana, 1960.

26   Furet, *Marx et la révolution française*, pp. 87–9.

27   See Doyle, *Origins of the French Revolution*, for bibliographical details.

28   John Dunn, *Modern Revolutions*, Second ed., Cambridge, Cambridge University Press, 1989, p. 3.

29   See Jacques Godechot, *La contre-révolution*, Paris, Quadrige/Presses Universitaires de France, 1961, for a good summary.

30   For an excellent example of this tendency see Georges Lenotre, *Le jardin de Picpus*, Paris, Librarie Academique Perrin, 1955.

31   Raymond Aron, *Mémoires*, Paris, Julliard, 1983.

32   *Ibid.*, p. 351.

33   Raymond Aron, *Essai sur les libertés*, Paris, Calmann-Levy, 1965.

34   Furet, *Penser la Révolution Française*, p. 173. Roland Barthes used Michelet in ways that Furet would not have liked, but rightly saw him as a national French icon, cf. Barthes, *Michelet*, Oxford, Basil Blackwell, 1987. Furet's view is that the choice has to be between de Tocqueville and Michelet, but that now the latter has found his proper place in the sun, rather than being 'plus cité que lu, et plus lu que compris' (Furet, *Penser la Révolution Française*, p. 31). In attacking Michelet, Furet was being very provocative, but this has paid off since Furet is now rather an icon himself!

35   Furet, *Penser la Révolution Française*, p. 201.

36   Alexis de Tocqueville, *De la Democracie en Amerique*, Paris, Garnier/Flammarion, 2 vols, 1981.

37   François Furet and Mona Ozouf (eds), *The French Revolution and the Creation of Modern Political Culture, Volume 3: The Transformation of Political Culture, 1789–1848*, Oxford, Pergamon, 1989, p. xvii and Mitchell, in same volume, p. 5.

38   Philippe Raynaud, 'Burke et les Allemands', in Furet and Ozouf, *The Transformation of Political Culture*, p. 68. For a discussion of Burke and Paine, see Trevor-Roper, *From Counter-Reformation to Glorious Revolution*, pp. 232–3.

39   Mann sums it by saying '[i]n some sense Germany itself was young, impressionable and receptive in those days. The events of the French Revolution left an indelible mark on German affairs and German thought', Mann, *History of Germany since 1789*, p. 49.

40   H. G. Schenk, *The Mind of the European Romantics*, Oxford, Oxford University Press, p. 3.

41   Karl Popper, *The Open Society and its Enemies*, London, Routledge and Kegan Paul, 1945 and Talmon, *Myth of the Nation*.

42   Geoffrey Best, *The Permanent Revolution: the French Revolution and its Legacy, 1789–1989*, London, Fontana, 1988; James Mayall, '1789 and the liberal theory of international society', *Review of International Studies*, 15, 1989, pp. 297–307.

43   See, for example, R. J. Vincent, *Human Rights and International Relations*, Cambridge, RIIA/Cambridge University Press, 1986 and Andrew Williams, 'Human Rights', in A. J. R. Groom and Paul Taylor, *The International Institutions at Work*, London, Pinter, 1988.

44   James Der Derian, *On Diplomacy*, Oxford, Blackwell, 1987 and Gerrit Gong, *The Standard of 'Civilisation' in International Society*, Oxford, Oxford University Press, 1984.

45   T. C. W. Mowat, *The Diplomacy of Napoleon*, London, Edward Arnold, 1924, p. v.

46   Albert Sorel, *L'Europe et la révolution Française*, 9 vols, Paris, Plon, 1885–1911.

47   François de Callières, *On the Manner of Negotiating with Princes*, Notre Dame (Indiana), Notre Dame University Press, 1963.

48   Mowat, *Diplomacy of Napoleon*, pp. 3–11.

49   Edward A. Whitcomb, *Napoleon's Diplomatic Service*, Durham (NC), Duke University Press, 1979, p. 3.

50   Geoffrey Best, *War and Society in Revolutionary Europe, 1770–1870*, London, Fontana, 1982, pp. 63–81.

51   *Ibid.*, pp. 87–91 and 114–17.

52   One of the interesting asides of Mowat's account of this is the continuing role of Switzerland: 'During this war, as indeed during all modern wars, Switzerland was the place where negotiations and subterranean intrigues of all sorts were concentrated', Mowat, *Diplomacy of Napoleon*, p. 14.

53   Sutherland, *France, 1789–1815*, p. 315.

54   Armstrong, *Revolution and World Order*, p. 91.

55   Schama, *Citizens*, p. 643.

56   Whitcomb, *Napoleon's Diplomatic Service*, pp. 23–4.

57   1797 according to *ibid.*, p. 21.

58   Schama, *Citizens*, p. 16.

59   Whitcomb, *Napoleon's Diplomatic Service*, p. 38.

60   *Ibid.*, p. 148.

61   Crane Brinton, *The Lives Of Talleyrand*, New York, Norton and Co, 1936, p. 285.

62   Bull, *The Anarchical Society*.

63   In Best, *The Permanent Revolution*.

64   In Best, *The Permanent Revolution*, p. 23.

65   Schenk, *Mind of the European Romantics*, pp. 15–18; Hans Kohn, *Nationalism*, New York, D. Van Nostrand and Company Inc., 1955.

66   Mayall, *Nationalism and International Society*, p. 43.

67   See F. H. Hinsley, *Power and the Pursuit of Peace*, Cambridge, Cambridge University Press, 1963, for an excellent description of these in the nineteenth century.

68   Mayall, *Nationalism and International Society*, p. 26.

69   Charles Tilly (ed.), *The Formation of National States in Western Europe*, Princeton, Princeton University Press, 1975.

70   Armstrong, *Revolution and World Order*, p. 80.

71   Henry Kissinger, *A World Restored*, New York, Grosset and Dunlap, 1964.

72   Richard Langhorne, *The Collapse of the Concert of Europe: International Politics, 1890–1914*, London, Macmillan, 1981.

73   See, for example, Furet, *Penser la Révolution Française*, and the special edition of *Espaces Temps*: 'Concevoir la révolution. 89, 68, confrontations', 38/39, 3e trimestre 1988.

The Russian Revolution

> People who boast that they *made* a revolution always see the day after that they had no idea what they were doing, that the revolution *made* does not in the least resemble the one they would have liked to make . . .
>
>   Engels to Vera Zasulich, 1885

> It is the invention of the religious order, as the determining fact in the life of a great nation, which is the magnet which attracts me to Russia. Practically that religion is Comteanism, the religion of Humanity . . . How can we combine religious action with freedom of thought? That is the question which we want to solve by studying Russia.[1]

Introduction

If the French Revolution can continue to arouse passions, then it is not surprising that the Russian Revolution does likewise. Few events have caused such disruption to the international system and such heated debate as those of 1917.[2] Although it has now been formally declared 'over' in that the Union of Soviet Republics (USSR) that it spawned (officially in 1923) was dissolved in December 1991, its reverberations will be with us for some time to come. This chapter will attempt the almost impossible task of defining what these shock waves have been. In particular, as in the previous chapter, I will concentrate on the impact on thinking about international relations (IR), on the practice of statecraft by both the USSR and its opponents, and on the international system as a whole. In the interests of coherence the time scale will concentrate on the period when the Soviet Union was unequivocally a 'revolutionary' state, that is to say from October 1917 until the abolition of the Comintern in 1943.[3]

An initial caveat when talking about the impact of the Soviet revolution on international relations has to be that Soviet claims that they had

developed an elaborate theory of international relations has been widely
disputed by (Western) scholars of Soviet theory and practice. As Margot
Light has pointed out, although Soviet thinkers and practitioners of
foreign policy constantly claim that their approach was 'scientific', as
opposed to the West's atheoretical approach, many Western commentators have disputed this claim.[4] The alternative explanation is that Soviet
behaviour in international relations was solely, or mainly, based on the
pursuit of power. Winston Churchill famously summed up this view of
Soviet motivation in October 1939 as:

> I cannot forecast to you the action of Russia. It is a riddle wrapped in a
> mystery inside an enigma: but perhaps there is a key. That key is Russian
> national interest.[5]

The thorny problem of how one can properly disentangle the element of national interest, common to all state behaviour, and that of ideological motivation in foreign policy, a problem common to the study of
all revolutionary states, is still far from resolved. Walter Carlsnaes comes
closest in saying that ideology is used in different ways to explain foreign
policy behaviour, 'as a set of ideas which reflects the culture of a society',
under which nationalism would constitute ideology; or to denote how
foreign policy is analysed, for example to espouse a particular kind of
'order'; or at a 'causal-explanatory level', as an 'input'. The Soviet Union
would score heavily on this last explanation, and has indeed been widely
blamed for it by commentators from Woodrow Wilson to Henry Kissinger.[6]
Perhaps the most illuminating aspect of this division is to show that those
who most widely criticised the Soviet Union (or other revolutionary
states) for their 'ideology' themselves had very strong belief (or 'ideological') systems that directed their activities as foreign policy commentators
and activists. Michael Hunt has even suggested that we can use a Gramscian
notion of cultural 'hegemony', and examine the political culture of the
American ruling class to explain why so many 'usually white males' have
made a distinctive impact on American relations with many revolutionary
states.[7] However, this chapter will continue to use the expression in the
third, causal-explanatory sense to avoid the (albeit entertaining) generalisations into which Hunt has a habit of falling.

The impact of the revolution on the theory of international relations

Marxism-Leninism became the basis for the ideology not only of the new
Soviet state, but also of a host of revolutionary movements until the

present day, successful or not. Divisions between Marxists have in themselves led to many internecine struggles and often the losing of revolutionary wars, with the Spanish Civil War of 1936–39 being one arguably seminal case, as was shown by George Orwell.[8] Marxism also has a profoundly practical agenda, and hence has appealed to those who wish an 'off-the-shelf' belief and action system. The Soviet Union, as the first state to adopt such a creed as its justification and blueprint, has demonstrated this and has often demanded that its foundationalist analysis takes precedence over newer versions, which have often been denounced as 'revisionist' or worse. Marxism, as interpreted through the prism of Soviet Communism, has come to represent one of the most enduring forms of 'consequentialist' cosmopolitan thought.[9]

As has been pointed out, Marx and Engels devoted little time or space to the relations between states, and mainly concentrated on the wider questions of the relations of the means of production and those who exercised them.[10] Miklos Molnar points out that Marx himself actually often evinced a very German sensibility in his likes and dislikes, referring to Slavs in most disparaging terms and considering Russia as lost to civilisation, and therefore to revolution, for the foreseeable future, a position he only started to moderate in the late 1850s under the influence of Vera Zasulich and Tchernyshevsky.[11] For Marx, as indeed for many political commentators before and since, Russia was *Asia*, predating those twentieth-century commentators, of the right, left and centre, who felt that no understanding of Russia was possible, given its asiatic or even 'mongol' characteristics. However, Marx was also an *internationalist*, indeed a cosmopolitan thinker, convinced of the integrating power of economic forces. He was also a polemical journalist and historian of some genius, one who was to prove the inspiration for several generations of international theorists, many of whom drew their own, and different, conclusions from reading him. Moreover, as Robert Tucker observed some years ago, Marx's views on distributive justice, modernisation, the 'inevitability' of the success of revolutionary struggle and the consequent 'end of history' have formed the basis of nearly all revolutionary creeds of the twentieth century. Allen Lynch summarised Marx's importance for us succinctly with 'Marx . . . was interested in the world as a whole rather than in international relations as such'.[12]

Lenin's (and of course that of other thinkers like Bukharin and Luxemburg) main contribution was to give practical application to Marx's ideas and to apply them to a particularly Russian context. Lenin's genius has been widely recognised as a pragmatic, even opportunistic, adaptation of a diffuse creed to a situation unforseen by Marx, a revolution in what can only be described as an 'underdeveloped' country, much like most, if not all, other countries of the twentieth-century revolutionary generation. The question that continued, until 1991, to hover over Leninist thought was whether the emphasis of Soviet Russia could always be one of 'Socialism in One Country' as Stalin put it, or whether the international aspirations of the Soviet Union must dominate. This ideological tension, and the costs that it inevitably imposed, must be seen as one of the main inherent flaws in Soviet policy. It was difficult to drop the aspiration to World Revolution without destroying the internal legitimacy of the Soviet state, but impossible to pursue this 'Two Camps' thesis while asking for economic help from the West.[13]

Lenin first developed a theory of a socialist state and, perhaps even more crucially, of a socialist party.[14] Marx's belief that a revolution would simply 'emerge' from the working class was replaced by the idea of a disciplined 'vanguard party', one that would lead the working class to victory, with little place for 'bourgeois individualism', and a great dislike of rival socialist ideas like syndicalism and 'labourism' (both strong features of socialist movements before and after 1917). Such 'revisionism' would not be tolerated, and the party would become the state. Lenin simultaneously also gave socialism a theory of revolution itself, because revolution was deemed impossible without the party. Lenin, it has been observed, took inspiration from other thinkers, including many who would later be assassinated or executed as 'revisionists', like Leon Trotsky and the Mensheviks, in their belief in the long-term nature of revolution, even its 'permanent' nature.[15] The onset of the war in 1914, and particularly the demise of Czarism in February 1917 none the less persuaded Lenin that socialism could be accelerated by an organised group like the Bolsheviks. His final distinctive contribution to revolutionary thought was to point to the importance of imperialism for capitalist development, although this is a claim that can arguably be given to Bukharin[16] or Luxemburg, some of whose work predated Lenin's *Imperialism: The Highest Stage of Capitalism* of 1916.[17] The link backwards to Marx lay in the focus on economic factors, the updated analysis taking account of the huge changes in international relations since Marx's death, and the stress being laid on the necessary link between capitalism, imperialism (its 'highest stage') and war. His was a 'system-dominant' analysis, one that has been developed by many Marxist and more broadly 'structuralist' thinkers since.[18]

Perhaps the most lasting legacy of Leninist thinking lay in his formulation of the Soviet relationship with the hostile capitalist world, a world with which he thought ultimate war was 'inevitable'.[19] This formulation was summed up in the Soviet doctrines of 'peaceful coexistence' (PC) (sometimes the word 'cohabitation' was used by Lenin himself) and 'proletarian internationalism' (PI). These contrasting and yet complementary expressions were used throughout the existence of the Soviet Union to explain how it was possible for the Soviet Union to continue in an international system characterised by a state of war without that war actually breaking out. Light points out that although PC was more or less constantly used throughout the period 1917–88, and that it was indeed the *policy* of the Soviet Union, 'whether that policy [was] always based on a *theory* of amity between socialists and capitalists is arguable'.[20] It was also a periodised policy, in that it was used out of necessity when the Soviet Union was weak (as between 1918 and 1921) or seen as desirable when capitalist knowhow was needed to rebuild the country (between 1921 and 1933 or so), or even as a matter of survival, as between 1941 and 1945. On the other hand it tended to wane as a principle for action when the Soviet Union felt at its most expansionist or aggressive, as between 1945 and 1953, or during the periodic invasions of its satellites, in 1956, 1968 or during the 'Second Cold War' (1979–84).[21] When such accommodation was not deemed so tactically or strategically necessary the other principle of PI would be stressed, one which vaunted the revolutionary leadership (or 'vanguard' role) of the Soviet Union or its support for communist parties in Western or developing countries.

During the inter-war period the two doctrines were often stressed *simultaneously* by Soviet or Soviet-dominated bodies (like the Comintern, see below), often to the confusion of the capitalist world or even of Soviet officials themselves. This was one of the factors which led to the deadly farces of the 'party line', which seemed to shift with amazing whimsy and which led to some memorable literary analogies, such as Orwell's *Animal Farm*.[22] It also led to periodic disillusion by non-Soviet communists, who took some while to understand that the priorities of Soviet 'socialism' moved mainly with the needs of Soviet internal and foreign policy, defined by the often paranoid or even senile incumbents of the Kremlin, not with the wider needs of the international proletariat.[23]

So while it may be doubted that Bolshevism, or Leninism, really gave birth to an original body of political *thought* it certainly gave rise to a body of original political *practice*. This tradition was carried on by other Marxist thinkers, such as Mao Tse Tung, Ernesto 'Che' Guevara and many others. Perhaps the most original feature of the Soviet system of thought is what it covered up with euphemism and downright lies. The Soviet penal system, the collectivisation process, the forced occupation of large parts of Europe, were all defended as historically 'necessary' and had their supporters in many countries (such as Britain, France and the United States) who would have fought to the last bullet to prevent such enormities happening in their own societies. This phenomenon, of non-communists 'fellow travelling' was an important part of Soviet theory and practice of international relations, one that has had its imitators in many other revolutionary states. Trotsky actually coined the term as one of derision, and it is hard to disagree totally with him. The 'targets' were always left-leaning, but usually liberal thinkers, whose preoccupation with the problems of their own societies (as during the 1930s) was used to encourage them to see the Soviet Union as a mythical land of plenty and opportunity.[24]

Many went to ludicrous lengths to defend the indefensible, some went so far as to emigrate to the Soviet Union, many acted as a kind of 'fifth column' for the USSR within the 'establishments' of the West. Some of the most famous intellectuals of the twentieth century figure among this group – George Bernard Shaw, Sidney and Beatrice Webb, Jean-Paul Sartre, Arthur Koestler, etc. Some who saw their error in time, as did Koestler or André Gide,[25] were vilified by many of their contemporaries. This blindness by intellectuals has led to some damage to the whole concept of an intellectual 'elite', especially in Britain and the USA. One explanation is of course that the period of greatest 'fellow travelling' was during the rise of Hitler, when Stalin's Russia was the only major power openly condemning his actions. Another is a more subtle one, a cultural reaction to the horrors of the trenches and the feeling that Soviet Russia represented a 'New Civilisation', expressed eloquently by Beatrice Webb at the beginning of this chapter and in over a thousand pages by her in 1935 as *Soviet Communism: A New Civilisation?* (the interrogative was dropped for the second edition).[26] David Caute called this phenomenon a 'Postscript to the Enlightenment'. It was certainly a warping of the Enlightenment project, and perhaps can be seen as a major contribution to the creeping disdain in which all rational and humanistic thought has come to be held by some, but by no means all, 'critical' and 'post-modern' thinkers.

Diplomacy and statecraft

When examining the credentials of a revolutionary state one of the main criteria that can be used is its declarations about, and practice of, diplomacy, as was discussed in the previous chapter. But whereas the early French revolutionaries developed some of the trappings of revolutionary diplomacy, the Bolsheviks turned this into a fine art form. The primary evidence of this is often quoted: Stalin's 'a diplomat's words must have no relation to actions – otherwise what kind of diplomacy is it? . . . Good words are a concealment of bad deeds. Sincere diplomacy is no more possible than dry water or iron wood';[27] or Lenin's '[p]romises are like pie crusts – made to be broken'.[28] The cynic might observe that this is not too different from the oft-quoted description that the diplomat is an 'honest man sent abroad to lie for his country'.[29] But it must be said that the level of organised deceit to which Soviet diplomacy sank went far beyond that of 'normal' diplomacy.

The first reason for this lies in the fact that the Soviet state, for most of its existence, considered itself to be in a state of war with the capitalist world. There was good reason for this belief initially. The Western powers – France, Britain, Japan and the USA – all erstwhile 'allies' until 1917, intervened militarily on the side of the Whites in the Civil War of 1919–21.[30] Their contribution did little but delay the final triumph of Bolshevism, as troop levels never went very high and the mandate of the forces involved was very limited, but their presence was skilfully exploited by the Bolsheviks and turned into a propaganda triumph. Many of the subsequent harsh actions of the 'War Communism' period (1919–21) and of the Collectivisation and Industrialisation period (especially during 1928–32, and described in Soviet propaganda as the 'Class against Class' period), were justified by a series of 'war scares', when the population was urged to take special care to work hard and to root out (generally imaginary) 'saboteurs' in order to fend off a supposedly imminent repetition of 1918–21. It is significant that nearly all revolutionary states (including France) have found it useful to have such a bogy man to frighten the population into acquiescence during difficult periods of the revolution.

However, the main external 'support group' for Soviet Russia in its early years had the Communist International, or Comintern, as its umbrella.[31] For a second reason for the deceitful nature of Soviet diplomacy lies in its split nature, at least for the first ten years of its existence. The setting up of the Comintern in 1919, a coalition of communist parties which was supposed to act as a kind of world government when the revolution had broken out in Germany, Britain and elsewhere, conducted its own 'neo-diplomacy' for much of the period 1919–35, often to the great irritation of the official Soviet diplomatic service, the People's Commissariat for Foreign Affairs (NKID or Narkomindel). This body, founded in October 1917, and first of all headed by Trotsky, was in some contradiction to the stated aims of the new regime, one which in effect denied the morality of, or even the need for, diplomacy, which was seen as a main reason for the outbreak of the Great War: hence Trotsky's dismissive comment 'I shall issue a few revolutionary proclamations and then close up shop.' Diplomacy would not be the centre of gravity of the new regime.[32] It went on to become much more than that, and quite quickly, since in 1918 Trotsky himself was forced to use a kind of diplomacy to discuss the end of the fighting on the Eastern front with the Germans, a discussion which led to the Treaty of Brest Litovsk. It also attracted some of the best minds among the Bolsheviks, not least of them Trotsky and his successors, Chicherin and Maxim Litvinov, all men with considerable experience of foreign countries. Many of them were to prove vulnerable to Stalin's purges of the 1930s and 1940s, as men who had been 'contaminated' by foreign ideas. But throughout the inter-war period, the Comintern and the NKID existed in uneasy collaboration as the conventional and neo-diplomatic arms of Soviet foreign policy, indeed as a key arm of Soviet *domestic* policy. This can be seen by a simple (and grossly simplified) graphic illustration of the main periods of Comintern and NKID activity and the main policies being pursued within the Soviet Union (see the table below).

Dates	Comintern	NKID	Soviet domestic policy
1919–21	Civil war	Brest Litovsk	'War Communism'
1921–27	'United Front'	Genoa	'New Economic Policy'
1928–32	'Class v. Class'		'Socialism in One Country' (SIOC)
1932–39	'Popular Front'	Collective security/LON*	SIOC cont./purges

* League of Nations

As all the above will have made clear, it is totally impossible to say where 'foreign policy' ends and a theory of justification for the entire Soviet state structure begins. As with the French Revolution, revolutionary diplomacy was in its essence a neo–diplomacy, appealing over the heads of governments to their peoples. The same questions can therefore be asked, especially as to whether the revolution was ever 'socialised' into international society. The implication of Light's PI and PC explanation above is that this never happened fully. PI, in its last formulation as the

'Brezhnev Doctrine' was not formally renounced until 1988, by Gorbachev, and, significantly, in a speech in Castro's Havana. This was the significance of the 'New Political Thinking' (NPT),[33] although of course NPT never really had a chance to show its possibilities as a modified revolutionary foreign policy doctrine, as its introduction coincided with the end of the Soviet system itself. It might also be argued that the NPT was in effect the culmination of a progressive jettisoning of PI that had started with Stalin's death.

For the reality of revolutionary foreign policy rhetoric and practice it might be argued that we have to go back to the Treaty of Brest Litovsk of 1918, the Genoa Conference of 1922 and other major points of confrontation between Soviet Russia and the West.[34] It is helpful here to bring out not only the formal positions taken by both 'sides', but also the more 'cultural' reactions that they inspired. The Soviet-German discussions that led to the Treaty of Brest Litovsk were the most celebrated episode of revolutionary diplomacy, during the Soviet republic's weakest hour, with German armies occupying one-third of the former Russian Imperial Empire. While the Germans grew ever more impatient, Bukharin and others in the Politburo urged a revolutionary war against Germany, in line with the belief that revolution would then spread like a bush fire across Europe. Lenin and the wiser head of Trotsky prevailed. Lenin's issuing of the '21 theses' that became the basis of entry into the Comintern for foreign communist parties specifically warned against revolutionary 'adventurism' that might threaten the new Soviet state and prepared the ground for a humiliating separate peace with Germany. With what Debo calls 'casuistry worthy of a seventeenth century Jesuit', Lenin had placed the 'national interest' of the Soviet Union above the imperatives of international revolution.[35] While this can hardly be seen as a 'socialisation' of the revolution, it indicated a trend towards 'national' Bolshevism and showed that 'peaceful coexistence' would always triumph over 'proletarian internationalism' when this was in the best interests of Soviet Russia.

This trend was confirmed as the 1920s advanced and Soviet Russia slowly started to talk to capitalist states.[36] The recent renewal of interest in the Genoa Conference of 1922 has been due mainly to a reappraisal of the entire post-First World War settlement and the various attempts to revise the Treaty of Versailles, as well as a renewed interest in the various possible lost opportunities for East-West *détente* since 1917.[37] Genoa was essentially an initiative by British Prime Minister Lloyd George to revitalise the European economy, that had sunk into a deep recession. The political results of this recession were being increasingly exploited by extremists of the Left and Right. The problem was that in order to counter this trend Lloyd George (rightly) believed that he would have to fully reintegrate Germany and Soviet Russia into international society, an idea that was anathema to the French, and, in the case of Russia, to the Americans. Genoa and its follow-up conference at The Hague, also in 1922, failed to attain Lloyd George's principal objective.

Previous to Genoa, in the first agreement signed with a capitalist state, Lenin had sent his *Polpred* (chief diplomatic representative[38]) Leonid Krassin, to London in March 1921 to sign a trade agreement with Britain. This and the 'New Economic Policy' in Russia, convinced Lloyd George that Russia was becoming normalised (or 'socialised', to use Armstrong's expression), and he explicitly often referred to the French Revolution as a useful parallel).[39] The other rationale he often used, one used by all Western commentators on revolutions, was that it was necessary to encourage the 'moderates' in Russia (Lenin and Krassin in particular) and discourage the 'extremists', with Trotsky and Litvinov as chief villains, a logic that had the major failure of wanting to see divisions where they do not necessarily exist. The Bolshevik emissaries, led by People's Commissar Chicherin, did have some hopes of economic success at Genoa, but mainly used the opportunity to voice their own propaganda and, most significantly, to sign a secret treaty with Germany at nearby Rapallo. It was clear almost from the outset that Lloyd George could not deliver any form of real plan for Europe in the face of American and French intransigence, although Rapallo sealed this and led everyone to blame the Russians for failure.

The Russians compounded their role as useful scapegoats by citing the precedent of 1789 for not wishing to pay their (pre-war and wartime Allied) debts.[40] But they in fact mainly offended by their style rather than by their substance and were held in almost open contempt by their Western counterparts. In a revealing letter, the FO representative at Genoa, Gregory, wrote:

> You never saw anything like the appearance of the Bolsheviks. There were two who came to the Plenary session, who looked for all the world as if they had stepped out of a Drury Lane Pantomime – real melodramatic cut-throats from the 'Babes in the Wood' – ! Chicherin looks the degenerate he is, and of course except for himself and Krassin I fancy they are all Jews. It is very unpleasant to reflect that the main interest here is centred on the future relations between them and ourselves.[41]

This tone of visceral rejection, often linked to anti-semitic comment[42] can also be found strongly represented in the Foreign Ministries of other

Western states at the time, particularly in Washington and Paris.[43] What was attempted by the Western states at Genoa was to bind the Russians to a 'code of conduct', often referred to as the 'Cannes Conditions', conditions which Soviet Russia could not fulfil then or, arguably, ever. They were (in abbreviated form) that: nations could not dictate to others what their form of government should be; foreign investors must have their property rights respected; all debts incurred by pre-revolutionary regimes must be respected; and adequate means of exchange must be provided; all nations must refrain from subversive propaganda; and all nations must refrain from aggressive action against their neighbours.[44] Soviet Russia breached all of these conditions at some time or other during the seventy-four years of its existence. Carole Fink's summary of the reason for failure at Genoa is a good one: '[b]elow the surface was the seemingly insuperable practical difficulty of accommodating national security and prosperity with international economic cooperation and peace.'[45] This could be used as a motif for subsequent dealings between the West and Soviet Russia right up to 1991.

But Genoa nevertheless showed that Russia could be tempted to the conference table by the use of economic incentives. Lloyd George held out the promise of glittering prizes for countries that would agree to the Cannes Conditions. Keynes, who was the *Manchester Guardian*'s correspondent at Genoa, agreed with Lloyd George that Russia might have been enticed back into international society by the promise of export credits and loans, and that this in time would have encouraged economic and even political convergence between East and West.[46] This was a logic pursued until the early 1930s, and occasionally after, by a series of political figures and parties in Britain, France and the United States, to be finally snuffed out by the economic nationalism and disintegration of the West itself in the 1930s. It was the economic side of the Cannes Conditions, especially those on the repayment of debt, that finally stymied the increased trade that would have really encouraged convergence, and it is arguable that a more intelligent interpretation of these clauses by the West might have saved a great deal of grief over the long run.[47] Economic statecraft of this kind is still being used against revolutionary states to encourage convergence, as the example of China, Vietnam and other states can be said to prove.[48]

The impact on the international system

Among the other horrors and upheavals of the period 1914–19, the Russian Revolution can be seen as the one that had the most lasting effect. By the end of the First World War attention understandably focused on the unresolved problem of what to do about a defeated Germany, and the prevention of renewed conflict. The botched compromise of Versailles, much criticised at the time and since, often unfairly, left Europe with no one key state in a position to impose or even to make heard a clear vision of the future. Britain and France fell out almost immediately over the Treaty, the United States withdrew into a kind of isolation and Germany only partially resumed its rightful place before being hijacked by the Nazis and plunging the world into renewed conflict. It is not surprising that it has now become a commonplace to talk of the 'European Civil War' or the 'Thirty Years War' of 1914–45, and to see the inter-war period as a mere respite.

The role of Soviet Russia in this maelstrom was never far from disruptive. The first immediate effect of the Bolshevik withdrawal of Russia from the war in 1917 was to leave the Allied alliance system in tatters and, arguably, to remove all semblance of a sensible foreign policy for France until the establishment of NATO in 1949. Given the disagreements between Britain and France, the only major democratic powers in the League of Nations (LON, 1919–40), Russia and the United States' absence from the League for most of the period, and the rising tide of fascism in Italy, Japan and Germany, there was no 'Centre' that could hold, to paraphrase T. S. Eliot's *The Waste Land*. The chances for mischief and disruption in such a climate were legion, and it is perhaps only surprising that Soviet Russia did not take more advantage of them than it did.

Unfortunately, one of the major contributions of the Soviet Union to the practice of international relations has been that of domestic and international terror. If the Bolsheviks can clearly not be blamed for introducing the notion of revolutionary violence, where, as Lenin put it, 'you cannot make an omelette without breaking a few eggs', they can none the less take the credit for both developing and enormously widening the use of such terror. Examples of Soviet crimes against their own population took some while to be fully realised by both Soviet citizens and the outside world, William Chamberlin's (1934) account of the horrors of collectivisation being an early and largely isolated case of such negative publicity, although countered by plenty of the opposite kind of 'good' (and mainly ridiculous) publicity, until at least the early 1940s.[49] We now have extremely detailed and shocking accounts of the crimes committed by Stalin's henchmen against the peasantry and many other sections of the population.[50] But during the formative period of the Soviet Union's interaction with other states, such accounts were rare, and rarer still those who believed them.[51] The only valid excuses for this lie in the destruction wrought on Russia by the war and the Civil War (1919–21) that followed it, and the insane economic and political policies followed in the late 1920s and 1930s by Stalin. If half the energy put into annihilating his own people had been concentrated on defeating capitalism then Soviet Russia would by now be being quoted as the most successful revolution of all time, not as a failed and bloody experiment. The epithet 'Stalinist' is consequently used to describe any rigid and malevolent form of socialism, naturally often inaccurately given the horrors of the original.[52]

In the post-Second World War period the nature of Soviet Russia had changed. No longer a revolutionary underdog, Stalin had transformed it into a 'superpower'. During the war itself there was a temporary accommodation of the West with Soviet Russia in the 'Grand Alliance', one which US President Roosevelt believed could be translated into peacetime alliance through the mechanism of the United Nations (UN). In fact a 'Cold War'[53] emerged that largely paralysed any hopes of 'collective security' through the UN. The Western response changed accordingly – with the policy of 'containment', first suggested by the pre-war American State Department critic of Soviet Russia, George Kennan, in his 'The Sources of Soviet Conduct', printed in *Foreign Affairs* in the summer of 1947.[54] Although he later claimed that his policy had been abused by the setting up of the North Atlantic Treaty Organisation (NATO) and several other regional treaty mechanisms that in fact brought into being the old Russian nightmare of 'encirclement', nearly all Western states (now widened to include all Western 'allies', most notably Japan) were enlisted in the fight against an international communist conspiracy. This was complemented by a not altogether successful economic containment that tried to stop the export of Western technology to the Soviet Union susceptible of 'dual' (i.e. military and non-military) use.[55]

It can be doubted that such a international communist conspiracy ever existed, given the sharp differences of ideological emphasis between nearly all communist states (see the chapter on China in this volume for some illustration of this), but the two 'military industrial complexes' of the NATO allies and their counterparts in the Soviet-led Warsaw Pact developed huge arsenals of nuclear and conventional arms in readiness for a war in Europe that never happened. Armstrong is right to suggest that this process unwittingly created a new impetus for the widening of international society to include all those states that agreed with the NATO view of the Soviet threat, thus including Japan and even, from 1970, (Communist) China.[56] This has of course been described at great length

elsewhere; its relevance for us lies in the shadow it shed over nearly all
liberation movements world-wide until the end of the 1980s and all the
subsequent case studies in this book.

The Soviet Union's attitude to what came to be called the 'Third
World' is therefore of great interest to us. Arguably, all American foreign
policy in much of this 'world' was in response to perceived Soviet expansionism. But might this, undoubtedly noisy, and often violent, activity
have been a cover for Soviet national interest, rather than evidence of
Soviet proletarian internationalism, i.e. the spread of an international
revolution? The problem for the analyst of both the motivations of Soviet and its allies' foreign policies was that the debate was usually seen
entirely through the prism of American concerns. For example, a review
of Cuban foreign policy in the late 1980s concluded that '[d]ebate has
become passionate only over the question of whether Washington should
become more hard-line or more accommodating with respect to relations
with Havana'. Other considerations, such as the role of Castro's personality, ideology, the specifics of Cuban nationalism, domestic sources of
foreign policy or Soviet influence, were lacking.[57] If this was the case with
Cuba, probably the most important of Soviet allies outside Europe, how
much more true was it of lesser friends in the Third World? Evidence
that the Soviet Union manipulated, or at least benefited from, Cuban
foreign policy of course exists (as in Angola), but there were large areas
of disagreement and the Soviet line was often not followed by Havana. In
the other area of great concern to the United States, the 'surrogate thesis'
is even less strongly supported: Nicola Miller commented that even the
Latin American Left had to accept that 'the Soviet Union [was] not going
to do what it did for Cuba for any other Latin American country'.[58] In the
inter-war period, 'help' given by the Comintern had proved as nearly
fatal for Latin American Marxism as it had for that of Spain and Germany in the 1930s. On a broader 'Third World' front, even a 'right-wing'
analysis of the same period came to the conclusion that although up to the
late Brezhnev period the need for ideological influence was seen as vital
by Moscow, control over 'Marxist-Leninist Vanguard Parties' was seen
as important mainly because they were 'regarded as a useful tool for
furthering the state interests of the USSR, which are dictated in large
measure by realpolitik concerns.'[59]

There are two imponderables that must remain: firstly, it remains to be
seen whether the logic of the international relations of revolutionary
states will be totally transformed by the removal of the wider umbrella of
Western-Soviet conflict that dominated the international system from

1947 to 1990, and arguably since 1917. Secondly, we might ask what will happen to the coherence of (the Western-based) international society in the absence of the Soviet threat. Will the institutions that have cemented this, such as NATO and the European Community (EC), lose their *raison d'être* or will they be transformed into something broader that will provide a new impetus for the ideals of 1688, 1776 and 1789, based on such resounding slogans as 'better governance', or are we headed for a situation that has been described as 'back to the future', where uncertainty will be the prevailing *leitmotif*?[60]

Notes

1 Ian Cummins, *Marx, Engels and National Movements*, London, Croom Helm, 1980, p. 162 and Beatrice Webb to her *Diary*, 4 January 1932, quoted in Andrew Williams, *Labour and Russia: The Attitude of the Labour Party to the Soviet Union, 1924–1934*, Manchester, Manchester University Press, 1989, p. 187.

2 Probably the most celebrated history of the Bolshevik Revolution is: Edward Hallett Carr, *A History of Soviet Russia*, 14 vols, London, Macmillan, 1950–1982. See also Richard Pipes, *The Russian Revolution, 1899–1919*, London, Collins Harvill, 1990.

3 Writing on the Russian Revolution has run into many thousands, perhaps millions, of volumes. There are several bibliographical volumes that a reader can refer to for the most significant scholarly contributions, such as Thomas T. Hammond, *Soviet Foreign Relations and World Communism: A Selected Bibliography*, Princeton, Princeton University Press, 1965. Here the concentration will inevitably be on the English-language contribution to this literature. The best collections of documents on Soviet foreign policy are: [in Russian] Andrei A. Gromyko (ed.), *Dokumenty vneshnei politiki SSSR*, Moscow, Progress Publishers, 21 volumes, 1957–77; [in English] Jane Degras (ed.), *Documents on Soviet Foreign Policy*, London, RIIA, 1953 and Xenia Eudin and Harold Fisher, *Soviet Russia and the West, 1920–1927*, Stanford, Stanford University Press, 1957. More documents are being released daily, so an up-to-date list is impossible, but few have as yet been translated into English.

4 Margot Light, *The Soviet Theory of International Relations*, Brighton, Harvester/Wheatsheaf, 1988.

5 He used, as did most other commentators until 1945, the expression 'Russia' to mean the Soviet Union. Churchill quoted in Robin Edmonds, *The Big Three: Churchill, Roosevelt and Stalin in Peace and War*, London, Penguin, 1991, p. 160.

6 Walter Carlsnaes, *Ideology and Foreign Policy*, London, Macmillan, 1986.

7 The main interest of Hunt's book lies in his analysis of US reactions to Latin America and China, and he is at his weakest on American attitudes to the Soviet Union; Michael H. Hunt, *Ideology and U.S. Foreign Policy*, New Haven, Yale University Press, 1987, p. 12.

8   George Orwell, *Homage to Catalonia*, London, Penguin, 1962 (first published 1938).

9   Chris Brown, *International Relations Theory: New Normative Approaches*, Hemel Hempstead, Harvester/Wheatsheaf, 1992, p. 46.

10   Miklos Molnar, *Marx, Engels et la politique internationale*, Paris, Gallimard, 1975; Vendulka Kubalkova and Albert Cruickshank, *Marxism and International Relations*, Oxford, Oxford University Press, 1985 and Allen Lynch, *The Soviet Study of International Relations*, Cambridge, Cambridge University Press, 1987.

11   Molnar, *Marx, Engels et la politique internationale*, p. 174.

12   Robert Turker, *The Marxian Revolutionary Idea: Marxist Thought and its Influence on Radical Movements*, London, George Allen and Unwin, 1970; Lynch, *The Soviet Study of International Relations*, p. 13.

13   George W. Breslauer, 'Ideology and Learning in Soviet Third World Foreign Policy', *World Politics*, XXXIX, 3, pp. 429–48, esp. p. 446; R. Judson Mitchell, *Ideology of a Superpower: Contemporary Soviet Doctrine on International Relations*, Stanford, Hoover Institution Press, 1982.

14   See especially Vladimir I. Lenin, *The State and Revolution*, Moscow, Progress Publishers, 1949 (first published 1917).

15   Trotsky's *History of the Bolshevik Revolution*, 3 Volumes, London, Shere, 1967 is probably the best account, if inevitably biased, of the revolution written by an insider.

16   Stephen Cohen, *Bukharin and the Bolshevik Revolution*, Oxford, Oxford University Press, 1980 (first published 1973).

17   V. I. Lenin, *Imperialism: The Highest Stage of Capitalism*, Moscow, Progress Publishers, 1975 (first published 1917).

18   For a good overview of a modern derivative, 'dependency' theory, see the chapter by Chris Brown in Margot Light and A. J. R. Groom (eds), *International Relations: A Handbook of Current Theory*, London, Frances Pinter, 1985.

19   P. H. Vigor, *The Soviet View of War, Peace and Neutrality*, London, Routledge & Kegan Paul, 1975.

20   Light, *Soviet Theory of International Relations*, p. 25.

21   For a discussion of this controversial view of the Cold War, see Fred Halliday, *The Making of the Second Cold War*, London, Verso, 1983.

22   George Orwell, *Animal Farm*, London, Penguin, 1984 (first published 1945).

23   For a wonderful recent fictional account of the confusion felt by Soviet agents at the changes of line imposed during the 1930s see Alan Furst, *Dark Star*, London, Grafton, 1991.

24   David Caute, *The Fellow Travellers: A Postscript to the Enlightenment*, London, Weidenfield and Nicholson, 1973.

25   Arthur Koestler, *Darkness at Noon*, London, Secker and Warburg, 1948; André Gide, *Return From the USSR*, Paris, Gallimard, 1936. See also Sylvia R. Margulies, *The Pilgrimage to Russia: The Soviet Union and the Treatment of Foreigners*, Madison, University of Wisconsin Press, 1968, for a description of the 'guided tours' given to foreign intellectuals in Russia.

26   For details see Williams, *Labour and Russia*, ch. 13.

27   Quoted by Vernon Aspaturian, *Process and Power in Soviet Foreign Policy*, Boston, Little Brown, 1963.

28   Quoted by Robert Jervis, *The Logic of Images in International Relations*, Princeton, Princeton University Press/London and New York, Columbia University Press, 1970.

29   Harold Nicolson, *Diplomacy*, London, Oxford University Press, 1939.

30   The best accounts are to be found in Michael Kettle, *The Road to Intervention, March–November 1918*, London, Routledge, 1988; and Richard H. Ullman, *Intervention and the War; Britain and the Russian Civil War; The Anglo-Soviet Accord*, 3 volumes, Princeton, Princeton University Press, 1961, 1968 and 1971.

31   Julius Braunthal, *History of the International*, London, Nelson, 1967; Anthony Cave Brown and Charles B. Macdonald, *On a Field Of Red: The Communist International and the Coming of the Second World War*, New York, G. P. Putnam, 1918; E. H. Carr, *The Twilight of the Comintern, 1930–1935*, London, Macmillan, 1982.

32   Teddy Uldricks, *Diplomacy and Ideology: The Origins of Soviet Foreign Relations*, London, Sage Publications, 1979, p. 17.

33   Mikhael Gorbachev, *Perestroika: New Thinking for Our Country and the World*, London, Collins, 1987; Richard Sakwa, *Gorbachev and His Reforms, 1985–1990*, London, Philip Allan, 1990.

34   Or even before, given the unoffical diplomacy between Colonel House and Trotsky during 1918; see Arno J. Mayer, *Political Origins of the New Diplomacy, 1917–1918*, New Haven, Yale University Press, 1959.

35   Richard Debo, *Revolution and Survival: The Foreign Policy of Soviet Russia, 1917–18*, Toronto and Liverpool, Toronto University Press/Liverpool University Press, 1979, p. 76.

36   For an overview of this period see George Kennan, *Russia and the West Under Lenin and Stalin*, Boston, Mentor, 1960 and Sally Marks, *The Illusion of Peace: International Relations in Europe, 1918–1933*, London, Macmillan, 1976.

37   Carole Fink, *The Genoa Conference: European Diplomacy, 1921–1922*, Chapel Hill, University of North Carolina Press, 1984; Stephen White, *The Origins of Détente: The Genoa Conference and Soviet Western Relations, 1922*, Cambridge, Cambridge University Press, 1985; Carole Fink, Axel Frohn and Jürgen Heideking (eds), *Genoa, Rapallo and European Reconstruction in 1922*, Cambridge, Cambridge University Press, 1991.

38   An office that was created in 1918, and confirmed in 1921, as the equivalent of Ambassador was intended to indicate that Soviet diplomacy was different from traditional diplomacy. The most famous Polpred in the early 1920s was in fact a Trade Ambassador, Krassin, who negotiated the Anglo-Soviet Trade Agreement of 1921 (see Andrew Williams, *Trading with the Bolsheviks: The Politics of East-West Trade, 1920–1939*, Manchester, Manchester University Press, 1992). In 1927 he (or she in one case, that of Alexandra Kollontai) was given absolute power over all other diplomats in a country posting and became the full

functional equivalent of a traditional ambassador. Quite a few of them were assassinated in the 1920s, and many more defected, often for the venal reason that they were engaged in corrupt activities (cf. Uldricks, *Diplomacy and Ideology*, p. 40, and ch. 3).

39 Stephen White, *Origins of Détente*, p. 97. Some of the best accounts of Anglo–Soviet relations in the 1920s can be found in: F. S. Northedge and Audrey Wells, *Britain and Soviet Communism: The Impact of a Revolution*, London, Macmillan, 1982; Gabriel Gorodetsky, *The Precarious Truce: Anglo-Soviet Relations*, Cambridge, Cambridge University Press, 1977; Stephen White, *Britain and the Bolshevik Revolution*, London, Macmillan, 1979.

40 Williams, *Trading with the Bolsheviks*, p. 111.

41 Andrew Williams, 'Lloyd George and the Politics of Recognition', in Fink, Frohn and Heideking, *Genoa, Rapallo and European Construction*, p. 43.

42 This kind of attitude was seen as much less unexceptional than it would be today. Even Keynes, who professed a certain admiration for Chicherin at Genoa, commented that Bolshevism was 'bred by the besotted idealism and intellectual error of the sufferings and peculiar temperaments of Slavs and Jews' (Keynes quoted by Robert Skidelsky, *John Maynard Keynes: The Economist as Saviour, 1920–1937*, London, Macmillan, 1992, p. 108).

43 See Stephen Schuker, 'American Policy Towards Debts and Reconstruction at Genoa, 1922', in Fink, Frohn and Heideking, *Genoa, Rapallo and European Construction*, p. 109 for a discussion of State Department anti-semitism; and Williams, *Trading with the Bolsheviks*, p. 123 for similar evidence from the French Ministry of Foreign Affairs.

44 White, *Origins of Détente*, pp. 55–6.

45 Carole Fink, 'Beyond Revisionism: The Genoa Conference of 1922', in Fink, Frohn and Heideking, *Genoa, Rapallo and European Construction*, p. 7.

46 Skidelsky, *John Maynard Keynes*, p. 108.

47 Williams, *Trading with the Bolsheviks*, and (for different views): Christine White, *Anglo-American Trade and Commercial Relations with Soviet Russia, 1918–1924*, Chapel Hill, University of North Carolina Press, 1992; Joan Hoff-Wilson, *Ideology and Economics: U.S. Relations with the Soviet Union, 1918–1933*, Columbia, University of Missouri Press, 1974.

48 David A. Baldwin, *Economic Statecraft*, Princeton, Princeton University Press, 1985.

49 William Chamberlin, *Russia's Iron Age*, Boston, Little, Brown, 1934.

50 One classic example being Robert Conquest, *The Great Terror*, London, Pelican, 1971. The first firm descriptions of the methods of the Terror that I have found are in: David Dallin and Boris Nicolaevsky, *Forced Labour in Soviet Russia*, New Haven, Yale University Press, 1947.

51 See Williams, *Labour and Russia*, for a discussion of this.

52 See Robert Tucker, *Stalinism: Essays in Historical Interpretation*, New York, W. W. Norton, 1977.

53 Herbert Feis, *From Trust to Terror: The Onset of the Cold War*, London, Anthony Blond, 1970 and Edmonds, *The Big Three*, 1991. On the question of how we can define the Cold War there is much vagueness. According to Wagner the Cold War was 'a vague, undifferentiated relationship of hostility between the United States and the Soviet Union' (R. Harrison Wagner, 'What was Bipolarity?', *International Organisation*, Vol. 47, No, 1, 1993, p. 80). According to Kenneth Waltz, in a celebrated article in *Daedalus* in 1964, it grew out of the Second World War, the first system transforming war ever, so that there can be no comparison with *anything* that occurred before. Walter Lippman, who invented the expression, saw the Cold War as basically a US/Soviet disagreement over Germany. For Wagner it can be best understood as a substitute for the Peace Conference that never was (Wagner, *International Organisation*, p. 80).

54 George F. Kennan, *Memoirs, 1925–1950 and 1950–1963*, 2 volumes, Boston, Little Brown, 1967 and 1972; David Mayer, *George Kennan and the Dilemmas of U.S. Foreign Policy*, Oxford, Oxford University Press, 1988; Anders Stephanson, *Kennan and the Art of Foreign Policy*, Cambridge, Mass., Harvard University Press, 1989.

55 Philip Hanson, *Western Economic Statecraft and East-West Relations*, London, Routledge/RIIA, 1988; Michael Mastanduno, *Economic Containment: CoCom and the Politics of East-West Trade*, Ithaca and London, Cornell University Press, 1992.

56 David Armstrong, *Revolution and World Order: The Revolutionary State in International Society*, Oxford, Clarendon Press, 1993, p. 156.

57 Tony Smith, ' "The Spirit of the Sierra Maestra": Five Observations on Writing on Cuban Foreign Policy', *World Politics*, XLI, 1, 1988, pp. 98–119, esp. p. 99.

58 Nicola Miller, *Soviet Relations with Latin America, 1956–1987*, Cambridge, Cambridge University Press, 1988, p. 57.

59 Francis Fukuyama, in Andrej Korbonksi and Francis Fukuyama (eds), *The Soviet Union and the Third World*, Ithaca and London, Cornell University Press, for Rand/UCLA, 1987, p. 43.

60 John Mearsheimer, 'Back to the Future: Instability in Europe after the Cold War', in Sean M. Lynn-Jones (ed.), *The Cold War and After: Prospects for Peace*, Cambridge, Mass., MIT Press, 1991; Andrew Williams (ed.), *Reorganising Eastern Europe: European Institutions and the Refashioning of Europe's Security Architecture*, Aldershot, Dartmouth Publishers, 1994.

Part III

Contemporary revolutionary states

5 *Stephen Chan*

Revolution, culture, and the foreign policy of China

What the Chinese call China has usually been translated into English as 'the middle kingdom'. The ideogram for 'middle' is unambiguous: a vertical slash seems to bisect all containable existence. In fact, the ideogram might be better translated as 'central', and here the visual rendition is of a pillar that holds up the world, that stakes the world to the ground, that prevents the world from becoming unattached and, thus, causes it to be 'real'. This supported world is given its credence. Over the past two hundred years, as Chinese migration into its non-Asian quarters took place, other countries were named after popular experience or perception. Britain thus became 'the strong kingdom', recognising its imperial pomp, and the US became 'the beautiful kingdom'. But there was still only one centre to the world.

Years later, in 1949, with the triumph of the revolution, Mao declared the People's Republic in Beijing. Looking down at the vast march-past of the liberation army in Tienanmen Square, he stood a metre back from a web microphone and, arms held rigidly at his sides, half sang, half declaimed, with the resonances of Western mourning, the birth of the revolutionary central kingdom. A British monarch could not have been crowned with more successful evocations of lineage and history. Mao's was the voice of the court poetry of yore. The poet-king was promising social, political and economic modernisation and transformation, using the literary style of antiquity.

Years later, in 1989, another drama unfolded in Tienanmen Square. Much of the literature that emerged after the massacre of students there has a curious quality. Whether books by student leaders involved,[1] or by older, 'established' dissidents,[2] they tell stories of a groping towards modernity, and its implicit freedoms – there is no freedom in these accounts without modernity – from the points of view of childhoods and adulthoods steeped firmly in Chinese articulations of the self. The self as subject is drawn from the customs and practices of antiquity, but is attracted to a modern and free object. The actual room this allows for a dialectical or dialogical process is small, since each can accommodate the other little and grudgingly. The German Sinologist, Wagner, reaches a similar conclusion in his extremely interesting article on the symbols and semiotics of political discourse in China. He comments that the students organised their protests in the historical forms established for student protest in the Han and Song dynasties, that neither the protests nor the official responses provided room for compromise, that the persistence of the student cause was prompted by the student conviction of their greater moral virtue and that, in the end, both sides could be described as participating in a unified 'process of intellectual desertification in China.' Mao's communism merely 'continued and systematised the pursuit of a core ideal of the traditional Chinese polity, the unification of thinking.'[3] There is, in short, no dialogue with power, but the occupation or retention of the centre of power, and both students and government fought and thought with this in mind.

Not everyone agrees with this. Commenting on Chinese military thought, Pollack, a Rand Corporation analyst of China, maintained that Chinese debate on military doctrine is often addressed through the 'problematic filter of CCP military history or allegorical writings based on Chinese dynastic history.' These devices are deliberately used in policy debates and are therefore 'politically tainted in ways which diminish their worth for the study of strategy per se.'[4] Wagner's view would be that, certainly, such usage has symbolic weight, and that such symbols are considerably weightier in Beijing than elsewhere. In other words, historical and allegorical reference points are an inescapable aspect of political discourse and debate. Debate is not tainted by this process. The process of debate is not tainted by its own process. The more central point that Pollack misses is that allegory and metaphor are not problematic filters, so much as constituents of a non-Western epistemology. This is how knowledge is constructed, not just how it may be problematically interpreted, and I shall return to this later.

It should be pointed out, however, that the antique does not always seek to blot out the modern. It seeks to incorporate it, or even invent it, on its own terms. Of the two precendental (and unsuccessful) revolutionary uprisings Mao could contemplate, the Tai Ping movement of the nineteenth century was an amazing ideological *tour de force*. Instigated by an itinerant petty trader who discovered in his hotel room some Christian missionary tracts, and who then authored a full-length Biblical text based on his deduction of what the Bible must be, as represented by the tracts, the Tai Ping preached social justice and equality for all, even for women. Its military and governmental structures, however, were based firmly on the allegorical motifs of Chinese folklore. The erstwhile trader, now a 'king', a brother of Jesus, and the husband of several wives, fielded an armed movement where, notwithstanding the invention of a 'Christianity', claimed its essential rights from divine appointment and virtue. The Boxer uprising of the early twentieth century, rather than inventing a 'new' doctrine, reinvented several old ones. Based on crash courses in the martial arts, with an admixture of magic and incantational initiations, evoking the purported vows of a mythicised Shaolin temple, its representation of what kung fu was meant to be was so successful that dozens of 'traditional' kung fu schools, almost a century later, are based only on the cannon-fodder training of the Boxers. For Mao, these precedents meant that a text, as we understand the term today, could be borrowed, appropriated, reinvented or bowdlerised, but that it could be used successfully only if freighted with, or as one instrument alongside, a range of antique symbols, in a semiotical system where every word was also an ideogram.

Some texts

In his latest book, Vasquez proposes that war is a social invention for the use of force. It being a social invention, war will have different cultural determinants and manifestations according to region or sub-system.[5] This point can be expanded, as it already has been in Western international relations theory. Here, firstly, war is based on a rationale, on a system of thought that encompasses not only violence but the power that the capacity for violence connotes, and its uses outside of violence itself. Thucydides has been incorporated into the foundations of Realism, to suggest not only a system of thought but its historical pedigree; by implication and association, the cultural foundations of the West, as they derive from Greek civilisation, are involved. Secondly, war is based on policy and, in Clausewitz's terms, is its extension by other means. War is neither gratuitous nor arbitrary, but policy objectives and scale of force coincide. War, in short, has firstly a rationale and is secondly rational. Its twentieth-century rationality, in the use or non-use of extreme force, has kept the world intact as the technological instruments of war have grown in destructiveness.

A history of this sort might, however, be differently constructed in a non-Western region. The Chinese, for instance, use a parallel to Thucydides as a historical gambit in explaining their current thought. The primary author in this usage has become well known, Sunzi Bingfa (usually anglicised as Sun Tsu or Sun Tzu), as has his work, *The Art of War*. The same exercise might be accomplished using other eighth-century BC writers, such as Zhan Guo Ce (*Annals of the Warring States*) and San Guo Zhi (*History of the Three Kingdoms*). During the years of liberation struggle, however, the Red Army used other literary references, expressing either a 'low-brow' taste on Mao's part, or a deliberate populist usage of literature. The thirteenth-century novel, *The Water Margin* – an abridged translation by Pearl Buck was published as *All Men are Brothers* – was indeed one of Mao's favourite books, and readings from it were a popular pastime in peasant China. It has, in its sense of just rebellion, a parallel in the Robin Hood stories, and, in its accumulation of just warriors from all walks of life, something of the Knights of the Round Table. In addition, however, it has a clearly expressed sense of natural law: that justice is inevitable; it is inevitable since Heaven wills it; the Heavenly mandate can be removed from those who rule unjustly and conferred on those who rebel on just grounds; that Heaven will express this will in the epochs that come after the novel; and that the just men who arise against the chaos and tumult of oppression will be born and act under a star.

Here, there is both a dialectic of history and a metaphysical note on man's nature. In history, Heaven's mandate is first earned then ebbs. The tension of its passing is characterised by oppression and rebellion. Righteous human agency earns its claim to government in a history structured by Heaven's will. Righteousness embodies the popular good, is carried forward by all men as brothers, and is sanctioned if not determined by natural law. In these circumstances, to rebel is to be blessed, and to fight is to anticipate the triumph of virtue.

Unable or unwilling to recruit on the basis of the Marxist dialectic, Red Army cadres would enter peasant villages and indicate the red star on their berets as proof of the novel's prophecy in the twentieth century.

Whereas Thucydidean 'realism' could be taken to precede a system of thought in international relations, various Chinese texts can be viewed in a continuum: in a dialectical clash of opposing poles, in which virtue is triumphant, before its quality ebbs away to necessitate a further clash in a succeeding historical epoch. The Western text describes and seeks to explain; the oriental texts determine and justify. Expressed baldly and generally in this manner they might still be viewed as folklore and colour-ful. Inoguchi *et al.*, however, have made a subtle contribution to thought on international relations. Whereas the Western school of Realism, of the centrality of the state and the exercise of its power, has been established in a twentieth-century history of inter-state wars approaching global scale, there is a parallel if not alternative twentieth-century history of people's wars of liberation, mostly in the non-Western Third World.[6] Here, the state is not the central actor but an alternative collectivity is; here, wars are fought and won not on the resources of power alone, but on the foundation resources of popular will, justice and historical inevitability. War, as a social invention, can be invented differently from west to east. Thought on war, and its place in social systems; thought on violence, resistance and overthrow can also differ from cultural base to cultural base. The foreign policy of a revolutionary state can express something beyond the fact of a political revolution having taken place.

Poles of power

Van Ness, as have others, identifies three contemporary periods of Chinese foreign policy.[7] These are, firstly, the period of 1950–57, when the young People's Republic enjoyed what seemed an ideological affiliation with the Soviet Union; secondly, the period 1960–70, in which there was a Chinese 'Third World line', and this is discussed below; and, thirdly, a period from 1978–88, in which internal modernisation led to an opening of a number of fronts with the West. Van Ness's depiction of these three periods is very interesting. The first period is described as premised on a world divided between capitalist and socialist camps; the second on a world dominated by two imperialistic superpowers; and the third on a world shaped by a 'superpower rivalry for hegemony'. Michael Yahuda, in his brief survey of modern Chinese thought on international relations, concentrating on works from the third of Van Ness's periods, remarks that Chinese theoreticians are largely concerned with poles of power.[8] The unifying question of all three periods has been, 'which pole of power constitutes the proper Chinese position?' Even in the largely post-revolutionary foreign policy of the third period, there has been a central concept of a divided world that is competitive in its divisions. A certain language has linked all three periods as well and, though less used at the present moment, it is still wheeled out for occasional effect. The Chinese attacks on the British Governor of Hong Kong, Chris Patten, in early 1993, made full use of a panoply of metaphor and insult that had once been far more commonplace. In the first two periods, however, the foreign policy of a self-consciously revolutionary state was anchored on a pole of power approach, and conceived as well as expressed in indigenous thought and language. In this chapter, the aim is to concentrate discussion on the second period – as the most 'Chinese' of them all – repeating in passing what has often been noted of the Sino-Soviet split that ended the first period, that the Chinese laid claim to a greater purity in the Marxist tradition, and that the virtue that accumulated from this was such that it could not possibly act only on the sufferance or behest of the less virtuous Soviet Union. An explanatory refinement, however, in the context of the present chapter, would say that the less virtuous could not be acknowledged as the more powerful. Virtue and power are here correlates of each other.

Three poles of power and the Three World Theory

The Chinese 'Third World line' in fact started earlier and finished later than Van Ness allows. Although it was not until 1974 that the Chinese articulated, to their satisfaction, how they viewed themselves in relation to the Third World, their interest in it had been instigated as early as 1955, at the Afro-Asian summit in Bandung. The Bandung format captured the Chinese imagination, and Africa was the first non-Asiatic Third World area of sustained Chinese foreign policy.

The first material interest in Africa, on the part of the People's Republic of China, was demonstrated in November 1956 – seven years after the Chinese revolution – by a $4.7 million grant to Egypt. Since then, China has continued to accord Egypt generous financial and technical assistance; Egypt enjoys a sort of 'most-favoured recipient' status along with Algeria, Congo, Morocco, Tanzania and Zimbabwe – a strange, sometimes contradictory assortment of nations, with both right and left wing governments.

A major Chinese diplomatic and political initiative, however, was attempted in the 1960s, with Premier Zhou Enlai's visit to Africa, which had been intended to culminate in Algiers, in a grand Afro-Asian conference, in which China hoped to mobilise African support against US actions in Viet Nam, strip Taiwan of diplomatic recognition among the newly-independent African nations, and initiate moves towards a formal alliance – a new organisation in the UN style, but without the USA or USSR. The Algiers conference was to be a bold gambit, whereby the Chinese, with a single strategy, hoped to generate enough momentum to install themselves as leaders of the Third World.

This sort of bold stroke clearly required much of Zhou Enlai's formidable gifts, but, from the very beginning, things went wrong for him. Zambia's President Kaunda complained bitterly of an Albanian pamphlet, of Chinese origin, accusing him of being an imperialist stooge. Zhou, miscalculating the African taste for revolution, orated on 'the exceedingly favourable situation for revolution' prevailing in the Third World, including Africa; this speech, delivered in Dar es Salaam, thoroughly alarmed the neighbouring Kenyans, who promptly accused him of exporting revolution. To round things off, Algeria's Ben Bella was overthrown, and the Chinese, rightly convinced that this time nothing would roll for them, called the conference off; Zhou went home, having reached his lifetime low as a diplomat.

The Chinese concluded that no simple strategy would win over the Third World, and Africa in particular. The Chinese, like the USA and USSR, perceived a power vacuum in Africa. In the space of a few short years, the continent's predominantly British and French political geography had been transformed. None of the major powers had any strategic conception of how to make friends in Africa, or, except near the Cape route and, possibly, the Horn, what use African friends could be. The continent's trade links and, hence, the disposition of its markets for minerals, had been conditioned by the colonial era. The search for African friends was a search for political allies or, more negatively, to prevent other powers from increasing their share of allies. In the absence of strategy for winning friends and influencing them, the USA, USSR, and China set about making friends wherever and however they could. For the Chinese, this was a particularly expensive campaign. Their own figures suggest that, over the years, they have spent $100 million in each African country (averaged out) and from 1970 to 1977 they spent $2 billion, or half of the total Chinese aid budget for that period, in Africa. These were the years of the Tazara railway and the 550-mile Somalia border road. These were also the years of Chinese support for UNITA (Union for the Total National Independence of Angola) in Angola, even after the OAU (Organisation of African Unity) had closed ranks behind the MPLA (Popular Movement for the Liberation of Angola) government; and the years when it was rumoured (though never proved) that China was selling reactor-grade uranium to South Africa. These were the years, bestriding these contradictions, of the Chinese Three World Theory.

The Three World Theory was meant to suggest Chinese solidarity with, and eventually allow Chinese leadership of, the Third World. It was the most complex development of Zhou Enlai's single, simple strategy of

the 1960s, and, since that strategy had floundered in Africa, it was to
Africa that the first overtures concerning the theory were made; as President Kaunda had been the first to find offence in the earlier Chinese
initiative, he was the first to whom the new theory was propounded. The
Chinese went one step further with Kaunda – who, by this time, had
established an international reputation for his interest in social philosophy. They let it be known that Mao first formulated the Three World
Theory in February 1974, during discussions with a visiting Third World
leader. Kaunda had met with Mao on the afternoon of 22 February 1974.
Without going so far as to say it in so many words, the Chinese implied
that the new theory was jointly authored by Mao and Kaunda, or that, at
least, Kaunda had crystallised the theory which had been formulating in
Mao's mind. This time round, the Chinese initiative would appear to be
both complex and collaborative. In fact, the actual theory had taken a
long time to formulate. Ten years earlier, Mao had granted an interview
to M. M. Ali of Zanzibar, in which he described the world as two
extremes, and two middle zones. The superpowers constituted the two
extremes. The first middle zone comprised the developing nations of
Asia, Africa and Latin America. The second middle zone comprised the
developed countries of Western Europe, Japan, Canada, Australia and
New Zealand. This description had, in turn, descended from Mao's
formulation of the world system, as he had described it to the American
journalist, Anna Louise Strong, in 1946. The imperialist drives of the
USA were resisted by the Soviet Union, with the rest of the world
between the two colossi.

The Three World Theory, as officially proclaimed by Deng Xiaoping
at the UN on 9 April 1974, postulated that the two superpowers, the
USA and the Soviet Union, together constitute a First World; the
developing nations together form a Third World; while the developed
nations in between comprise a Second World. China belonged, Deng
said, firmly in the Third World.

In the theory of international relations, this was a new development.
The world, according to Mao and Deng, was not bipolar. In fact, far from
constituting two opposing poles, the USA and the Soviet Union were
equal partners in a combined pole of capitalist and social imperialism.
The world was multi-polar and, in so far as two major poles could be
identified, they were the poles of the imperial First World and the self-
liberating Third World. It was not really a theory at all – more an
assertion. It was also, simultaneously, idealistic and nostalgic; romantic
and firmly rooted in Chinese chauvinism.

The Three World Theory suggests a united front against the super-powers. The Third World is united against them. The Second World is capable of being united against them. This was, in international terms, a refurbishment of Chinese Communist strategy during the Chinese civil war and in the war against the Japanese, of 'developing the progressive forces, winning over the middle forces, and isolating the diehard forces'.[9] This strategic concept never left Mao's mind.

Essentially, the Three World Theory was a vehicle for Chinese leadership on at least part of the international stage; simultaneously, it was a device whereby China could be protected, or at least surrounded by allies, in the face of superpower machinations. The Chinese had been, for many years, in international isolation. While China was recognised by many countries, she was not recognised by the USA. Because of this, she had been unable to emerge as an actor on the world stage, with the same importance and recognition as other major actors. For instance, she had been unable to take her seat on the UN Security Council, or to be a member of the UN at all. During this time, Chinese commentary on US foreign policy was shrill. The Chinese considered, however, that US expansionism in Asia would always stop short of encroaching upon Chinese territory itself. Her alliance with the Soviet Union was regarded as a guarantee that the USA would not, for instance, invade China from Taiwan. When China and the Soviet Union quarrelled, and the Soviet barrier to US ambitions was withdrawn, China realised that she required a framework by which she could view the world, and *through which she could be viewed*. A theory, therefore, through which China could be viewed as the pre-eminent Third World leader, would bolster Chinese prestige at least, suggest international Chinese influence, and appear to suggest a potential for mobilising international power. The theory was meant, therefore, to address a situation of *realpolitik*; its strategy was based on Mao's wartime formula, but it was also intended to provide scope for Chinese opportunism.

As it stood, the theory might have been seen as a world view in which the superpowers could have their ambitions diminished by third world solidarity. In fact, while propounding the theory, the Chinese actively sought to play one superpower off against the other. It was an elastic theory,

> delineated to meet the PRC's requirements of the time, and these in turn were determined by Chinese perception and analysis of the overall situation in the global system. In essence, the Three World Theory was a dynamic concept which could be modified and adapted to new situations by changing

or shifting the composition of political forces in the 'three worlds'. The concept itself was therefore part of and an instrument of Beijing's global strategy.[10]

If the elements of the theory could be manipulated, and would be manipulated whenever advantage could accrue to Beijing, how faithful would China be to the interests of the Third World?

This question can be answered by examining the cultural components of the theory – which drew from traditional Chinese literature and the traditional Chinese world view. The theory originated from the mind of a guerilla leader who had been an academic librarian and poet.

Elasticity

As noted above, the Three World Theory is elastic. It requires constant manipulation to meet constant change. The concept of constant change was a feature in Mao's favourite historical novel, *The Water Margin*, in which its thirteenth-century author, Shih Nai-An, writes: 'All that is clear is that time passes, and all the time there is continual change going on.' Without great extension, this idea accorded well with the Marxist dialectic of change. Each country, therefore, contains contradictions and the likelihood of change. In each country, the people desire change. At this stage, however, a major extension is introduced: the country which leads the many countries desiring change is in a position to manipulate some of the international preconditions for that change.[11]

Intentionality

To state that change is natural, and that one will be in charge of change, is a traditional device in formal Chinese rhetoric. That is, a statement of principle requires to be reinforced by a statement of intention or position. For instance, Lin Piao, in a speech delivered on 3 September 1965, berated the Soviet Union for its fear of war: 'First we are against them (imperialist wars), and secondly, we are not afraid of them (unlike the Soviet Union)'.

Strategy and opportunism

Although the ancient strategist, Sunzi Bingfa, is chiefly remembered as a protagonist and theorist of unconventional warfare, his maxims and principles were not necessarily confined to war. Since war extends the pursuit of policy, it is governed by the strategy and tactics of policy. Thus, if cunning and stratagems are useful in, say, diplomacy, they will also be useful in combat. Throughout his work, *The Art of War*, Sunzi seldom praises violence and heroism; but cunning and stratagems – opportunism – are applauded.

In the Three World Theory, the traditional devices of elasticity, Chinese leadership (following the logic of Chinese rhetoric) and opportunism are all apparent. These devices were of Chinese origin and formed a theory that sponsored a Chinese world outlook. This is not to say that little was done for those nations that were part of the Chinese cosmos. As noted above, the Chinese record in foreign aid has been generous. The point is that this was incidental to the essential purpose of the Three World Theory – the components of which suggest that the theory was impeccably chauvinist.

The theory and practice

Although the Three World Theory was put abroad as evidence of a liberal, if not revolutionary, Chinese foreign policy, the planning and application of Chinese foreign policy in the Asian region was evidence of something entirely different. Although China sought a theory through which she could be viewed, she also built a regional structure through which, in very concrete terms, she could be defended. Having quarrelled with the Soviet Union, a defensive structure was erected against her erstwhile ally. Although commentators noted the ability of Chinese nuclear weapons to strike Soviet targets, these weapons were not, in themselves, a defensive structure; they were, however, the hinge to the Chinese defensive strategy. In fact, the creation and deployment of the Chinese nuclear force had followed conventional deterrence theory pretty faithfully; and had added to it the classical European doctrine of limited force and limited objective. Sufficient nuclear weapons (limited force) to convince the Soviets that a nuclear attack would mean a nuclear reply, forcing the Soviets to attack, if ever they came, in conventional strength – thus allowing the Chinese resistance to follow its carefully planned strategy of cutting supply-lines and letting the wastes of Northern China swallow the invaders (limited objective).[12]

Strategy of the same conceptual origin was at play towards the end of 1979, with the invasion of Viet Nam by Chinese forces. Ostensibly, this was to 'teach a lesson' to the Viet Namese for their expansion into Kampuchea. Many observers also took it that the invasion was intended to draw Viet Namese divisions out of Kampuchea, to meet the Chinese threat and, thereby, relieve the Khymer Rouge. Gerald Segal's analysis, however, suggests that the action did not highlight military objectives, but political ones; exposing to the Viet Namese the shallowness of Soviet support, as well as cautioning them against further regional adventurism.[13] In other words, the action had again a classical Western 'feel' about it:

the deployment of limited power to achieve clearly defined, politically-conceived, limited objectives.

In any case, Viet Nam was a Third World nation. The Chinese action hardly accorded with the idealism of the Three World Theory. The Chinese themselves understood this, and when, in December 1979, the Soviet Union invaded Afghanistan, the Chinese abandoned the theory. The invasion of Afghanistan thoroughly alarmed the Chinese. Third World solidarity, whether led by China or not, was scarcely enough to deter the 'die-hard' Soviets in a determined mood. The theory could not protect China. Moreover, China, by her own regional conduct, had undermined the theory. Finally, Chinese defensive preparations revealed that neither international solidarity nor cultural romanticism could compete against traditional military strategy. The only point of wonder is over the degree of schizophrenia the Chinese had induced for themselves – linked simultaneously to romance and the realities of the world. The invasion of Afghanistan shook them on to the side of reality. 'China in its alarm turned increasingly to the West, in particular to the United States.'[14] To some extent, this had been a trap of China's own making. Having used the Three World Theory as a cover by which she sought to play off one superpower against the other, she now felt compelled by events to play much closer to the USA than she had ever intended.

The Chinese had sought to build themselves an international security through the Three World Theory. The construction of that theory was itself representative of China's isolation in the world, or of its cultural detachment from the world. It was a theory rooted in historical romance, in idealism and in the effort to overcome Zhou Enlai's diplomatic failure of the mid-1960s. These factors indicated a Chinese stubbornness that required the dramatic events of Afghanistan to change it.

A debate on culture

Such an account of a critical period in Chinese foreign policy would not command universal support. Gladue, however, suggests in his non-culturally-based account of Chinese foreign policy that, in Africa at least, Chinese policies 'have always been limited by the Chinese tendency to generalize . . . related to the human propensity to see oneself as central to other people's behaviour.'[15] In this chapter, the argument has been to locate this centralising tendency in something more specific than 'the human propensity'. Even so, to talk of a cultural base is to talk of something very wide and capable of selective usage (or misuse) in debate.

Gong has sought to locate a specific point in time as being critical to Chinese cultural self-esteem. China's entry into the international system was not only against the terms and concepts of its own 'traditional Chinese world order', but was forced upon her, was felt to be traumatic and seemed illogical. The system of 'unequal treaties', through which Western powers asserted extraterritorial rights over parts of China, and which lasted from its first assertion in 1842 to abrogation in 1943 (and in which Hong Kong is seen as residue), meant (a) a perception of international inequality which ended only recently, (b) a first major encounter with international law to which the Chinese could not respond on their own terms, and (c) 'a cultural humiliation for the Middle Kingdom, the shattering of China's tradition of cultural superiority'.[16]

Even with 1842 as a point of departure, the history of Chinese foreign policy, under the People's Republic, can be read as a series of reactions to events. A communist republic was always going to be allied to the communist Soviet Union. The crumbling of that alliance naturally led to a search for a new alliance elsewhere. Coinciding roughly with the divorce from Moscow was the first assemblage of Third World nations at Bandung. It seemed sensible, at that time of Third World assertiveness and optimism, for the Chinese to explore the development of links with it. There followed a period of aberration with the Cultural Revolution of 1966, but a period of greater pragmatism was already being shadowed in 1972, with Nixon's visit to China. The Three World Theory that followed from 1974–79 was a sentimental and rhetorical device, harking back to a history of cultural chauvinism, briefly resurrected in modern Maoist colours in 1966, but which had no real relevance to the world as it then really was. After only five years, it was seen as no defence against reality and was abandoned. It could therefore have had no real depth. Looking at textbook recitations of Chinese history,[17] one might surely be forgiven for taking such a view.

There is also the very strong case for examining Chinese history, particularly revolutionary history, not so much from the point of view of culture, as from an enquiry into the structural conditions of Chinese society and commerce. Skocpol has done this brilliantly.[18] In addition, one might take the case of Taiwan, view the Chinese government there as having, until 1949, a shared history with China proper, agree with Bobrow and Chan that its foreign policy performance has been abnormal,[19] but wonder at the relative absence of cultural referents or even anything remotely resembling a cultural determinism. Finally, in any case, the literature on culture and international relations, culture and foreign policy, can be provocative but astonishingly generalised.[20] Is this at all a positive avenue down which to travel, or might it be better to give the anthropologists another hundred years before we can have reliable criteria that link domestic histories to foreign policies shorn of their rhetoric? Even then, might anyone truly discriminate between real and imagined, physical and metaphysical? Even that old metaphysician, Malraux, in his fictionalised self-history, didn't pretend to understand Mao – when he spoke of destroying the whole of the Chinese past (everything that the Chinese culture had produced), so that China could be truly China again (culturally pure and animating).[21]

A cultural reading of the revolution

Thirty years ago, when uni-dimensional views of Chinese policy formulation were still common, Porter was suggesting the dualities in Chinese thought.[22] One possible duality was, on the one hand, a communism that 'derives as much from the Confucian dialectic as from Marx', said to denote the thought of Mao and Zhou Enlai, and 'the fanatical doctrinaires' of Marxism-Leninism on the other. Taking this approach, one could read modern Chinese history as a succession of dualisms: Confucian Marxism struggling with Marxism-Leninism; Confucian Marxism attempting a full-blown Maoism; residual Maoism and a conservative pragmatism; an entrenched conservatism confronting aspects of modern liberalism; conditional liberalism versus the demand for full-scale reform. This approach at least establishes a dynamism. However, looking back thirty years, it is instructive to be reminded how recently the Western view of China has attained nuance. Politically, at least, it is a recent development. Thirty years ago, even to suggest duality could be a bold statement. Felix Greene called one of his books, *The Wall has Two Sides*, just so a basic message could be portrayed on the cover. Other works were uni-dimensional in their condemnation of Chinese policy, or were without nuance in the Chinese defence. The latter provided a rich vein of enthusiasms, varying in sophistication from Edgar Snow to Rewi Alley, but united in their desire to establish a plain obstacle to the prevailing, unsympathetic and hugely but simply critical view of China. On Chinese history as a whole, before the communist era, it is still only recently that Joseph Needham constructed his immense exposition of the history of Chinese science and knowledge. So that, to an extent, much of our interpretation of Chinese policy has been made possible only from the accumulated struggle of scholarship being able to provide a platform for hindsight. In this hindsight, there are certain caveats to be observed, the foremost being the recent emergence of China into international society, an emergence fraught with trauma and resistance lasting from 1842 to perhaps 1980, but probably onward going. The resistance to external society can only proceed with a full freighting of referentialism to the history of internal society – so that, say, Skocpol may be correct in her structuralism, that Chinese society was structured in such a way that a peasant movement could not take place without gentry support, indeed organisation and leadership; but, here, the question should be not just how a peasant movement took place, but with what permissions and precedents it took place. If rebellion, or revolution, was impossible in Chinese history, then no amount of historical cajoling would have fielded the Red Army. The more external forces encouraged Chinese resistance, the more self-referential policy responses became, so that in the 1950s and, particularly, 1960s, they seemed shrill, strident and disconnected from the external world – which, in a sense, they were. By contrast, the Taiwan Chinese were not resisting the external world, indeed were cosseted by the USA, and conceived and enunciated foreign policy differently. Both Van Ness and Yee consider that, post-1980, a pragmatism has taken hold of Chinese foreign policy formulation and that, indeed, it is now a largely 'normal' process.[23] The hypothesis of this chapter is that, running through all three of Van Ness's periods, though particularly the period of Third World attachment, has been a culturally-derived vocabulary and conceptual apparatus. Even as China struggles towards a modernity, with the freedoms to match, each symbol of that free modernity, if drawn from the West, has a matching symbol from the Chinese past. There is a dialectic but as much a constant and clumsy accompaniment. Here, Wagner's observations are again of interest. Looking at the 1989 uprising in Tienanmen Square, Wagner considers the students' 'Goddess of Liberty', and other artefacts of their protest, and finds an international/national, universal/Chinese dualism in them all.[24]

In the construction of the Three World Theory, there were several steps involved: (a) the struggles of the actual past, and the struggles of the past – as mediated by the historical imagination – provided both precedent and a form of determinism; righteousness would defeat injustice and oppression; (b) these struggles were represented in texts, both in strategic manuals and in historical romances, so that there was both a mode of operation and a metaphysical colouring of the combatants; (c) the struggles of the Red Army were not only successful in the twentieth-century sense, but confirmatory of the ancient texts, and Mao's writings on guerilla war added to their canon; (d) the idea of opposing poles of power, each with a clear moral colour, the notion of struggle and the triumph of

those with superior morality, greater virtue, confirmed the Marxist dialectic and was in turn confirmed by it; (e) successful guerilla strategy,
including winning the middle ground, was transformed into an international political strategy, the latter being confirmed by the success of
the former. The dualism of the Three World Theory, therefore, lies not
just with a 'Chinese' theory on the one hand, and the actual world on the
other, but with a theory that was layered by a series of chauvinisms,
constructed so tightly that it determined the sort of world which it was
capable of interpreting.

Here, there is a most unusual foreign policy of a revolutionary state, in
that 'revolutionary' may be taken as the overthrow of a state with change
possible by revolving. One revolves towards the future, but rolls past
one's own history as a condition for forward movement. In the end,
however, the most pertinent metaphor remains the construction of the
ideogram for 'middle' or 'central'. Even now, in post-revolutionary China,
both conservative and 'Western' schools of international relations are
fixated on theories to do with poles of power.[25] Where is China's position
today – on which pole of power? The defunct Three World Theory
answered this simply. Leading the Third World, it was the pole of power
that staked the earth to the ground; it was the pole that held up the
heaven; it was the pole that grew out of Mao's declamation on the mandate
of heaven in the Square of Heaven's Peace.

Notes

1   E.g. Li Lu, *Moving the Mountain: My Life in China from the Cultural
Revolution to Tiananmen Square*, London, Macmillan, 1990.

2   E.g. Liu Binyan, *A Higher Kind of Loyalty*, London, Methuen, 1990.

3   Rudolf Wagner, 'Political Institutions, Discourse and Imagination in China
at Tiananmen', in James Manor (ed.), *Rethinking Third World Politics*, London,
Longman, 1991, p. 144.

4   Jonathan D. Pollack, 'The Evolution of Chinese Strategic Thought', in
Robert O'Neill and D. M. Horner (eds), *New Directions in Strategic Thinking*,
London, Allen & Unwin, 1981, p. 140.

5   John A. Vasquez, *The War Puzzle*, Cambridge, Cambridge University Press,
1993.

6   Hayward R. Alker Jr, Thomas J. Biersteker and Takashi Inoguchi, 'From
Imperial Power Balancing to People's Wars: Searching for Order in the Twenti-
eth Century', in James Der Derian and Michael J. Shapiro (eds), *International/
Intertextual Relations*, Lexington, Lexington Books, 1989.

7   Peter Van Ness, *China as a Third World State: Foreign Policy and Official*

National Identity, Canberra, Department of International Relations Working Paper 1991/5, 1991, p. 5.

8 Michael B. Yahuda, 'International Relations Scholarship in the People's Republic of China', in Hugh C. Dyer and Leon Mangasarian (eds), *The Study of International Relations: The State of the Art*, London, Macmillan, 1989, p. 322.

9 Mao Tse Tung, *On Tactics against Japanese Imperialism*, Beijing, Foreign Language Press, 1965.

10 Herbert S. Yee, 'The Three World Theory and Post-Mao China's Global Strategy', *International Affairs*, 59, no. 2, 1983.

11 See Arthur Huck, 'China and the Chinese Threat System', *International Affairs*, 49, October 1973.

12 See Harry Gelber, *Nuclear Weapons and Chinese Policy*, London, International Institute for Strategic Studies Adelphi Paper 99, 1973.

13 Gerald Segal, 'The PLA and China's Foreign Policy Decision-making', *International Affairs*, 57, no. 4, 1981.

14 Yee, 'The Three World Theory'.

15 E. Ted Gladue Jr, *China's Perception of Global Politics*, Washington, DC, University Press of America, 1982, pp. 77–8.

16 Gerrit W. Gong, 'China's Entry into International Society', in Hedley Bull and Adam Watson (eds), *The Expansion of International Society*, Oxford, Clarendon, 1989.

17 E.g. Daniel S. Papp, *Contemporary International Relations: Frameworks for Understanding*, New York, Macmillan, 1988, pp. 299–323.

18 Theda Skocpol, *States and Social Revolutions: A Comparative Analysis of France, Russia & China*, Cambridge, Cambridge University Press, 1979.

19 Davis B. Bobrow and Steve Chan, 'Understanding Anomalous Success: Japan, Taiwan and South Korea', in Charles F. Hermann, Charles W. Kegley Jr, and James N. Rosenau (eds), *New Directions in the Study of Foreign Policy*, Boston, Allen & Unwin, 1987.

20 E.g. Ali A. Mazrui, *Cultural Forces in World Politics*, London, James Currey, 1990.

21 André Malraux, *Anti-memoirs*, Harmondsworth, Penguin, 1970, p. 431.

22 Brian Porter, *Britain and the Rise of Communist China*, London, Oxford University Press, 1967, pp. 17–18.

23 Yee, 'The Three World Theory' and Van Ness, *China as a Third World State*, p. 17.

24 Wagner, 'Political Institutions', esp. pp. 133–4.

25 For a survey of Chinese theoretical literature on international relations, in both English and Chinese, see Stephen Chan, 'International Relations Theory Outside the North-West: Six Eastern Examples', in A. J. R. Groom and Margot Light (eds), *Contemporary International Relations: A Handbook of Current Theory*, London, Pinter, 1994.

The Democratic People's Republic of Korea and its foreign policy in the 1990s: more realist than revolutionary?

By the mid-1990s there were five states which appeared to the United States to threaten its security and which, in the view of a number of US policy makers and academics posed a threat to the stability of the entire international system. Three of these states – Libya, Iraq and Iran – were troublesome not simply because of their domestic ideologies which in one way or the other challenged the legitimacy of the view that only representative democracy offered a suitable model of domestic political development and not only because these states' foreign policy demonstrated a tendency to independence (of US tutelage). These states were of importance to the United States and the West in general for strategic/economic reasons, and specifically for their control over vast oil resources.

The other two states which appeared to cause problems for US foreign policy makers were in many senses hangovers from another era; that of Cold War politics where the world was divided between crusading free traders led by the US and a congeries of socialist experiments led by the former superpower, the USSR. Cuba and the Democratic People's Republic of Korea (DPRK) remained the last two important states professing a socialist vocation as at 1993. These small states were similar in that both had been led by strong, charismatic leaders for some time. Both states resisted pressures to 'democratise' along the Western model of representative democracy, although by 1993 there were some signs that Cuba would move down this path, and both developed severe economic problems by the mid-1990s. There the similarities probably stopped. Cuba's domestic development took place within the context of Latin American, Catholic culture and within close proximity to an oppositional hegemon which until the revolution in 1959 was to all intents and purposes its colonial metropole. The cultural context of Korea (north and south) is of Buddhism and Confucianism and the DPRK was created only recently, in 1948, as one half of a divided country, in the aftermath of thirty-five years of Japanese occupation, anti-Japanese guerrilla warfare and subsequently a war against UN forces led by the United States, of such violence that it is no exaggeration to decribe the country as having been 'levelled' by saturation bombing by 1952.[1] Thus the inhabitants of the DPRK have within living memory the experience of foreign occupation and foreign invasion from two external powers. These factors inevitably helped to create the siege mentality which arguably is characteristic of north Korean society.

This chapter, however, offers an overview of how the DPRK has operated, not domestically, but in international relations. It considers how the DPRK's unique domestic political trajectory has influenced its foreign policy and diplomacy and considers how the DPRK's policy makers may have changed in terms of their approach to other states in the system and whether this represents a fundamental shift in foreign policy philosophy. This chapter also investigates how, as analysts, we can best explain and understand the DPRK's foreign policy. The suggestion made here is that we can best understand the DPRK's foreign policy as having evolved from that underpinned by a 'revolutionary' perspective through to that which is more or less better explained by the classical conceptual framework of Political Realism.[2]

A brief historical survey of the strategic objectives and rationale of DPRK foreign policy is presented here. The survey will *not* specifically focus on foreign policy objectives in respect of the Korean war (1950–53), partly because these were fairly clear – to unify the country – and partly because this relatively short period in the DPRK's history has been well covered elsewhere.[3] This brief review is followed by a synopsis of current foreign policy priorities for DPRK decision makers. The empirical review is accompanied by some commentary on the changing conceptual underpinnings of DPRK foreign policy.

Subordination to self-reliance: 1945–54

The DPRK was established in September 1948, three years after the partition of Korea and three months before the Soviet army which had liberated the country from Japanese occupation withdrew its troops from the north of the peninsula.

The story of the three years between partition and the establishment of two separate states – the DPRK north of the 38th parallel and the Republic of Korea (ROK) in the south – and the years leading to the Korean war is relatively well known, but its basic elements bear repeating given their implications for future DPRK foreign policy.[4]

Japan had occupied Korea from 1910 to 1945, expropriating land and resources and ruling through physical repression. The aim was to suppress resistance and suspected resistance by violence and at the same time to try to eradicate the Korean identity by measures which included the banning of Korean in schools and the forcing of Koreans to take Japanese family names.[5] During the war Korean women were sent to the front lines and many forced into prostitution – the so-called 'comfort-women' – for the Japanese army.

Koreans resisted the occupying forces, but because of the efficiency of Japanese repression Korean guerrillas were forced to establish bases outside the country – mainly in the nearby Chinese province of Manchuria. The future DPRK President Kim Il Sung emerged as a leader from the anti-Japanese liberation movement based outside the country – firstly as a fighter with a Chinese unit – then after 1940 as a Captain in a Soviet-led offensive against the Japanese in Korea. DPRK hagiography today both exaggerates and obscures the importance of Kim as a revolutionary leader, but nevertheless it would be a mistake to underestimate Kim's significance and support. Kim Il Sung was entrusted with a leadership position by older and more experienced Korean guerrillas and by both Chinese and Soviet leaderships.[6] Gavan McCormack has noted in his commentary on Kim Il Sung's important military victory over the Japanese at Pochonbo in June 1937 that 'its political significance has perhaps been under-estimated (because exaggerated by Pyongyang)'[7] and similarly it is perhaps best to remain cautious about dismissing all of Pyongyang's public emissions as pure propaganda.[8]

Notwithstanding the above, Kim's accession to power in the emergent DPRK was made possible by the Soviet Red Army. Early DPRK foreign policy pronouncements reflected an acknowledgement of Soviet support, although at the same time there were some indications of an inchoate policy of Korean self-reliance – later systematised into the north Korean *Juche* philosophy.[9] As Gordon White has noted, public homage to the Soviet Union diminished after the end of the Korean war and the concept of *Juche*, formalised by Kim Il Sung in 1955, brought more to the fore.[10] *Juche* emphasises political independence; economic self-sufficiency particularly in key strategic industries and non-alignment in foreign relations; this was a policy of autarky as opposed to its stronger relation of autarchy.[11] As one consequence, the DPRK, unlike Cuba for instance, developed a foreign economic policy which, again unlike Cuba, deliberately set out to be, as far as was possible, independent of major allies.

Post-1948 foreign policy objectives were to

> strengthen solidarity with the international democratic forces to enhance the
> international position of the Republic and create the international conditions
> favourable for national reunification and to contribute to international peace
> and security and to the development of the world revolution through a
> vigorous anti-imperialist struggle.[12]

The DPRK intended to carry out this policy, according to Kim Il
Sung, by establishing relations with 'freedom-loving countries that respect
the liberty and independence of our nation and approach us on an equal
footing'.[13] Kim specifically condemned 'the revival of Japanese imperialism' and uncompromisingly stated that 'the imperialist countries that are
attempting to revive Japan as an imperialist aggressive state will all be
considered enemies of our nation.'[14]

In 1949 the DPRK applied to join the United Nations on the basis
of its support for the UN charter – declaring that it was the legitimate
representative of both north and south. Not surprisingly the United
Nations, dominated as it was then by the United States, rejected the
application.

Early DPRK foreign policy therefore was characterised by the drive to
unify the country and the Korean 'nation', by hostility to Japan and the
United States and by a commitment to a global anti-imperialist struggle.
It did not, however, entirely reject participation in the post-war structures
which had been created by the victorious allied powers.

Conceptually early DPRK foreign policy emphasised a commitment to
the unity of the Korean 'nation' where nation strictly referred to a group
of people bound together by a common culture, language and sense of
history. The concept was not used to denote a meaning more or less
synonymous with the concept of 'the state' – much less the DPRK as a
state. DPRK foreign policy also stressed the priority given to the anti-
imperialist struggle and arguably gave a lesser priority to its objective of
developing relations with other states on a basis of equality.

This conceptual downgrading of the state as the focal analytic point
and the upgrading of the commitment to a global anti-imperial struggle
rejected the normal rules of the international game where sovereignty,
non-interference (on any grounds) and the inviolability of a state's territory and borders are considered *sine qua non* for participation in the world
game of international relations. Here class and imperialism were the key
variables and the international scene was understood – not as the Political
Realists would have it, as a realm of interacting sovereignties within an
anarchical society, but as 'a world divided not into states but into class

antagonisms and a dichotomy of riches and poverty, with imperialism and economic and political asymmetrical penetration affecting the fortunes of millions of people.'[15] This is what Tony Thorndike has characterised as the 'revolutionary' approach to international relations.[16]

The revolutionary approach in practice: 1955 to the 1980s

The post-Korean war period saw the consolidation of the *Juche* policy both domestically and in the sphere of foreign policy. In terms of the latter the *Juche* idea provided both rationale and strategic objective for economic and political policies. Self-reliance or the policy of *Juche* did not mean a commitment to a policy of international isolation. Instead the emphasis was on economic independence as providing for the principle of all-round independence in international relations – identified as the principle of *Chajusong*. In 1975 for instance Kim Il Sung told a party gathering that

> Self-reliance in the economy is the material basis of Chajusong. Failing economic independence, subordination to another country is unavoidable and freedom from colonial slavery is impossible. Economic dependence leads to political subordination, and economic inequality leads to political inequality.[17]

Economically the DPRK was forced to reassess its foreign policy given that trading patterns had dramatically changed as a result of both the Second World War and the Korean war. Prior to 1945 Japan had been by far the dominant trading partner for Korea – taking 93 per cent of Korean exports and providing 94 per cent of its imports.[18] Soviet aid supported reconstruction in the north in the early post-1945 period, although Soviet suggestions that the DPRK should 'co-ordinate' with the Soviet Union as a supplier of raw materials in return for Soviet machinery were rejected. The DPRK reindustrialised – aiming for self-reliance – although it still relied on Soviet and later Chinese aid to pursue its goals. DPRK insistence on independence caused some friction with the Soviet Union although not enough to prevent the DPRK from applying for and receiving observer status at the Council for Mutual Economic Assistance (COMECON) in 1957.

By the end of the Korean war in which it was of course assisted by the Chinese 'volunteers' the DPRK was closely aligned with the Socialist bloc countries both diplomatically and economically. In the unlikely event that the DPRK would have wished to become a participant in any of the Western economic institutions it would have been unable to do so because of the continued economic sanctions (still extant) imposed by the United States. Nevertheless its 'selective participation' in COMECON gave it 'most of the advantages of the CMEA (original name for COMECON) (barter trade, no need for convertible currencies) while avoiding the major disadvantage . . . the loss of economic and therefore politial independence involved in the "socialist international division of labour".'[19]

The DPRK also maintained economic relations with the West in that trade was developed with Japan and west European countries. In the early 1970s the DPRK made a determined effort to buy, among other things, new technology from Western countries – to the extent that in 1974, 54 per cent of all the DPRK's imports originated in the West (compared to 1969 when just 27 per cent of all DPRK trade was with the West).[20] The DPRK had intended to finance these imports with earnings from mineral exports and loans, but as commodity prices fell and interest rates rocketed in the early 1970s the DPRK's response was to stop paying. The accumulated debt has been estimated as $1,400 million as at 1992.[21] Other indications that DPRK foreign economic policy maintained some intention and hope of developing economic relations with the West included the 1984 Joint Venture Law and the meeting of international bankers in Pyongyang in the same year.[22]

In political terms DPRK foreign policy priorities remained that of unification and a commitment to international anti-imperialism, but the alliances chosen to pursue these policies became more diversified. The DPRK attempted to maintain good relations with the Socialist states and to build relations with newly independent states via the non-aligned movement. The DPRK acknowledged differences within the Socialist bloc but warned against the development of what it termed 'organisational splits'. The DPRK made clear its rejection of any type of 'Brezhnev Doctrine' (i.e. a limited sovereignty under Soviet leadership) and insisted that relations with other socialist countries be based 'on the principle of non-interference in other's internal affairs, mutual respect, equality and mutual benefit.'[23]

The non-aligned movement (NAM) was seen as an important vehicle for co-operation between non-hegemonic states – a co-operation which was based on 'the principle of complete equality and noninterference in each other's internal affairs'.[24] Co-operation was sought with states of varying political hues within the NAM. Kim Il Sung stressed that 'to fight against the common enemy, the new-emerging countries should attach prime importance to unity and subordinate everything to this, and should closely bond together, transcending the difference in the social system, political view and religious belief.'[25]

Throughout the 1950s and 1960s the DPRK had attempted some contacts with the south. It offered emergency food aid after natural disasters such as floods affected the ROK in 1956, 1957, 1961 and 1963.[26] No significant progress was made, however, until July 1972 when the governments of the DPRK and the ROK agreed a Joint North–South statement and the formation of a North–South Coordination Commission. The DPRK's understanding of the agreement was that it was based on the three principles of 'independence, peaceful reunification and great national unity'. As far as the DPRK was concerned the agreement committed both sides to first of all

> reunify the country independently without relying on foreign forces and free from interference of outside forces; secondly, to reunify the country peacefully without recourse to arms; and thirdly, to achieve great national unity regardless of the difference in ideology, ideal and social system.[27]

The statement resulted in little concrete progress towards unification and the Commission ceased operations in 1975 after ten meetings had taken place. North–South talks held under the auspices of the Red Cross also ended in failure to agree.[28] Lack of progress was partly a result of the two sides' differing understanding of the necessary priorities in terms of implementation of the agreement. The DPRK insisted on resolving military and political issues as a priority and the ROK insisted on giving priority to 'confidence-building'. Because of the emphasis on 'great national unity' the DPRK also refused to consider supporting any proposals for simultaneous admission to the UN – the so-called 'two Koreas' policy.

In 1980 the DPRK proposed a five-point plan for the reunification of Korea based upon a confederal solution. The plan called for a non-aggression treaty between the DPRK and the ROK; a peace agreement between the DPRK and the US to replace the 1953 Armistice agreement which ended the Korean war; troop reductions in the north and the south to less than 100,000 each; and nuclear weapons and foreign troops (i.e. the US military) to be withdrawn from the Korean peninsula.[29] The major obstacle to unification, at least according to the DPRK, was US interference in (pan-)Korean affairs particularly as manifested by the joint US/ROK military exercises which have taken place in the peninsula since 1969 and which became the annual 'Team Spirit' exercises in 1976.[30]

The most celebrated incident in the DPRK's chequered relations with the United States was in 1968 when the DPRK captured a US frigate, the USS *Pueblo*, which strayed into its territorial waters. Its crew were released after signing a written 'apology' to the DPRK for spying. In the following year the DPRK shot down a US plane leaving thirty-one people dead. Jon Halliday and Bruce Cumings report that 'Nixon and Kissinger at first recommended dropping a nuclear bomb on the North but later backed off'.[31]

The DPRK became a member of various international organisations and from the mid-1970s was an active participant in various UN agencies such as WHO and UNESCO. The DPRK adopted an activist international policy – sending official delegations abroad and encouraging visits by heads of state and foreign delegations to the country. Kim Il Sung attended the Bandung conference in 1955 and became an active proponent of the non-aligned movement (NAM) after the DPRK joined that organisation in 1975.[32] In 1960 (according to DPRK material) the state was a member of 49 international organisations, by 1970 some 106 such organisations and by 1975 was a member of 141 international organisations. These organisations ranged from the International Telecommunication Organisation through to the 'Group of 77' through to the Inter-Parliamentary Union.

As the DPRK worked to consolidate its independence and sovereignty – one aspect of its *Chajusong* – via its state to state relationships through bilateral and multilateral contacts so it at the same time worked to advance the more controversial aspects of *Chajusong* – that of fighting imperialism. The principle of 'internationalism' in foreign activities meant not just a process of solidarity with communist and 'newly independent' *states* but also a commitment to work for the

> cohesion of the international communist movement . . . supporting the anti-imperialist national liberation movement of the peoples in these regions [Asia, Africa and Latin America] and the revolutionary movement of *the peoples of all countries*, and waging an active struggle for world peace and the progress of mankind against the imperialists' policy of aggression and war.'[33]

A vociferous anti-US rhetoric accompanied the DPRK's foreign policy activities with the US replacing Japan as the major enemy. Dr Li Sung Hyok, the Director of Pyongyang's International Relations University argued that

> US imperialism violated our sovereignty, interfered in our affairs and made obstacles to the reunification of our country. The US have demanded that we reduce the level of propaganda against them. Yet given the historical aggression of the US and the obstacles placed by them to our unification

it is natural that our people should have an antipathy and hatred to the aggressors. We say that they should stop their aggression and interference in our internal affairs and then we will not issue anti but pro–US propaganda.[34]

The tactics involved in the promotion of the DPRK's foreign policy objectives of anti-imperialism included the promotion and encouragement of various groups for the study of *Juche* abroad. Asian, African and Latin American groups materialised, as did such groups in Europe.[35] Western governments became convinced that in this period the government of the DPRK had also resorted to more sinister methods in support of its policies. These included the bombing and killing of south Korean cabinet ministers meeting in Rangoon in 1983 and the bombing and destruction of a (south) Korean Airlines flight in 1987.

DPRK foreign policy in this period can therefore be characterised by its attempts at the state to state level to (i) maintain good relations with the socialist countries; (ii) to develop wide-ranging ties with the smaller countries within the international system – whatever their ideology – through the vehicle of the NAM; and (iii) to join international organisations within which the state could enter on terms of formal equality. In terms of links with non-state actors the DPRK attempted to deal with Western institutions such as banks and business to the extent needed to further its domestic goals. The DPRK also maintained its anti-imperialist, internationalist policies through its promotion of the *Juche* idea abroad and support for communist parties internationally.

Foreign policy rationale thus reflected the policy of self-reliance and the stress on *Chajusong*. The principle of *Chajusong* in the political sphere appeared to emphasise the defence of state sovereignty in its classic sense: that the state was the superior authority at home and that it should, on a reciprocal basis, respect the independence and equality of other states in the international system, regardless of ideology. However, the principle of *Chajusong* also stressed that these principles of state equality and independence were embedded within a domestic context which understood the realisation of these principles as only being possible within the context of a socialist transformation of society – specifically in the domestic sphere and by implication elsewhere.

In essence therefore, DPRK foreign policy of this period displayed two contradictory ideas. One was that of an emphasis on the principle of state sovereignty which according to most understandings would preclude (with rare exceptions) interference in the internal affairs of another state. Kim Il Sung's pronouncements very closely reflected the conventional view of international relations which relies on the classical concept of sovereignty. In this reading states should respect each others' independence and equality within the international system.

On the other hand DPRK foreign policy continued to express 'revolutionary' aims at least in the area of rhetorical anti-imperialism, with its involvement in terrorist activities, and with its support for groups which actively sought to propagate 'Kim Il Sungism'.

The proposition advanced here, however, is that during this period DPRK foreign policy displayed a practical and *conceptual* reorientation towards that of Political Realism and away from revolutionary ideas (at least in relation to foreign policy). The aspect of *Chajusong* which emerged most strongly in the actual practice of foreign policy was that of independence and equality of states within the international system. This emphasis on the classical ideas of sovereignty could most clearly be seen in the DPRK's attitude to working within the NAM – an attitude which publicly rejected ideology as a basis for co-operation and prioritised state to state co-operation links. Anti-imperialist rhetoric remained but policy development reoriented itself to operating on a state to state level using diplomacy and aid (in relations with the south) to establish influence and economic links. It is also suggested here that further study based on classical balance of power theory may well reveal some insights into DPRK foreign policy particularly in regard to its two powerful neighbours – China and the former USSR.[36]

This chapter does not seek to argue that the DPRK's foreign policy did not contain some elements of 'revolutionism' in its foreign policy. Its involvement in acts of terrorism would indicate that it was prepared to move outside the norms of diplomacy and international relations on certain occasions. However, speculative hypotheses may be put forward which if sustained would tend to support the overall argument made here.

Firstly, it is by no means apparent that the DPRK conducted a campaign of terrorist actions as part of a sustained and conscious policy chosen by the state. Its steady and increasing involvement at the state to state level and its innumerable pronouncements about the necessity to respect 'independence' and 'equality' and 'non-interference' would suggest the opposite. One hypothesis which might serve to offer some explanation of the Rangoon bombing and the Korean Airlines incident might be that derived from the 'bureaucratic politics' school of foreign policy analysis. Here analysts argue that organisations within states develop goals of their own and unless checked carry out actions according to 'standard operating procedures' (*sops*) which develop an organisational logic of their own not *necessarily* compatible with the interests of the state.[37] Given that internally the DPRK is both a national security-centred state *and* its institutions are heavily compartmentalised and separated from each other and appear to have difficulties in communication and co-ordination between each other, it may be that security agencies operating according to *sops* took the lead in planning and implementing the Rangoon and Korean Airlines outrages. As indicated this is an inevitably speculative hypothesis, but it may offer some way out of the puzzle as to the apparent contradiction in DPRK foreign policy.

Another, less tenable, hypothesis is that DPRK foreign policy makers conceptualised these activities against the south as *internal* to the nation and therefore outside the bounds of international law and norms of conduct. This is a less tenable hypothesis not because the DPRK recognised the existence of the south as separate state. It did not. The hypothesis is not persuasive because such terrorist actions would be equally inadmissible whether conducted *intra*-nationally or *inter*nationally.

There were of course other aspects to the 'revolutionary' nature of DPRK foreign policy – most notably the promotion of study groups abroad. These were, however, innocuous developments and represented inchoate efforts at cultural diplomacy. The aims of these groups were little different from those pursued by the French in their support for the promotion of French culture abroad via the *Alliance Française* or the Germans via the Goethe Institutes and the Friederich Ebert and Karl Adenauer Foundations (or Britain via the British Council).

The rocky road to (Political) Realism: the 1990s

The end of the Cold War did not have a major impact on the DPRK's orientation towards the rest of the world which remained based on the necessity to maintain economic independence and which was summarised in DPRK pronouncements as being shaped by an adherence to the principles of 'independence, peace and friendship'. The DPRK did not ignore the changing international configuration of forces but argued that the setbacks to the development of socialism were temporary. In the DPRK's reading the end of the Cold War did not mean the victory of one side over the other but rather

> the nullity of power politics, and this can be viewed as a major precondition for independence to prevail in the world. If one side assumes that it has a monopoly of world power because it has defeated the other side and attempts to maintain and expand the outmoded order of domination and

subjugation by means of power politics, it will not only meet the resistance of the peace-loving people of the world but also be deserted by its partners and ultimately invite its own collapse.[38]

Foreign policy in the early 1990s was shaped by domestic exigencies related to the necessity to modernise the economy. The DPRK particularly sought to respond to consumer demand for more varied and better quality consumer goods.[39] The reasons for this may have been that despite the DPRK's confident approach to the durability of its socialist system, the DPRK's policy makers could not have been unaware that part of the reason for the collapse of socialism in eastern Europe and the Soviet Union was due to the lack of consumer choice and economic inefficiencies as much as for political reasons. Like their socialist neighbours in the People's Republic of China the DPRK tried to modernise without losing political control.

DPRK policy makers promoted three 'revolutions' within north Korean society as frameworks for domestic development. These were the ideological, cultural and technical revolutions. The aim of the technological revolution was to

build up in a short space of time the solid production foundation of the engineering, ultraminiature electronics and robot industries by concentrating great efforts on their development and to produce and supply various up-to-date machinery and equipment, electronic and automation elements and devices needed for the technical reconstruction of the economy.[40]

Because the DPRK had more or less reached the limit of extensive growth, it sought to expand its productive potential through attempts to purchase new technology from abroad. Some attempts had been made to obtain technologically more advanced goods from eastern Europe in the mid-1980s and attempts had also been made to reinvigorate contacts with the West.[41] But it was the end of the Cold War and the increasing commercialisation of international relations as all states sought to expand trade links to cope with a vicious international recession, which brought some opportunities for growth in economic and technical exchange, which the DPRK was keen to pursue. For instance, the post-USSR Russian Federation continued to trade with the DPRK which provided a market for, among other things, Russian arms.[42]

In foreign policy 'proper' terms the objective of reunification of the 'nation' remained the top priority even if the strategy chosen to achieve the objective appeared to undergo a reassessment which was as much a response to the rapidly changing international scenario as it was to domestically inspired changes of policy. DPRK foreign policy also attempted to deal with other important foreign policy problems in the early 1990s – most of them in some way related to the reunification issue. Foreign policy developments included the decision to join the United Nations; moves to try to resolve conflicts with the international community over north Korea's nuclear programme; the start of direct talks with the United States; and the unsuccessful attempts at normalisation of relations with Japan.

The underlying principles in respect to the DPRK's approach to unification remained unchanged. The DPRK remained committed to what it identified as

> the three principles of independence, peaceful reunification and great national unity . . . we hold that on these principles the country should be reunified by founding a confederacy based on one nation, one state, two systems and two governments.[43]

The end of the Cold War, which was welcomed in public pronouncements as a contribution to 'easing of tensions', was seen as an opportunity for DPRK foreign policy. The DPRK argued that, because the division of Korea was a product of the Cold War, the partition of Korea was 'anachronistic'. But the DPRK also rejected what it termed 'reunification by absorption', 'unification of systems' or 'reunification by prevailing over communism'.[44] In making such statements the DPRK was making explicit its repudiation of the German example and offering a (not so) veiled warning that any attempt by the ROK to implement a similar policy towards the north would be met with resistance.[45]

The changing international balance of forces did, however, force one change in north Korean tactics, if not in the strategy of reunification policy. DPRK policy had consistently opposed a 'two Koreas' policy or 'cross-recognition' which would have permitted the ROK and the DPRK to join the UN as two separate states. The policy could be maintained because of support from the USSR and China. By the early 1990s – with economic pressures forcing both the Soviet Union (later Russia) and China into closer trading relations with the ROK – the DPRK could no longer rely on these two permanent members of the Security Council for support. In 1991 therefore the DPRK executed a volte-face and agreed to apply for UN membership and in September 1991 both the ROK and the DPRK were admitted to UN membership. The DPRK argued that

> As the South Korean authorities insist on their unilateral UN membership, if we leave this alone, important issues related to the interests of the entire

Korean nation would be dealt with in a biased manner on the UN rostrum and this would entail grave consequences.[46]

On the substantive issue and despite the often acrimonious public debate between the north and the south of Korea very rapid progress was made in the early 1990s, at least in comparative terms, on moves towards reunification. Between September 1990 and September 1992 eight rounds of talks were held between the north and south Korean governments. The talks made some progress in that at the sixth round in February 1992 both sides ratified the 'Agreement on reconciliation, nonaggression, co-operation and exchange between the north and the south', and the 'Joint declaration on the denuclearisation of the Korean peninsula'.[47] In September 1992 the composition of the Joint North-South reconciliation Committee was agreed and further protocols were signed on the implementation of the February agreements.[48]

The DPRK raised within the negotiations the question of the ROK's National Security Law which among other things made it a criminal offence for south Koreans to visit the north and called for the release of the Reverend Mun Ik Hwan and the student Rim Su Gyong, two south Koreans imprisoned after visiting the DPRK in 1991.[49] The DPRK also raised the question of the 'Team Spirit' exercises in the peninsula which the DPRK had consistently cited as an obstacle to negotiations between the north and the south. Although in 1992 the US and the ROK had agreed to discontinue that year's 'Team Spirit' exercise, the DPRK charged the south with a violation of the spirit of the non-aggression agreements because of the staging the US/ROK 'Focus Lens' military exercises in the south in the same year.[50]

Thus, when the United States announced in October 1992 that it was considering resuming joint US/ROK military exercises in 1993 the DPRK responded by breaking off all high level contacts with the south. The DPRK charged the ROK with breaching the denuclearisation accord, saying that 'Team Spirit 1993' was in effect a nuclear war exercise. In March 1993, as 'Team Spirit' began, Kim Jong Il, the President's son, designated successor and Supreme Commander of the Korean People's Army (KPA), placed the country on a war footing, claiming that the US and the ROK intended to launch 'a surprise, pre-emptive strike at the northern half of our Republic'.[51]

Part of the reason for the DPRK's strong reaction was because of the fear that the United States might indeed use the occasion to militarise the diplomatic war of words between both countries in respect to the concurrent conflict over the DPRK's nuclear programme. Indeed the DPRK had some past precedents which might give good grounds for apprehension. The October 1983 US invasion of Grenada had been preceded by large-scale military and naval exercises. Large-scale US/Honduran military manoeuvres had also taken place on a regular basis in locations close to the Nicaraguan border during the years of the Reagan administration's aggressive policies towards the Sandinista governments.

Initially, the ostensible reason for US hostility arose from the DPRK's tardiness in respect of fulfilling its obligations under the Nuclear Non-Proliferation treaty which it had signed in December 1985. The DPRK did not comply with its obligations under the Treaty to sign the Nuclear Safeguards Agreement (NSA). The north Koreans argued that they did not possess nuclear weapons and were not developing them. At the same time they attempted to make its signing of the NSA conditional on the withdrawal by the United States of the more than 1,000 tactical nuclear weapons which the DPRK claimed had been situated in the south since 1976.[52] There appeared to be some amelioration of the dispute after President Bush announced in September 1991 that the US would withdraw short range nuclear arms from its overseas bases – an initiative which the DPRK publicly 'welcomed' in October 1991.[53] The DPRK signed the NSA in April 1992 and in May admitted the International Atomic Energy Authority (IAEA) for the first official inspection of the DPRK's nuclear facilities.

By March 1993, however, after six IAEA inspections of DPRK nuclear facilities, relations had deteriorated to such an extent that the DPRK announced that it intended to withdraw from the Nuclear Non-Proliferation Treaty (NPT). The DPRK alleged that the IAEA was acting contrary to the provisions of the NSA in its demand for a special inspection of what the DPRK claimed were non-nuclear installations. The north argued that the United States, whose intelligence information the IAEA was utilising to provide the foundation for its request to visit the disputed locations, had 'fabricated' evidence in order to step up the war of words with the DPRK. This then was the background, along with the resumption of the 'Team Spirit' exercises, to the announcement that the DPRK would be placed on a semi-war footing on 8 March 1993.[54]

Despite belligerent rhetoric by both the DPRK and the US on this issue, including an aggressive statement by President Bill Clinton on a visit to the Panmunjon border area, by mid-1993 both sides appeared ready for a climbdown. The DPRK had already demonstrated, since early

1992, some signs of wanting an accommodation with the US. In January 1992 DPRK representatives met with US government officials in New York, inaugurating a series of talks which allowed for some progress in DPRK/US relations. In May 1992 the remains of a number of US soldiers killed in the Korean war were returned to US forces – indicating that the DPRK was giving serious consideration to shows of 'goodwill' towards the United States.

Team Spirit 1993 had brought an abrupt halt to such conciliatory moves but did not appear to have ended the possibilities for dialogue between the DPRK and the US. In June and July 1993 these countries made sufficient progress at bilateral meetings to issue joint statements which attempted to reach a mutually acceptable resolution to the conflict over the north's nuclear programme. Face was saved all round when the DPRK informed the US that it was 'out of the question' for the north to return to the Non-Proliferation Treaty while at the same time it agreed 'to suspend the effectuation of its withdrawal from the NPT'.[55]

The DPRK/US talks caused some uneasiness within Japan which although interested to a certain extent in a normalisation of relationships with the DPRK, had expressed public concern about what it perceived as a potential nuclear threat from the north. The DPRK for its part had also made some cautious attempts to improve relations with Japan at the same time as denouncing what it decried as Japan's own process of 'nuclearisation'.

Efforts to improve Japan/DPRK relations included the 28 September 1990 agreement between the Workers' Party of Korea (WPK), the governing party, and the two major Japanese political parties, the Liberal Democratic party and the Japanese Socialist party. This contained a commitment by all three political organisations to work towards normalisation of relations between Korea and Japan.[56] In February 1991 a delegation comprised of senior WPK members visited Japan and met with senior government representatives including the Prime Minister, Toshiki Kaifu.[57] Talks between representatives of the two governments took place in Beijing but made slow progress. The DPRK had raised several issues including reparations for Japanese historic 'crimes'. Chief of these was the question of recognition and restitution *vis-à-vis* the 'comfort-women', that is the Korean women who had been forced into sexual slavery for Japanese armed forces during the Second World War; and the alleged moves by Japan in the direction of developing nuclear armaments. The north also called for Japan to be refused a seat on the UN Security Council. Japan on the other hand raised issues pertaining to the DPRK's potential nuclear capabilities and the question of Japanese women said to be forced to remain in the DPRK against their will.

The DPRK maintained its policy of collaboration with elements of the international communist and socialist movement but in the early 1990s this aspect of DPRK foreign policy appeared to be diminishing in importance. A declaration published in Pyongyang in April 1992 on the occasion of the President's birthday by seventy such parties entitled 'Let us defend and advance the socialist cause' was notable mainly because of its moderation. The United States was not mentioned at all by name and the calls to anti-imperialism stressed the autonomy of societies to work out their own indigenous paths towards socialism. The call to 'defend and advance socialism on an international scale' was qualified by the insistence that socialism must be 'carved out and built within a country or national state as a unit.'[58]

The underlying rationale for DPRK foreign policy in this period was enunciated as being based on a policy of independence, peace and friendship. Independence and sovereignty were stressed and the strident commitment to anti-imperialism replaced by the less controversial objective of promoting 'friendship' between states and peoples. It was not the duty of socialists to 'export' revolution but to work for socialist change within one's own country. Non-intervention in the affairs of states was stressed and the necessity for each nation 'to build socialism which suits its own situation'.[59]

Anti-US rhetoric remained in DPRK foreign policy statements, but the rhetoric appeared to be increasingly focused on the rights and duties of the US as a *state* in the international system and less on the US role as the leader of an imperialist system involving a world-wide, interlocking state/society system of imperialism. A prevalent view by June 1992 was that - 'Like the United States, the Democratic People's Republic of Korea is an independent and sovereign state and has the legitimate right to choose its ideology, ideal and system.'[60]

From revolutionism to (Political) Realism?

The basic concepts of a Political Realist approach have been outlined by thinkers following in the tradition of Thucydides, Machiavelli, Hans Morgenthau and Henry Kissinger.[61] The fundamental approach is of a picture of the world as that of interreacting sovereign states whose governments respond to the protection and pursuit of the national interest by a due regard for the maintenance of power. The dominant morality *of states* (not of individuals) should be of prudence and a wise foreign policy maker should be careful not to allow messianic tendencies (such as those characterising either Woodrow Wilson's idealism or Lenin's anti-imperialism) obscure the primary goal of foreign policy which is of preservation of the sovereign state. The idea of sovereignty with its logical corollary of non-intervention in the affairs of other states based on the principle of reciprocity is central to the Political Realist vision. A foreign policy based on such principles, at least according to the Political Realists, will produce a 'rational' policy and in all possibility a beneficient one in terms of protecting the state's national interest *and* at the same time the stability of the international system. Stability is likely because the adherence to these basic principles allows for a degree of predictability and order in the system.[62]

The argument presented here is that the DPRK's foreign policy has increasingly shown signs of operating according to these classical Political Realist principles. This is not to say that the DPRK may never again engage in 'revolutionary' foreign policies but rather that, given the current domestic and international context, DPRK foreign policy is more rather than less likely to choose more conventional approaches to the management of its international relations than it may have adopted in the past.

The consequences for foreign policy decision makers elsewhere are that in their contacts with DPRK officials at the bilateral or at the multilateral level there may be improved possibilities of forging sustainable relations based on conventional principles in international relations. It would be foolish, however, to be too optimistic about the normalisation of the DPRK's relationship with the rest of the world. Unresolved internal divisions in the DPRK may as well make for unpredictability in the DPRK's international relations as much as a 'rational' foreign policy may make for predictability.[63]

In conclusion this analysis has sought to show that the DPRK's foreign policy is not necessarily benign but – contrary to received impressions – it is explicable.

Notes

1   This is the word used by Jon Halliday and Bruce Cumings, in *Korea: The Unknown War* (New York: Pantheon, 1988), p. 172.

2   For the classic exposition of Political Realism as a framework for the understanding of international politics see Hans Morgenthau, *Politics Among Nations:*

the Struggle for Power and Peace, Sixth edition (New York: Alfred A. Knopf, 1985). For a brief but useful discussion about Political Realism and other frameworks used to understand and interpret international politics see Michael Banks, 'The Inter-Paradigm Debate', in Margot Light and A. J. R. Groom, *International Relations: A Handbook of Current Theory* (London: Pinter, 1985), pp. 7–26.

3   See for instance Jon Halliday and Bruce Cumings, *Korea: The Unknown War* (New York: Pantheon, 1988) and Max Hastings, *The Korean War* (London: Michael Joseph, 1987). On the causes of the war see also I. F. Stone, *The Hidden History of the Korean War* (Boston: Little, Brown and Company, 1952).

4   A useful overview of the period 1945–54 can be found in European Ecumenical Network on Korea, *The Reunification of Korea: The Background* (London: KEEP/CIIR, 1989), pp. 13–19.

5   Jon Halliday, 'The North Korean Enigma', in C. Carciofi *et al.* (eds), *Revolutionary Socialist Development in the Third World* (Lexington: University Press of Kentucky, 1983), p. 117.

6   Gavan McCormack, 'Mists Clearing: Forecasts for the Past and Future History of the DPRK', paper given to the First Pacific Basin International Conference on Korean Studies, Honolulu, Hawaii, July/August 1992, pp. 2–3.

7   *Ibid.*, p. 3.

8   Although the official emissions are written in such a manner as to create disbelief to say the least. For the official version of the Pochonbo battle, for instance, see Party History Research Institute, *History of Revolutionary Activities of the Great Leader Comrade Kim Il Sung* (Pyongyang: Party History Research Unit, 1983), pp. 115–25.

9   Gordon White, 'North Korean Chuch'e: The Political Economy of Independence', in *Bulletin of Concerned Asian Scholars*, Vol. 7, No. 2, 1975, p. 45.

10   *Ibid.*

11   The *Juche* idea underlies all state policies in the cultural, economic, technical, political, social and personal aspects of north Korean society. See Kim Jong Il, *On the Juche Idea* (Pyongyang: Foreign Languages Publishing House, 1982); and for a critique see White, 'North Korean Chuch'e', pp. 44–54. For current north Korean thinking see the regularly published journal *Study of the Juche Idea* (Tokyo: International Institute of the Juche Idea).

12   Kim Han Gil, *Modern History of Korea* (Pyongyang: Foreign Languages Publishing House, 1979), p. 245.

13   Kim Il Sung, quoted in *Ibid.*

14   *Ibid.*

15   Tony Thorndike, 'The Revolutionary Approach: The Marxist Perspective', in Trevor Taylor (ed.), *Approaches and Theory in International Relations* (London: Longman, 1985), p. 56.

16   *Ibid.*, pp. 54–99.

17   Kim Il Sung, *On the Non-Aligned Movement* (Pyongyang: Foreign Languages Publishing House, 1982), p. 15.

18   White, '*North Korean Chuch'e*', p. 46.

19 Halliday, 'The North Korean Enigma', p. 133.

20 European Parliament, Committee on External Economic Relations Draft Report *on the Community's trade relations with North Korea*, PE 99.748, Rapporteur: Michael Hindley, 17 July 1985, p. 12.

21 Foreign and Commonwealth Office, Background Brief, *North Korea: Joining the World?*, June 1992, p. 1. These figures are inevitably somewhat speculative. A 1982 South Korean estimate of the DPRK's total foreign debt including that to the then USSR and China was of some $3,000 million. See European Parliament, *on the Community's trade relations with North Korea*, p. 15.

22 European Parliament, *on the Community's trade relations with North Korea*, p. 15.

23 Kim Han Gil, *Modern History*, p. 542.

24 Kim Il Sung, *On the Non-Aligned Movement*, p. 59.

25 *Ibid.*, p. 42.

26 Kim Han Gil, *Modern History*, p. 509.

27 Party History Research Institute, *History of Revolutionary Activities of Kim Il Sung*, p. 658.

28 For the DPRK's view on the 1972–75 north-south talks see Kim Han Gil, *Modern History*, pp. 510–21.

29 The proposal can be found in *Korea Today*, No. 4 (403), Pyongyang, 1990. pp. 2–3. My original discussion of this is in Hazel Smith, 'An End to Isolation? North Korea in the 1990s', in *LSE Magazine*, Vol. 2, No. 3, Autumn 1990, p. 34.

30 For the DPRK's assessment of ROK/US/Japanese military co-operation see Foreign Languages Publishing House (FLPH), *'Team Spirit': Nuclear War Game* (Pyongyang: FLPH, 1986).

31 Halliday and Cumings, *Korea*, p. 216.

32 Kim Han Gil, *Modern History*, pp. 553–5.

33 *Ibid.*, p. 540, my italics.

34 Li Sung Hyok, author's interview, Pyongyang, May 1990.

35 These study groups have adopted various names such as Groups for the study of Kim Il Sung's works, Groups for the study of Kim Il Sung's revolutionary idea. In Britain the group calls itself the 'Society for Independence Studies'.

36 For a useful analysis of balance of power theory see Hedley Bull, *The Anarchical Society* (London: Macmillan, 1977), pp. 101–26.

37 The most well-known exponent of theories of bureaucratic politics is Graham Allison. See Allison, *Essence of Decision: Explaining the Cuban Missile Crisis* (Boston: Little & Brown, 1971). The theories were developed within the framework of a study of foreign policy making within a democratic polity but there appears to be no reason why the theories could not be applicable to an authoritarian state.

38 Kim Il Sung, 'Answers to Questions Raised by a Delegation of Journalists of *Washington Times* from the United States – April 12, 1992', in *Study of the Juche Idea*, No. 59, October 1992, pp. 1–2.

39 The efforts to improve standards of living are stressed in various

pronouncements including Kim Il Sung, 'New Year Address, January 1, 1991', reproduced in *Study of the Juche Idea*, No. 53 (Tokyo: Shuhachi Inoue, April 1991) and Hong Sung Un, *Economic Development in the DPRK* (Pyongyang: FLPH, 1990), pp. 63–5.

40   Hong Sung Un, *Economic Development*, p. 66.

41   European Parliament, *on the Community's trade relations with North Korea*, p. 13.

42   *Bulletin D'Information*, Délégation Générale de la RPD de Corée en France, No. 28/1292, 24 December 1992, p. 4.

43   Kim Il Sung, *For a Free and Peaceful New World* (Pyongyang: FLPH, 1991), p. 6; see also New Year Address of Kim Il Sung, *Bulletin*, No. 01/0193, 1 January 1993, p. 3.

44   *Bulletin*, No. 2/191, 28 January 1991, pp. 4–8.

45   *Ibid.*, p. 6.

46   *Bulletin*, No. 11/591, 28 May 1991, p. 1.

47   The text of the 'Agreement on reconciliation' can be found in *Bulletin D'Information*, Délégation Générale de la RPD de Corée en France, No. 27/1291, 13 December 1991, pp. 1–2. The text of the 'Denuclearisation' agreement can be found in *Bulletin*, No. 05/0292, 20 February 1992, p. 3.

48   *Bulletin*, No. 20/0992, 22 September 1992, pp. 2–3.

49   *Bulletin*, No. 16/0892, 24 August 1992, p. 3.

50   *Ibid.*, p. 1.

51   Order of Marshal Kim Jong Il, *Bulletin*, No. 09/0393, 8 March 1993.

52   FLPH, *'Team Spirit'*, pp. 12–15.

53   *Bulletin*, No. 22/1091, 1 October 1991, p. 5.

54   *Bulletin*, No. 09/0393, 8 March 1993.

55   *Bulletin*, No. 19/0693, 29 June 1993, p. 8.

56   The text of the agreement can be found in *Bulletin*, No. 12/1090, 5 October 1990, pp. 6–7.

57   WPK Delegation's visit to Japan, report issued by the Paris Mission of the DPRK, no date.

58   *Bulletin*, No. 08/0492, 23 April 1992, pp. 2–3.

59   Kim Il Sung, 'Answers to Questions', p. 3.

60   *Bulletin*, No. 12/0692, 30 June 1992, p. 1.

61   For a good overview of this dominant approach to understanding international relations see Banks, 'The Inter-Paradigm Debate', pp. 7–26.

62   For a development of these themes see Bull, *The Anarchical Society*.

63   I utilise the term 'rational' here in the sense of Graham Allison's identification of the traditionalist or Realist approach to international relations as that of the foreign policy actor as a unitary, purposive actor which seeks optimal gains from a series of known preferences. See Allison, *Essence of Decision*.

7 *Philip G. Philip*

The Islamic revolution in Iran: its impact on foreign policy

Introduction

The Islamic revolution in Iran can be considered as one of the major events of the twentieth century. Few revolutions have shocked the world with such intensity or set in motion such a search for causes. The objective of this chapter will not be to analyse the contending theories of revolutions and their application to the upheavals in Iran; substantial work on this aspect can be found elsewhere.[1] The main emphasis will be to examine the overall impact that the revolution had on Iranian politics and international relations, particularly on the evolution of its foreign policy over the last decade, i.e. 1979–89. The chapter will also address the question of continuity and change by examining the elements which continue to shape Iran's foreign policy, and those elements which have given its post-revolutionary foreign policy an identity of its own.

Section one will study the extent to which Islam transcended its populist boundaries to become a geopolitical reality and the driving force behind Iran's foreign policy; section two will examine the evolution of Iran's foreign policy and diplomacy and the interaction between internal and external political developments; and section three discusses the nature of Iran's revolutionary foreign policy and signals the way it demonstrated itself in the foreign policy practice of that country.

While certain primary sources of information (interviews, Iranian foreign ministry press releases and Iranian press cuttings) have been used, all subsequent analyses of the policies and practices of the Islamic government in Iran will include the diverse interpretations of scholars and political scientists in the field.

The impact of ideological Islam on Iran's political process

In order to understand the religious factor (ideology) in the Iranian revolution and the role it played in the creation of an Islamic republic, it
is important to put into perspective a combination of certain unique
elements which transformed Iranian society and politics. This exercise
will not necessarily contribute something new towards the ongoing discussions in academic circles, but may help to dispel the popular myth that
labels the Iranian political experience as being nothing more than 'fundamentalist' in nature.[2]

More importantly, the religio-political dimension which continues to
play a leading role in the political process of the Islamic Republic of Iran
has not only created a new scope of study in the behaviour of Third
World countries, but has also affected the geopolitics of the region, by
condemning the existing international order as being exploitative and
imperialist in design.

Professor R. K. Ramazani,[3] addressing the issue of why Iran's political
behaviour is often seen as incomprehensible, has said 'If [one] fails to
acknowledge, for example, the religious influence of the Calvinist cast of
mind on Woodrow Wilson's concept of world order, how can [one] possibly understand Khomeini's concept of an Islamic world order?'[4] For
this reason the present section tries to describe both the secular interpretation of the ideological transformation which took place in Iran and
the religious or Islamic aspects of the actual government which was
formed following the upheavals of 1978–79.

The role of ideology in the political transformation of a society can be
viewed as problematic. The 'middle class' has many ideas but no ideology
of its own. It sets out to revolutionise the dominant ideology (usually
dependent capitalism) by means of a borrowed ideology (usually nationalism or the native religion). The existing dominant ideology is generally
conservative and tends to fix or otherwise distort the real essence of the
existing order. Thus, the emerging dominant ideology must not only
offer a more objective analysis of reality but must also engender change.
In addition, it must also be able to create a melange between theory and
practice. Dogmatism and rigidity are the common enemies of such an
ideology, which needs to be open and critical.[5]

In the case of Iran, ideological transformation faced two parallel developments. Firstly, the delegitimisation of the old dominant ideology and
secondly, the adaptation of the borrowed but all-persuasive ideology to
the specific needs and interest of the 'middle class'.[6] In the case of Iran,

the borrowed ideology was Islam. Although Islam was all-embracing as a religion long before the political revolution of 1979, its subsequent adaptation as an ideology of the state followed only after the displacement of the Pahlavi monarchy,[7] and not before both secular and religious forces jointly participated in removing all ideological and other vestiges of the Pahlavi state.[8]

However, in the immediate post-revolutionary phase, contrary to the predictions of the Western media,[9] the Islamists or clerical element of the revolution gained the upper hand over the secular elements, comprising nationalists, socialists, leftists and liberals. What then was the reason for the triumph of the Islamists and the subsequent adoption of Islam as the dominant state ideology?

The revolution was initially supported by a coalition of groups having different and even opposing backgrounds, goals and ideologies.[10] Ironically, in the ensuing struggle for power, groups helped to crush each other only to become victims themselves. For example, all groups helped to fight Mehdi Bazargan (November 1979, Khomeini's first appointed Prime Minister); those who remained then joined in disqualifying Ayatollah Kazem Shariatmadari (1980, leader of the five million Turkish-Azari speaking Iranians and also a high-ranking cleric).[11] The others helped the clerics in bringing down Abolhassan Bani Sadr (summer 1981, President of the Islamic Republic) and with him the Mojahedeen.[12] Those who still remained helped in removing Sadeq Qotabzadeh (summer 1982, foreign minister) who was executed later that year.[13] The remainder – and among them Huyjjatiyyah (the most strictly orthodox religious grouping) helped in the crackdown on the TUDEH (communist party) in the spring of 1983.[14] Finally, the radical clerics belonging to the Khomeini factions turned against the Hujjatiyyah in August 1983.[15] Thus, from what started out as working within a political alliance, Khomeini's supporters gradually achieved exclusive power within Iran.[16]

Having come to power in 1979, the revolutionary government, consisting mainly of clerics, concentrated on the consolidation, institutionalisation and, if possible, perpetuation of clerical rule. It was recognised that to implement Khomeini's revolutionary ideology it was necessary to rally a popular front which would actively support the clerics and maintain a critical level of revolutionary zeal. In addition, power would have to be concentrated within revolutionary institutions and active and potential opposition kept at a minimal level.[17]

In realising these goals, the leadership faced difficulties on various levels. Firstly, given that Islam is cross-class in nature, its interests naturally extended beyond the interests of any one class; this resulted in inter-class and intra-class conflicts. The fragmentation of Iranian society due to this conflict into several factions, each with different interests and motivations, rendered Islam problematic as an all-embracing ideology.

At a more general level, the leadership faced difficulties inherited from the previous regime: centralism, corruption, etc. It is therefore not sur-prising that there are demands for the rectification of these errors and for popular participation.[18] The inability of the revolutionary government to decentralise decision-making, planning and formulation of policy outside of a few 'Revolutionary Institutions' (Nichadha-ye-Enghelabi) has been partly attributed by some authors to the fact that 'the old military (op-posed to federal) and sectorial (opposed to regional) structure of the state remains largely intact'.[19]

These shortcomings, however basic they may be to consensus-based politics, were not too great to be sacrificed by the Iranian leadership at the altar of ideological Islam. This attitude led to the alienation of a wide spectrum of supporters for whom Khomeini was the undisputed leader. According to some authors, at the present time, the regime has no active supporters beyond ideological Islamists . . .[20]

Impact of ideological Islam on Iran's foreign policy

In the words of Shireen T. Hunter,[21] Iran's foreign policy since the revolution

> has been more deeply affected than before by ideological considerations, as a relatively well-defined set of beliefs has guided its actions. The Iranian leadership has been divided over the interpretation of different components of this broad ideology, but no key political figure has challenged the validity of the basic framework. Because of its principal motivations, the Islamic regime has seen itself as representing not just Iran's state interests but also those of a much broader Islamic movement. Thus, in the process, it has acted not only as a state but often as the spokesman of a cause.[22]

Ayatollah Khomeini's world view consisted of establishing an Islamic World Order, the basis of which would be an integrated ummah (congre-gation of believers). The role of Iran in this Islamic World Order is based on its commitment to providing the necessary material and spiritual guidance to Moslems in their struggle to replace the world imperialist governments with a just and divine government of the meek.

Article 3, Section 16 of the Constitution of the Islamic Republic states that the Islamic government of Iran would engage all provisions to realise the formulation of a foreign policy based upon 'Islamic criteria, brotherly commitment to all Moslems and unqualified protection of all the deprived of the world'.[23]

One of the direct consequences of the internal political system and the external perceptions and objectives of Tehran in terms of policy towards other states, especially in the region, has been the export of the revolution. This had a two-fold purpose: to destabilise the political situation in those areas and create a hostile environment for Western interests and, in addition, Iran, an Islamic revolutionary state of Shi'ite political persuasion, was primarily interested in liberating its Shi'a brethren in the Gulf States, Lebanon and Iraq, which continue to suffer deprivation under the predominantly Sunni ruling classes. Therefore for Iran, Western interests which were in favour of maintaining the *status quo* in the name of political stability and an uninterrupted supply of oil to the West, meant continued political deprivation and oppression.

Use of terror tactics against the French and US embassies in Lebanon and the taking of hostages were also motivated by the above factors. Iranian government functionaries like Mohsen Rafiqdoost, Minister of the Revolutionary Guards, explained yet another socio-political dimension of his country's involvement in Lebanon to Robin Wright, journalist and author. Rafiqdoost told her: 'We wanted to transfer our culture to Muslims in Lebanon. I saw the corrupted culture there. We started to show Muslims in Lebanon our way of living and our way of fighting.' When queried about his organisation's alleged involvement in the suicidal bombing of the American marine barracks and hostage-taking in Lebanon, Rafiqdoost replied:

> We only trained the Lebanese (Shi'ites) to defend their country. When we heard about the bombs – which killed two hundred and forty one American troops – we were happy. But we didn't plan it. It was their right. Ask yourself, why were the Americans in Lebanon?'

Not, he implied, to help the Muslim community.[24]

One of the main reasons why the Iranian style of protest did not develop into a wider revolutionary movement in the region was because it was Irano-Shi'a centric. Moreover the infighting within the clerical ranks in Iran demoted the infallible nature of the revolution into a mere political movement in the eyes of many Muslims. Nevertheless, the revolution still had a number of adherents especially among those who were disenchanted by the decadence and pro-Western tendencies of Muslim rulers.

Certain authors believe that the Iranian revolution has failed to have, or is unlikely to have, any long-term international impact in the same way as the American, French and Russian revolutions.[25] It is easier to agree with the latter part of the above opinion as it is still too early to measure the historical contribution made by the Iranian revolution towards the politics of the Middle and Near East and to the Muslim world in general. However, to argue that the revolution has had *no* international impact is difficult to accept. For one thing, 'the very act of overthrowing the most powerful monarchy in the region and its replacement by a republican regime challenged the legitimacy of the remaining dynasties in the Gulf and, moreover, exposed the fragility of these regimes and the feasibility of overthrowing them'.[26]

The export of the revolution being an integral part of Iran's revolutionary foreign policy necessitated the formulation of both short- and long-term strategies by the leadership. In the first instance, supporters were encouraged to demonstrate against the ruling cliques which, if monarchical or involving hereditary succession, were condemned as being anti-Islamic and invalid. Some of these protests in the Gulf countries did result in serious breaches of internal security and obliged governments to adopt repressive measures.[27] Long-term strategies involved steps to radicalise the entire Muslim ummah against what was considered as their illegitimate governments and rulers and against Western, especially American, domination of the affairs of the Middle East and the Muslim world.

For example, Khomeini argued that the annual pilgrimage to Mecca (Haj) was not only to be considered as an act affirming devotion to God, but an opportunity for Muslims to demonstrate and rid the Muslim world of foreign domination. This would remind Muslims of their social and political obligations and fulfil the real purpose and spirit of the pilgrimage just as God had intended. Khomeini's call to use the Haj as a tool of political protest resulted in violent clashes between Iranian pilgrims and Saudi militia in July 1987, causing the death of several hundred pilgrims. On the international level this led to mutual recriminations and the cutting off of all diplomatic ties between the two countries.[28]

In the period after the Haj tragedy, the speaker of the Iranian Parliament in a speech in October 1988 admitted that there existed serious differences among the world congregation of Muslims (ummah) especially along political and religious lines. This disunity was even more apparent among Shi'as and Sunnis, and any vision of achieving the ideal of a united ummah, Rafsanjani concluded, would have to be preceded by 'a high mindedness (se'eh-sadr)' which does not exist.[29]

It is important to note that Iranian leaders themselves have recognised the failure of tactics used to implement their strategies connected with the export of the revolution. Rafsanjani, in describing Iran's revolutionary position *vis-à-vis* other countries in the world political arena, clearly states: 'One of our incorrect measures was that, in the revolutionary atmosphere, we made enemies . . . We created enemies for ourselves. Those who could have remained indifferent were made to transform their indifference into hostility, and we did not attempt to attract the friendship of those who could have been our friends.'[30]

Another aspect of ideological Islam on Iran's foreign policy process was manifested in its allegiance to the principles of non-alignment. On the one hand revolutionary Iran remained within the movement, while on the other it questioned the concept of non-alignment and its functions.

Non-alignment can be considered as a built-in component of Iran's revolutionary foreign policy, and the Iranian revolution being primarily directed at a regime which was an active client of a superpower and one in which no foreign power was involved 'provided tremendous confidence, self-righteousness, and exuberance to the new regime'.[31] Non-alignment, which is generally understood as a positive concept based on passive resistance to superpower politics was not fully acceptable to the Iranian regime. Iran sought to revolutionise this philosophy and saw the movement as a platform for direct confrontation with the superpowers.

Dr A. H. H. Abidi of the School of International Studies, New Delhi, and a specialist on Iranian affairs states that 'According to the Iranians, the tendency of alignment/non-alignment is the external manifestation of the state of mind of a given ruling elite'. The Iranians argue that 'true non-alignment is possible only when the thought process of people and leaders are completely emancipated from political oppression, economic exploitation, cultural manipulation, mental slavery, and all other causes of fear and alienation'. From the Islamic perspective, this is possible when 'one is subservient only to God and to no other power on earth',[32] and in this context, Prime Minister Hossein Musavi has stated that many countries and peoples 'regard the Islamic Revolution [Iranian Revolution] as a historical experience and model for revolt against the western and eastern imperialists'.[33]

On one level Iran's stance on non-alignment was a revival of Mossadegh's 'negative balance' in the sense of following neither East nor West. Dr Jamshid Hagoo, a Deputy in the Foreign Ministry during the early days of the revolution when the nationalists were still in government, stated that the 'Neither East nor West' policy espoused by Khomeini (Na Sharki, Na Gharbi) did not 'mean self-ostracization . . . but independence,

self-reliance, resourcefulness, as well as political and economic independence'.[34]

On another level Iran viewed non-alignment or the neither East nor
West ideal as a basis for conducting its foreign relations by 'preserving
the principle of non-compromise'. Hossein Musavi, who can be considered as a staunch Islamist following Imam Khomeini's line, described the
foreign policy system of the Islamic republic as one which 'negates compromise . . . despite various pressures and crises imposed by imperialism
. . .'[35] At the seventh non-aligned summit held in New Delhi, Musavi added
that member governments who based their policies on non-alignment
'*cannot* and *shall not* think of anything in the international political scene
but winning true independence for all, and annihilating all forms of
dependence on the Big Powers and political and economic empires which
have divided God's earth into zones of influence'.[36]

In practice, however, maintaining the 'neither East nor West' policy
strictly led to certain ambiguities in Iran's foreign policy formulation.
Take, for example, the following views of the Iranian Foreign Ministry
on economic relations. In an interview, Ahmad Azizi, the under secretary
for economic affairs, stated that in establishing relations his country 'would
give priority to those who do not have ties with the superpowers' or
intend to 'impose their economic or political views on Iran'. He added,
however, that although Iran was 'constantly trying not to have any special
tendency towards any certain blocs . . . economic ties with the Eastern
bloc are to the extent that we can call them rational and reasonable' (sic).[37]

A partial explanation of the above contradiction in terms of policy
would be that, on the periphery of the neither East nor West posture,
Iran adopts 'a basically benign view of the Soviet Union, favouring close
co-operation with Eastern bloc countries'. This ambiguity in the view of
certain authors has rendered Iran's post-revolutionary foreign policy both
'dualistic and contradictory' in character.[38]

A lack of a proper mix of ideology and pragmatism made Iran's
approach to non-alignment politically unviable and Khomeini's advice to
the movement to revolutionise the dominant orders untenable for the rest
of the grouping. Dr Abidi, in presetting a non-religious analysis of Iran's
perception of the Non-Aligned Movement, states that 'the Iranians show
a lack of understanding of the socio-politico-dynamics of the diverse
societies of the Third World'. Adding that non-alignment 'cannot be seen
only in black and white terms' but within the wider context of 'the hard
realities of international politics', Dr Abidi concludes by saying that they
are not prepared to rise above religion in order to tackle the intricacies of

politics or economics'. He described their approach as 'emotional, rather than rational'.[39]

The evolution of Iran's foreign policy and diplomacy

During the rule of the Pahlavi monarchy, the nature and direction of Iran's external relations underwent considerable change, reflecting both developments within Iran and events in the international arena.

The underlying principles of Pahlavi Iran's 'national independent' foreign policy as stated by the leadership were

(i) adherence to the Charter of the United Nations and respect for international law;
(ii) establishment of friendly relations with all countries regardless of their economic and social system.

In fact, it would not be incorrect to state that without jeopardising Iran's special political and economic relations with the West, the former sought to maintain diplomatic and economic relations with as many socialist, Western and Third World countries as possible.

By the mid-1970s Iran's special relationship with the Western allies suffered considerable setbacks due to its leading role in increasing the price of oil and its rapid military build-up. This led the West to scrutinise carefully Iran's record on human rights which hitherto was not an issue governing the relationship between the two. In addition, the military component of Iran's foreign policy caused much concern to the West, which felt that it directly affected the pro-Western Gulf Arab states and sought to further radicalise the anti-Western movements in the region. Albeit, Iran remained firmly within the Western camp, given its deep involvement with the former in the economic, political and military fields.

This situation created the impression among many that Iran was openly a pawn of the West, carrying out the imperialist game plan in the Persian Gulf region. Opposition groups both secular and religious were against Iran's membership in CENTO (Central Treaty Organisation) and its relations with Israel and South Africa, which further seemed to prove their country's domination by outside powers.

With the advent of the revolution there was general disagreement regarding relations with the West. The nationalist elements favoured maintaining links with the occident and the United States as opposed to the demands of the left and the clerical factions who were not in favour of it. In order to reach a middle ground, the Shah's last government led by the late Shapour Bakhtiar declared it would leave CENTO and sever relations with Israel and South Africa, a decision which was acceptable to all groups.

In the period preceding the declaration of Iran as an Islamic Republic, Mehdi Bazargan's provisional government was not able to bring about any change in Iran's foreign policy at the official level. By attempting to follow a moderate policy of non-alignment, Bazargan was suspected of wanting to move closer to the United States by the left and the Islamists. A direct consequence of this was the hostage crisis, which was a move to reverse this perceived trend.

The hostage crisis, while successfully alienating the West from Iran, opened a new chapter in Iran's foreign policy and diplomacy, one which was characterised by violence and greatly affected by Islamic revolutionary ideas. Although the direction of post-revolutionary Iran's foreign policy has often been determined by the changes in the configuration of power among internal groups, pragmatic considerations dictated by strategic and economic necessities have been said to be the prime mover of Iran's foreign policy. This has urged a line of reasoning (much to the chagrin of Iranian Foreign Ministry officials) that the pre- and post-Shah regimes have maintained a degree of congruence in their foreign policy objectives differing only in method. For example some analysts argue that the two regimes 'share a striking similarity in their perception of Iran's regional role', which is motivated by the 'unyielding determination to assert Iran's supremacy throughout the Gulf'.[40]

This view is not subscribed to by Iranian Foreign Ministry officials, who believe that Iran has no desire to assert itself militarily in the Persian Gulf region. They add that one of the main outcomes of the 'Islamic Revolution' was to relinquish its role as gendarme of this region.[41] This, of course, leaves the question of Iran's quest for spiritual/ideological leadership in the Persian Gulf region. It has been argued that Iran's war with Iraq was a direct outcome of this quest, but with acceptance of Security Council Resolution 598 in July 1988 it is argued that 'Iran's world view had completed a cyclical reversal from the revisionist dream to shape the Gulf along Islamic lines to acquiesence in the status quo established by the Shah in the mid-1970s'.[42]

There is a chance, however, that these arguments tend to simplify the nature and relationship between particular dimensions of pre- and post-Shah foreign policy. In the context of these views, it may be said that the chances of outside misperceptions are possible given the deep ideological gap between the pre-revolutionary monarchic regime and the post-revolutionary Islamic regime. It may therefore prove much more fruitful to study the orientation of Iran's foreign policy through its different phases and based on its actual practice, with reference to domestic determinants.

The orientation of revolutionary Iran's foreign policy

In an interview with Dr Mahmood Sariolghalam,[43] he stated that, in order to understand the Iranian revolution and the political processes it set in motion (of which the formulations of foreign policy assume a crucial part), it is necessary to pose certain questions and take into account certain variables. For example,

(i)   Which strata of the Iranian population have become the decision makers after the revolution?

(ii) What are their characteristics, what are their beliefs, thoughts and traditions? And how do they relate to the international system?

Of the variables that contribute to post-Shah political development, (a) the Islamic religion, (b) the impact of historical events and enduring perceptions of the past, and (c) the transformation of the clergy from a potential to an actual elite group are the most significant. The last variable is particularly important as it was 'the existence of well-established, semi-organisational, traditional and religious linkages in the pre-revolutionary period that provided the clergy with capabilities to rise above other intellectual groups and set the foundations of a new structure'.[44]

In order to gain a general picture of the decision making apparatus in post-revolutionary Iran and some of its characteristics, Dr Sariolghalam points out that the Shah's regime had alienated 'the majority of the population'. This majority and the clergy, he argues, have been asked to become decision makers in the new structure after the revolution. Hence in true revolutionary fashion 'formerly alienated and inexperienced and presently revolutionary decision-makers are learning and adapting to the requirements of national statecraft.'[45] Crisis management, trial and error and constant modification of ideas have characterised the decision making process in the last decade and in all this the Islamic clergy performs a crucial role. Dr Sariolghalam is of the view that 'as the clergy develops, learns, adapts and changes, the population in turn will change and adapt'. Portraying the clergy as a source of change in itself, he concludes by stating that 'the conceptual, orientational and evolutionary changes within the clergy will be the major determinants of the trends and patterns of Iranian politics in the coming years.'[46]

The question of how the Islamic government and its proponents seek to establish and structure a religious state within a secular international system has raised considerable conceptual problems for Iranian decision makers and continues to have a direct impact on the orientation of Iran's foreign policy. For example, while rejecting superpower politics and the concept of balance of power in the international system on the one hand, Iran adopted the creed of violence as a corrective measure in its foreign policy orientation on the other. In this context Khomeini told his followers that, because the superpowers 'are responsible for all world corruption', Muslims 'should mobilise the oppressed and chained nations so the superpowers can be pushed out of the scene and the governments can be handed over to the oppressed'. But this must be done in a way that teaches the superpowers a lesson . . . 'they must be slapped in the face . . . Through violence the satanic majority will be made to submit to the righteous few'.[47]

The termination of the Iran-Iraq war and the reconstruction phase which is under way in Iran have brought other ways of looking at the above-stated dilemma. Decision makers and academics believe that the conceptual task facing them is to bring into congruence 'divine norms and laws with the conventional interpretations of nationality in the contemporary international system'.[48]

Iran's geopolitical situation has necessarily influenced its perceptions of the outside world and continues to have great influence on its external relations. The Pahlavi regime's obsession with security arising out of the East-West ideological competition over power in the Persian Gulf region was shared by the nascent revolutionary regime. Iran's ex-President, Abolhassan Bani-Sadr has been quoted as saying in this context that, because Iran historically has found itself 'between two opposing powers . . . It has always been a battlefield. At the beginning of this century, Iran found itself wedged between Tsarist Russia and the British Empire. Toady it is between the Soviet Union and the United States'.[49]

Following from this perception, there exists a 'constant fear of disintegration and dismemberment . . . haunting Iranians', and many Iranians of both regimes believe that 'no foreign power wants to see Iran strong and independent'. In the aftermath of the revolution in 1979, new forces came into play. The Asian Republics bordering Iran being predominantly Muslim and the existence of oppressed Shi'a populations in the Persian Gulf states provided adequate tinder to destabilise seriously the *status quo* in the region. Ayatollah Khomeini, describing the new situation, has been quoted as saying:

With the victory of the Nation of Islam ... the attention of all the big powers centred on Iran, and their agents started conspiracy after conspiracy to prevent the realisation of this Islamic Republic. Because this Islamic Republic which started in Iran, and reached other Muslim and non-Muslim countries without doing any correct propaganda and merely by virtue of its message, is threatening those countries which are either under American or Soviet influence.[50]

In 1982, Foreign Minister Velayati stressed that 'creating unity among the World Muslims was a strategic objective' of his ministry. Dr Velayati added that his ministry sought to create a 'unified Islamic front against imperialism and Zionism' in which 'non-Islamic countries which had common views with Iran ... could also co-operate ...'[51]

Conclusion: the nature of Iran's revolutionary foreign policy

The nature of Iran's revolutionary foreign policy is made easier to understand if the writings of Ayatollah Khomeini on Islamic government are taken as a backdrop. Probably the best known of Imam Khomeini's works is a collection of lectures given by Khomeini at Najaf in Iraq between 21 January and 8 February 1970, and the following points give some idea as to where and how policy, whether domestic or foreign, originated.

 (i)　All political power should be subordinate to Islamic goals, precepts and criteria.
 (ii)　It is the solemn duty of religious scholars to assume the political mantle (the concept of Vilayat-e-Faqih described earlier on in this chapter).
(iii)　The faqih should be recognised as necessary and self-evident.
(iv)　The faqih should design the programme for the establishment of the Islamic government.

These points, taken together with the conviction that (i) imperialists have no religious beliefs, whether Christian or Islamic, and that (ii) Islam is the religion of militant individuals who are committed to truth and justice and are in continual struggle against the imperialist yoke, give rise to what some authors have described as an orientation of contemporary Muslim thought that 'seems to derive its main justification from the concept of Islam being belief and law (aqida wa shariah), religion and state (din wa dawla), and a system of values for spiritual and temporal affairs (din wa dunya)'.[52]

Following from this Islam-centric view, the contemporary international system and its institutions were regarded as suspect. The United Nations, epitomised by the politics of the Security Council and the existence of the veto, was considered as an instrument of American foreign policy and rejected.[53] The hostage crisis may be considered as a prime example, where Iran flouted international law on the grounds that it saw the ensuing struggle between itself and the United States as a war between Islam and blasphemy. At one stage, Foreign Minister Velayati said that his country would reconsider relations with countries which had voted against Iran on the issue of human rights adding that those countries were not in favour of human rights, but only intent on exerting political pressure on Iran.[54]

The nature of Iran's foreign policy, as preceding sections demonstrate, was one which continued to emerge from a highly centralised government that allowed its citizens minimal influence in deciding on policies that affected them directly. However, the revolution itself replaced the spiritual core which had been lost during the monarchy, and this in turn saw the exit of materialism as the main motor behind the formulation of policy. The example set by Ayatollah Khomeini, whose frugal approach to daily living and constant urging that hardship was the road to piety and a test of faith, became the underlying standard for general conduct in matters of personal life and state. Members of society who chose not to make this a way of life believed that this was a way of subordinating society to the will of the mullahs (who they believed led licentious lives), on the one hand; while on the other, they believed that it formed part of a grand conspiracy on the part of the United States who, in collusion with the government, preferred that the true potential of the Iranian people should not be realised.[55]

Myths like these are what fuelled a national consensus that America is in one way or another the 'Great Satan' and, more selectively, that the world is divided into those who follow the 'path of God and belief' and those who follow the 'path of Satan and disbelief'.[56] The polarised vision of the world includes that more universal revolutionary belief utilised by Ayatollah Khomeini, namely that further divisions exist between those countries and peoples who have the power to dominate and oppress others, namely the 'Mustakbarin' and those who lack power and are subject to oppression, namely the 'Mostazafin'.[57] In addition there is widespread belief in Iran and among revolutionary Muslims that there is an ongoing global conspiracy led by the West to plunder their wealth and weaken Islam in the process.

It can be assumed from the above that the political psychology of those committed to the revolution and the direction it had taken were in no doubt that their faith was the only means of resisting outside forces, which were continually trying to defeat their real purpose. Iranian officials have described their chosen path as a 'River of no return'.[58] This approach to international politics went against an 'extremely powerful and pervasive American belief system about the nature of foreign policy, how it is conducted and how it affects American life. This belief system is troublesome because of the hold it has in shaping political strategy and defining 'normalcy' in foreign affairs, even when it falls far from the mark in reflecting 'reality'. One analyst concludes by stating that 'At best foreign policy and military strategy based on this system of belief is ineffective. At worst it is detrimental to American interests'.[59]

Other authors have pointed out that American labels 'liberal conservative, fanatic and moderate – are ill-chosen for Iranian politics ... A conservative or economic policy may be a radical on social standards and ambivalent on foreign policy;' adding that, 'The American view is contorted by emotions over Iran's revolutionary excesses and continuing confrontations. Toward the United States, Iran displays equal or greater ignorance, conceptual difficulties, and emotional obstacles'.[60]

As stated earlier in this chapter there is a belief that under the ideological garb of revolutionary Iran's foreign policy lie the same geopolitical considerations which guided the Shah's foreign policy, albeit against an altered regional and global vista. Authors like Efraim Karsh differentiate between pre- and post-revolutionary Iran's quest for supremacy in the Persian Gulf region as between one which was restricted to political/military method during the Shah's time and one which made use of militant Islam in the period after that. Karsh himself said that, unlike the post-revolutionary situation, the Gulf states secretly endorsed Iran's role of policeman of the region, seeking 'a free ride from Iran's power'.[61]

In the post-revolutionary scenario, the single-mindedness with which Iran's leaders sought to revolutionise the Muslim people of the Persian Gulf region came to characterise a new phase in international politics, that of resurgent Islam. Muslim countries which had a resident Shi'a population were almost immediately affected. Iraq, which actually has a majority of Shi'as, was soon feeling the wrath of militant Islam. The attempted assassination attempt on the life of foreign minister Tariq Aziz and Saddam Hussein's crackdown on the Shi'a opposition were crucial factors which led to the outbreak of the full-scale war.

Lebanon, which like Iraq was linked to Iran by religion and an interconnected clerical network, was also a target. With the last vestiges of a confessional state in shambles, it provided Iranian militants with an opportunity to liberate their brethren who hitherto were the least emancipated among all the religious and ethnic groupings in the region. The large Western presence in the state was an added incentive for the newly-trained Lebanese groups who were out to prove their revolutionary credentials. Kidnapping and hostage-taking by the Hezbollah and Amal, both having their organisational and ideological roots in Iran, opened a new chapter in international relations and transformed the politics of the region. Towards truly revolutionising the Lebanon, Tehran has invested heavily in men (Revolutionary Guards), materials (arms and logistics) and funds. Lastly, the geographical proximity to Israel provided these fighters in the Lebanon with the holiest objective of all – the liberation of Jerusalem.[62]

Among the other Muslim countries in the region, Saudi Arabia was considered during the Haj pilgrimage as the ideal place to show up the incompatibility of being a true Muslim and yet following in the path of the Western countries, as Khomeini accused the Saud family, guardians of the holiest place in Islam, of doing. The active politicisation of the Haj by Iranian pilgrims resulted in the death of many of them at the hands of the Saudi forces in August 1987.[63] Political activism in other countries in the region, which has been discussed earlier in this chapter under the heading of 'export of the revolution', largely lost momentum before the mid-1980s.

Another departure from pre-revolutionary Iran's stance in international politics has been the overall attitude to the West, particularly the United States of America. In almost every speech of an official or statement from the Foreign Ministry, condemnation of the West, especially the United States, has been a permanent feature. The Foreign Minister in most of his speeches in public or conferences has gone to great lengths to show how the nexus between American imperialism and Zionism conspires to destroy Islam.[64]

In conclusion it may be argued that revolutionary Iran faced some of the most powerful states in a modern nuclear world and, given the circumstances it found itself to be in, imposed its dictate for what seems to be specific short-term goals, such as achieving the reputation of a defiant middle power while finally shrugging off the yoke of centuries of foreign interference and domination.

Notes

1   See Farrokh Moshiri, *The State and Social Revolution in Iran: A Theoretical Perspective*, New York: Peter Lang Publishing Inc., 1985. The author has made a

scholarly attempt to apply available social science theories to the Iranian revolution of 1978–79, after utilising a range of theories from Ted Gurr's Relative Deprivation thesis (see T. R. Gurr, *Why Men Rebel*, Princeton: Princeton University Press, 1970), Chalmers Johnson's notion of 'accelerators' (see Johnson (ed.), *Ideology and Politics in Contemporary China*, Seattle: University of Washington Press, 1973), to the more recent works of Theda Skocpol (T. Skocpol, 'Rentier State and Shi'a Islam in the Iranian Revolution', *Theory and Society*, vol. 11, no. 3, May 1982, pp. 265–83) and Charles Tilly (C. Tilly, *From Mobilisation to Revolution*, Reading, Massachussetts: Addison-Wesley, 1973), who proposes his own model of the Iranian Revolution. The work is a *mélange* of behaviourist models of revolutions and the history, politics and events which led up to the revolution in Iran in 1978–79.

2   For example, there are some authors who, while acknowledging the international dimensions of 'Islamic fundamentalism', stop short of enquiring into the socio-political transformation which Iranian society and politics went through. See Mohammad-Reza Djalili, 'The International Dimensions of Fundamentalism', *World Link*, no date. While warning Muslim and non-Muslim countries of the 'transitional character' of fundamentalism, the author calls upon nations to 'formulate efficient counter-strategies' against a movement which threatens 'the international system' and whose chief architect (Khomeini) has encouraged 'his followers to take out their sabres and chop up corrupt people'. This kind of sensationalism accorded to statements made by Khomeini or any other leader is often quoted out of context. According to others the word 'fundamentalist' itself is often used loosely. 'In the strictest historical sense fundamentalism refers to a movement in American protestantism arising out of a coalition of theologically conservative Evangelicals that came together about 1920 to struggle against the tendencies commonly labelled "Modernism" or "Liberalism" '. See article by William Shepard, 'Fundamentalism, Christian and Islamic', *Religion*, vol, 17, 1987, p. 356. The author prefers to describe the movements in the Islamic world as 'an ideological orientation', pp. 357–8.

3   Professor R. K. Ramazani of the University of Virginia, has written prolifically on Iran's government, politics and foreign policy, both during and after the Pahlavi monarchy.

4   R. K. Ramazani, *Revolutionary Iran: Challenge and Response in the Middle-East*, London and Baltimore: The Johns Hopkins University Press, 1986, p. 19.

5   See June Nash, Juan Corradi and Hobart Spalding, Jnr (eds), *Ideology and Social Change in Latin America*, New York: Gordon and Breach Science Publishers, 1977.

6   A number of authors have described the middle class as the prime mover in the Iranian revolution of 1979. This has been attributed to their superiority in numbers and also because a majority of the Iranian intelligentsia critical of the Shah's policies were among the middle class. Though a good number of the participating intelligentsia were socialist in colouring, a number of them, both

religious and secular, were nationalistic and basically reform-minded. Hossein Bashiriyeth, *The State and Revolution in Iran.* London: Croom Helm, 1986. Robert Graham, *Iran: The Illusion of Power*, New York: St Martin's Press, 1979, see chapter 12.

7   Mansour Farhang, 'How the Clergy Gained Power in Iran', in Barbara Freyer Stowasser (ed.), *The Islamic Impulse*, London: Croom Helm, 1987.

8   This crusade entailed a range of activities, for example, the dismantling and complete purge of the imperial forces, the abolition of judicial and security apparatus of the state, etc.

9   Yann Richard, 'The Relevance of "Nationalism" in Contemporary Iran', *Middle East Review*, vol. xxi, no. 4, Summer 1989. The author, who was in Iran during the revolution, recalls that most of the Western media 'seemed to think that the Revolution was going to turn to the benefit of the National Front (Jebhe-ye-Melli)' p. 27.

10   For a well laid out description of the secular, religious, nationalist and ethnic groups which were active in the aftermath of the revolution, see Nozar Alaolmolki, 'Iranian Opposition to Nozar Khomeini and the Islamic Republic', *Australian Outlook*, vol. 23, no. 2, August 1984, pp. 99–105.

11   Ayatollah Shariatmadari was one of the early opponents of the clergy's participation in politics as well as in the institution of the *vilayat-e-fagih* (government of the jurisconsult, office of Ayatollah Khomeini). The clerical community of Qam (holy city in Iran) then convened and stripped Shariatmadari of the title of Ayatollah in 1982.

12   In June 1987 the Mojahedeen (armed guerillas) rallied their support behind the ousted President Bani Sadr. Ironically the Mojahedeen had spoken in favour of Khomeini and the Islamic Republic, despite the fact the Khomeini never accepted the Mojahedeen as a legitimate Islamic organisation. See Alaolmolki, 'Iranian Opposition to Khomeini and the Islamic Republic', pp. 99–100.

13   In mid-April 1982, Qotabzadeh appeared on national television and confessed to conspiring to destroy all the heads of the Islamic government including Khomeini. He also confirmed that he had enlisted the support of a group of military officers and that of Ayatollah Shariatmadari, *ibid.*, p. 100.

14   See Zalmay Khalilzad, 'Moscow's Double Track Policy, Islamic Iran: Soviet Dilemma', *Problems of Communism*, vol. xxxiii, January-February 1984.

15   See the varied examples of leading orthodox clerics who were removed from their positions because of their opposition to Khomeini's views on religion and politics, Alaolmolki, 'Iranian Opposition to Khomeini and the Islamic Republic', p. 101.

16   Some authors also attribute the triumph of revolutionary Islam as the state ideology in Iran, to the uncompromising stance it took on all issues, by contrast with the leftist or nationalist ideologies which were willing to accept compromises. Moreover Islam, as a religion with universal scope, tended to be internationalist and even assume certain supranational dimensions.

17 See, for example, Cheryl Bernard and Zalmay Khalilzad, *The Government for God: Iran's Islamic Republic*, New York: Columbia University Press, 1984.

18 The most outspoken critic of the Islamic Government in Iran is the ex-president of the Islamic Republic of Iran – Abol Hassan Bani-Sadr. Through his newspaper *Islamic Revolution*, in a column titled the 'President's Diary', he condemned corruption and equated the Islamic Republic Party (IRP) with the single party of the Shah's regime, the Rastakhiz. In the period before being removed from office, Bani-Sadr sent a letter to Khomeini warning that the latter's trust in the IRP amounted to committing suicide. See Dilip Hiro, *Iran Under the Ayatollahs*, London: Routledge and Kegan Paul, 1985, pp. 179–85.

19 Hooshang Amirahamadi and Manoucher Parvin (eds), *Post-Revolutionary Iran*, London: Westview Press, 1988, p. 235.

20 Homa Katouzian, 'Islamic Government and Politics: The Practice and Theory of the Absolute Guardianship of the Jurisconsult', in Charles Davies (ed.), *After the War: Iran, Iraq and the Arab Gulf*, Chichester, West Sussex: Carden Publications Ltd, 1990.

21 Shireen T. Hunter is Deputy Director of the Middle East Programme at the Center for Strategic and International Studies in Washington.

22 Shireen T. Hunter, *Iran and the World: Continuity in the Revolutionary Decade*, Bloomington and Indianapolis: Indiana University Press, 1990, p. 36.

23 *The Constitution of the Islamic Republic of Iran*, Tehran, no date, p. 22.

24 Robin Wright, 'A Reporter at Large: Tehran Summer', *The New Yorker*, 5 September 1988, p. 42.

25 This was the opening comment of Patrick Bannerman, arguing the case against the Iranian Revolution as being a Historic Revolution at a Conference convened by the Royal Institute of International Affairs on 'The Iranian Revolution, Ten Years After', held at Chatham House, London on 19–20 January 1989.

26 Efraim Karsh, 'From Ideological Zeal to Geopolitical Realism: The Islamic Republic and the Gulf', in Efraim Karsh (ed.), *The Iran Iraq War: Impact and Implications*, London: Macmillan, 1989, p. 29.

27 See *Keesing's*, vol. XXXIII, 1987, pp. 35289–91.

28 *Ibid.*

29 *FBIS*, South Asia, 1 November 1988.

30 *BBC, SWB*, July 1988 (ME/0195/A/4).

31 A. H. H. Abidi, 'Revolutionary Iran's Perception of Non-Alignment and the Non-Aligned Movement', *Non-Aligned World*, vol. 2, no. 3, 1984, p. 351.

32 *Ibid.*, p. 352.

33 *Kayhan International*, 16 January 1984.

34 *Kayhan International*, 13 November 1980.

35 *Kayhan International*, 18 August 1981. Musavi was especially against compromising on issues which faced the Muslim world, like the question of Palestine and the common military and economic strategic interests of both Western Europe and the United States towards the region.

36 Quoted in Abidi, 'Revolutionary Iran's Perception on Non-Alignment and the Non-Aligned Movement', p. 356. Emphasis added.

37 *Kayhan International*, 18 August 1981.

38 Hunter, *Iran and the World*, p. 43.

39 Abidi, 'Revolutionary Iran's Perception on Non-Alignment and the Non-Aligned Movement', p. 361.

40 Karsh, 'From Ideological Zeal to Geopolitical Realism', p. 26.

41 Interview with ex-deputy Foreign Minister Mohammad Javad Larijaani, *In Tehran*, November 1990.

42 Karsh, 'From Ideological Zeal to Geopolitical Realism', p. 27.

43 Dr Mahmood Sariolghalam is a professor of International Relations at the Shaheed Beheshte University in Tehran.

44 This is an excerpt from a paper read by Dr Mahmood Sariolghalam at a BISA (British International Studies Association) Conference held at the University of Kent, Canterbury, in December 1989, entitled 'Islamic Revolution of Iran: Sources of Change and Challenges for Adaptation'.

45 *Ibid.*

46 *Ibid.*

47 Quoted in Martin Kramer (ed.), *Shi'ism, Resistance and Revolution*, Boulder, Colorado and London: Westview Press, 1987, p. 52.

48 Sariolghalam, 'Islamic Revolution of Iran'.

49 Quoted in Shireen T. Hunter, 'Iranian Perceptions and a Wider World', *Political Communication and Persuasion: An International Journal*, vol. 2, no. 4, 1985, p. 397.

50 Quoted in *ibid.*, p. 398.

51 *Kayhan International*, 13 January 1982.

52 Ali Merad, 'The ideologisation of Islam in the Contemporary Muslim World', in Alexander S. Cudsi and Ali E. Hillal Dessouki (eds), *Islam and Power*, Baltimore: Johns Hopkins University Press, 1981, p. 8.

53 Commenting on a United Nations resolution condemning Iran as a violator of human rights, Prime Minister Mir Hossein Musavi stated that the resolution was a 'US plot and we view the UN vote as a pat on Saddam's shoulder for his fight against our nation', *Kayhan International*, 15 December 1985.

54 *Ibid.*

55 The above was the belief of those Iranian citizens who, while not supporting the Islamic regime, had no wish to allow their country to come under American influence. Most of these citizens were highly nationalistic and believed that Iran could be among the most developed nations in the world if only allowed to develop without being dictated to. Discussions in Tehran, October 1990.

56 Quoted in Hunter, *Iran and the World*, p. 37.

57 The concept of 'Mostazafin' is widely used to mobilise the many million Iranians, especially those from the rural areas who had hitherto lived a life of deprivation. There is even an organisation called 'Bonyad-e-Mostazafin' or

'Foundation for the Oppressed' which helps people who, in their view, fall into this category. It may be said that, notwithstanding certain cases of corruption, the foundation is one of the most successful of the revolutionary institutions in Iran.

58 Phrase used by an Iranian diplomat to the United Nations in discussions with author.

59 William O. Beeman, 'Double Demons: Cultural Independence in US-Iranian Understanding', *The Iranian Journal of International Affairs*, vol. II, nos 2 & 3, Summer and Fall 1990, p. 320. The author also describes the belief system in which Iranian foreign policy operates, akin to what has already been discussed in preceding sections.

60 Henry Precht, 'Ayatollah Realpolitik', *Foreign Policy*, no. 70, Spring 1988, p. 109.

61 Karsh, 'From Ideological Zeal to Geopolitical Realism', p. 28. The author here is referring to the situation when, although the Gulf states condemned Iranian 'intervention in Oman, yet they were secretly relieved at Iran's assistance' to the sultanate which was under threat from the Dhofar rebels.

62 By designating the last Friday in the Muslim holy month of Ramadan as the Day of Qods (Jerusalem), the then Minister of Foreign Affairs Mir Hossein Musavi stated 'we want our foreign policy to have an unshakeable connection with the struggle against Zionism in the region. This will be considered the main pivot of our political movements'. *Kayhan International*, 9 July 1981.

63 In all 407 people were killed, a majority of them being Iranian.

64 While addressing a ministerial meeting of the Islamic Conference Organisation, Iranian Foreign Minister Velayati demanded Pan-Islamic sanctions, including an oil embargo against the US for aiding Israel in the invasion of Lebanon in 1982. *Kayhan International*, no date.

The conservative approach: Sandinista Nicaragua's foreign policy

Nicaragua's revolutionary movement, led by the Sandinista National Liberation Front (FSLN) gained state power on 19 July 1979. It relinquished that power in what literally hundreds of international observers described as one of the fairest elections in Latin America's history, on 25 February 1990.[1]

In their eleven years in government the Sandinistas, as they were universally known, attempted with varying degrees of success to implement a political project based on three principles; political pluralism, a mixed economy and non-alignment. The last of these, non-alignment, was intended to guide foreign policy and was based on commitments made as far back as 1969 when the then liberation movement, the FSLN, had issued its 'Historic programme' where it had set out its vision for a future liberated Nicaragua.[2] This chapter therefore, *inter alia*, offers an assessment as to how far revolutionary Nicaragua managed to maintain its non-aligned stance in its diplomatic practice.

A tentative analysis is also offered as to how revolutionary Nicaragua's foreign policy can best be explained. The suggestion is made here that, somewhat surprisingly, Sandinista foreign policy in practice can, at one level of analysis, best be understood through a theoretical prism articulated by an English Political Realist writer, albeit a Grotian in leaning. Hedley Bull's views, expressed in *The Anarchical Society*, are examined and related to the Sandinistas' theory and practice of foreign policy making and implementation.[3]

Because US foreign policy had a crucial agenda-setting function for Nicaraguan foreign policy, US foreign policy towards Central America is also analysed and it is argued here that the US approach to the region is best understood as being based on a view of world politics most famously articulated in theoretical terms by Kenneth Waltz in his *Theory of*

International Politics.[4] It will further be argued that an understanding of international politics derived from a Bullian perspective provided a better guide for foreign policy makers in Nicaragua than the Waltzian perspective provided for US policy makers.

In conclusion, the inadequacies of the various Political Realist accounts of the way states interact within the international system are discussed in regard to Sandinista foreign policy. Other theoretical approaches are also evaluated. It should be emphasised that it is not suggested here that either Nicaraguan or US policy makers were consciously guided by theory emanating from Bull, Waltz or anyone else; simply that their actions can be explained to a greater or lesser extent by the theoretical frameworks provided by these and other scholars.

The foundations: pragmatism and praxis

In the 'Historic programme' the Sandinista Front declared that once in government it would consolidate national sovereignty through the pursuit of an independent foreign policy. The 1969 document prefigured the programme of the revolutionary government, including its commitment to diversified foreign relations. The 'Historic programme' stated that a future revolutionary government would accept technical or economic aid from any country as long as this did not entail political compromise. The Sandinistas insisted that the future revolution would 'put an end to the Yankee interference in the internal problems of Nicaragua and will practice a policy of mutual respect with other countries and fraternal collaboration between peoples'.[5]

The reason for the emphasis on 'Yankee interference' was that the single most significant external factor affecting Nicaragua's domestic and foreign policies since the mid-nineteenth century, when it was the British who were the most important foreign influence in Nicaragua, was the United States.[6] Throughout the twentieth century the US has regularly both directly and indirectly sought to control the Nicaraguan polity in order to maintain stability in a country which was perceived as being located in a vital geo-strategic position in respect of United States security interests.[7]

In the early twentieth century, the United States sent in the marines on several occasions to try to control insurgent movements. In 1933, however, a successful campaign by a peasant army led by General Augusto César Sandino forced the marines to withdraw. General Sandino, however, was murdered in 1934 on the orders of Anastasio 'Tacho' Somoza

who assumed the Presidency in 1936, a position which was held or controlled by the Somoza family until the 1979 revolutionary victory.

The Somoza family presided over a particularly unpleasant family
dictatorship at home, and abroad subordinated Nicaragua's sovereignty to
the interests of the United States. Somoza's Nicaragua supported the US
diplomatically, for instance in UN votes, and in the military arena. The
Somozas supported the CIA-financed and organised military coup which
toppled elected Guatemalan president, reformist Jacobo Arbenz in 1954.
The US-sponsored invasion of Cuba in 1962, the Bay of Pigs débâcle,
was launched from Nicaragua's east coast and the Somozas offered to
send a Nicaraguan platoon to Vietnam, a proposal which was vetoed by
the United States.

The FSLN approach to foreign policy was inspired by Sandino's
writings and philosophy which had situated the anti-US struggle within
an anti-imperialist, Latin American, nationalist framework which also
incorporated calls for social justice.[8] Sandino had managed to evoke world-
wide sympathy for the Nicaraguan cause; it was indeed the French socialist Henri Barbusse who had bestowed on Sandino the now well-known
appellation, 'General of Free Men'. The FSLN developed their own
international strategy along lines derived from Sandino; anti-imperialism,
Latin American solidarity and the defence of national sovereignty were
the key principles. This was somewhat different from the domestic strategy
which in addition to the philosophical heritage of Sandino incorporated
elements derived from Marxist theory and liberation theology.

The tactics chosen by the FSLN to implement the international strategy
in the two years prior to the 'Triumph' of the revolution (as the revolutionary victory is popularly known within Nicaragua) were twofold. A
diplomatic offensive was launched whose objective was to gain support
from governments and international organisations; and in countries whose
governments were not sympathetic to the Sandinistas, solidarity was organised via non governmental organisations. The FSLN argued that

> it was necessary to win everybody's support, not the support of the left-wing
> sectors alone. The Sandinista Front made it a point to set up an infrastruc-
> ture of solidarity in each country, seeking, firstly, the support of all; and
> secondly, the support of those who best understood our problems.[9]

The diplomatic offensive was led by Sergio Ramirez, the future
Sandinista vice-president, who in 1977 organised a group of twelve
middle-class intellectuals, *Los Doce*, to mobilise international support for
the FSLN. This group was crucial in securing diplomatic approbation

and financial aid from a wide range of Latin American leaders, including José Figueres and President Daniel Oduber of Costa Rica, Carlos Andrés Pérez of Venezuela, José López Portillo of Mexico, General Omar Torrijos of Panama, and Fidel Castro of Cuba. Multilateral support came from organisations like the Socialist International and the Organisation of American States (OAS).

Diplomacy, however, provided only one of the instruments adopted by the FSLN to achieve victory. International diplomacy was backed up by the use of military force to try to defeat Somoza's combined army and police force, the National Guard. Military victory was seen as essential as diplomatic success. Humberto Ortega, the FSLN and later UNO Chief of Staff of the armed forces, was to argue that prior to the revolution, the FSLN was able to forge alliances with a very broad spectrum of what he termed 'progressive forces' internationally because 'we had a political program that was, to a certain extent, of interest to them and . . . we had military power'.[10]

Foreign policy in practice

When the FSLN achieved state power in 1979 it therefore had considerable practical diplomatic experience and a highly diverse international network of support and contacts. The FSLN in government continued with this pragmatic approach of garnering broad-based alliances abroad in support of the revolution. It attempted to synthesise tactical pragmatism within a strategy based on the foreign policy principles inherited from Sandino of nationalist, Latin American, anti-imperialism.

The Nicaraguan government intended to follow an independent political and economic policy at home, and an independent, nationally determined policy abroad. Political and economic pluralism domestically was to be complemented by a conscious policy of diversification of international relations, in order to try to maintain the broadest possible alliance in support of the revolution.

Perhaps surprisingly, there was little trace of idealism in the FSLN's foreign policy either as a liberation movement or party of government.[11] Calls to aspirational principles, particularly from 1982 with the intensification of the war waged by US-backed mercenaries, the 'contras', took second place to the pursuit of peace based on the vindication of Nicaraguan sovereignty.

This is not to say that Nicaraguan ministers ignored the world outside. Daniel Ortega placed Nicaraguan foreign policy within a global struggle against imperialism in his speech to the Havana meeting of the Non-Aligned Movement in Havana in 1979, expressing revolutionary Nicaragua's solidarity with 'the struggle of peoples against imperialism, colonialism, neocolonialism, apartheid, racism, including Zionism and every form of oppression.'[12]

FSLN foreign minister, Maryknoll catholic priest Miguel D'Escoto also took up the theme of global solidarity when he argued in a 1982 speech to the General Assembly of the United Nations that

> there can be no peace if the vast majority of the inhabitants of this planet are without bread, education, decent housing, security and political rights. There can be no peace without justice. There can be no peace while certain countries cling to outmoded systems of domination and dependence and stubbornly endeavour to prevent third-world countries at all costs from adopting measures they consider imperative and necessary to overcome underdevelopment and want in the exercise of their right to self-determination and independence.[13]

But these rather general statements of principles were not typical of the tenor and content of Nicaraguan foreign policy for the rest of the decade which became much more specifically geared towards stopping the war against Nicaragua. There was thus good reason for D'Escoto to add, in the same UN speech, that 'we have turned the struggle for peace into the guiding principle of all we do in the political realm.'[14]

Alejandro Bendaña, the senior civil servant at Nicaragua's Foreign Ministry during the Sandinista years argued in retrospect that 1982 was a major turning point.

> The stages [of foreign policy] are marked by the changes in the degree and kind of US actions to subvert, destabilize and put an end to the Nicaraguan revolution. The revolution had to develop new, ever more powerful strategies. I think one decisive stage was in mid-1982, when we could no longer doubt the Reagan administration's objectives . . . Then with the invasion of Grenada in October 1983, we realized that the [US] administration neither feared nor hesitated to carry out a direct invasion.[15]

Foreign policy objectives coalesced therefore in 1982, around three related goals. The first was to prevent the US from succeeding in its objective of international isolation and delegitimisation of the Sandinista government. The second was to gain support for Nicaraguan and Latin American peace initiatives for Central America. The third was to try to isolate the US administration diplomatically, and in a counterpoint to US policy to Nicaragua, to try to delegitimise internationally US policy towards Central America. The government engaged in active international diplomacy to try to accomplish these objectives. It also developed its military capacity to provide what it viewed as an essential complement to its international diplomatic strategy.

Military defence was based on the Sandinista Peoples' Army (EPS) which had a small professional core, supplemented since 1983 by battalions made up of conscripts carrying out two years' national service. Farmers and communities in the war zones also formed their own self-defence militias, as the contras made agricultural co-operatives and civilian communities targets for attack. Alejandro Bendaña argued in 1988 that

> success in foreign policy is basically a function of success in military policy. Had we three times the creativity and brains . . . but somehow on a military level we faltered, somehow our people did not stand up to the military and economic pressure, all of this would have collapsed. Foreign policy in and of itself would not have been able to sustain it . . . of course the diplomatic battlefield has been crucial in helping to avert a United States intervention. You could also say that it wasn't successful enough to be able to stop the war and to stop 28,000 Nicaraguans from being killed.[16]

Diversifying international relations

The non-alignment policy was institutionalised when Nicaragua joined the Non-Aligned Movement (NAM) in September 1979 and Nicaragua pursued its policy of non-alignment by establishing diplomatic relations with states of diverse political hues. These diplomatic ties extended through Latin America, Africa, Asia, the Socialist bloc countries, and the rest of the world.

Relations with the Soviet Union and other Eastern bloc countries were initiated but these remained politically low key for both sides. The Soviet Union supported the various peace initiatives of the 1980s and provided economic aid but did not commit themselves to such intensive support of Nicaragua as that given to the Cuban revolution. However, from 1984 when oil supplies from Mexico were cut off due to Nicaragua's inability to keep up with outstanding credit payments, the Soviet Union became increasingly important as the major supplier of petroleum, so much so that the post-Sandinista government of Violeta Chamorro attempted to keep Soviet, later Russian, oil supplies flowing to Nicaragua. Cuba gave vast amounts of material aid to the revolution, as well as help with military assistance and advisers.

Good relations with Western Europe were seen as important, not just because these relatively wealthy countries could provide economic co-operation, but increasingly for political reasons. It was argued that 'Western

Europe could be the needed equilibrium factor ... in the efforts to achieve Peace in Central America.'[17] The West Europeans consistently offered economic support, although some were more enthusiastic supporters of the Nicaraguan revolution than others.

War and international law

It might have been expected that on coming to power the FSLN would have reacted strongly against the United States. The US had been a longstanding ally of the Somoza dictatorship, providing it with military and economic aid; US military support had been used primarily to wage war against the FSLN and most of the economic assistance had found its way into the Somoza family's bank balances. Instead, however, the Sandinista government under the guidance of foreign minister, Miguel D'Escoto, set about trying to create good relations with a wide range of international partners, including the United States.

Attempts to establish friendly relations with the US included the visit of a top level Nicaraguan delegation to the United States in September 1979 to request assistance for reconstruction. Bendaña, perhaps rather disingenuously, commented that 'The hope was that Nicaraguan–US relations could develop into a model of mutual respect between a revolutionary nation and the dominant power of the western hemisphere.'[18]

Nicaragua requested assistance from the United States government to help train the country's new defence forces. There was some sympathy in the Carter administration to this request, on the basis that US assistance might prevent the Sandinistas from turning to the Socialist bloc countries for military assistance. But a proposal to include $5.5 million in military aid as part of the Carter administration's economic aid package to Nicaragua was rejected by Congress at the committee stage. The Sandinista delegation was instead offered a derisory $23,000 to purchase binoculars, and to pay for a visit by six Nicaraguan army officers to US bases.[19]

These Nicaraguan approaches to the United States government suggest the efforts that were made towards compromise, but such conciliatory approaches did not meet with success. Only $60 million of the $75 million loan which had been negotiated with the Carter administration was disbursed, as the incoming Reagan administration embarked on an offensive against the revolutionary government.

The Reagan administration adopted a policy whose aim was to oust the Sandinistas from office. The preferred foreign policy instrument was the military; massive funding was allocated to the direct arming of the contras, the construction of modern military bases and airports in Honduras, equipping the Honduran army and additionally for the regular large-scale US military and naval exercises which took place in the region throughout the 1980s.

The Reagan strategy had not seemed inevitable in the early 1980s. Initial bilateral relations with the Reagan administration appeared to show some signs that an understanding between both parties could be brokered. US ambassador Lawrence Pezzullo had tried to forge a working agreement between the new Reagan administration and the Sandinistas until his resignation in April 1981. Thomas Enders, the Assistant Secretary of State for Inter-American Affairs, engaged sceptical Sandinista leaders in secret talks in Managua in August 1981, promising a non-aggression pact in return for a halt in the supposed arms flow to the opposition forces in El Salvador and a cutback in the Nicaraguan military. These negotiations broke down in October, when the United States launched joint military exercises with Honduran armed forces on Nicaragua's border, the 'Halcon Vista' manoeuvres. The Nicaraguans saw these exercises as a preliminary to an attack on Nicaragua and said so. The US administration portrayed Nicaragua's accusations as anti-US rhetoric and stopped talking to the Sandinista government.[20]

Nicaragua made calls for further bilateral peace talks with the United States, on the basis that,

> all of the Central American nations as well as the United States, have the right to seek guarantees that will protect the security of all, including non-aggression pacts, agreements to refrain from aiding forces attacking other governments, and prohibitions on foreign military bases in Central America.[21]

The United States, however, had decided on the use of military force rather than diplomacy to solve the Nicaraguan 'problem'. Despite calls by Latin American leaders like Mexican President José López Portillo for a negotiated peace and warnings that any US intervention would constitute 'a gigantic historical error', the US stepped up its financial support for the contras in 1982. In that year contra forces attempted to blow up the country's major oil refinery and chemical plant and bombed Managua's international airport, killing three people.[22]

Bellicose speeches by President Reagan threatening military action against Nicaragua were followed by invasion, not of Nicaragua, but tiny Grenada, on 25 October 1983. The Grenada invasion had been preceded by large-scale US naval exercises in the Eastern Caribbean. In February 1983 the US began troop exercises in Honduras, the 'Big Pine 1' manoeuvres. The US Congress voted an additional $24 million for the contras in November 1983, and in February 1984 the US and Honduras carried out more large-scale troop manoeuvres, 'Big Pine 11', near the Nicaraguan border with Honduras. In February and March 1984 the US mined the ports of Corinto and El Bluff, and in April 1984, began more military exercises, 'Granadero 1' in Honduras. These military exercises were followed by intensive US naval exercises off Nicaragua's coast, involving 30,000 troops and 350 ships.

The United States' allies were concerned about the escalation of the contra war against Nicaragua. They feared that too great a US involvement might transform Central America's regional conflicts into a global war, involving both superpowers and Western Europe. Even Thatcher's Britain, normally so supportive of US policy, condemned the mining of Nicaragua's ports. US public opinion consistently expressing dissatisfaction with the administration's Nicaragua policies, and in the context of the upcoming November 1984 US presidential elections, the US administration seemed to have felt that it ought to make some diplomatic efforts to try to regain international and domestic support for its Central American policy. The US therefore agreed to hold bilateral conversations with the Sandinista government, in Manzanillo, Mexico.

The Manzanillo talks started in June 1984, and ended in January 1985, when the United States government unilaterally abandoned the negotiations after nine meetings had taken place. The United States' priority had been to try to secure political change within Nicaragua and to persuade the Sandinista government to negotiate with the contras. The Sandinistas were adamant that internal affairs could not be the subject of such negotiations, but they were willing to address the security concerns of the United States. In fact, in the later meetings, many observers commented that the Nicaraguans had come close to meeting these US security concerns, providing that the US agreed to disband the contras. The US suspended talks on the grounds of Sandinista 'inflexibility', and commented that it did not want to substitute a bilateral agreement for multilateral negotiations, and so undermine the Contadora-led peace process.[23]

But diplomatic relations with the US were maintained despite the worst provocations, including the mining of Nicaraguan ports. Concerned to find ways to end the war, Sandinista foreign policy makers still attempted to maintain good relations with sectors of United States society, viewing domestic opinion in the United States as a key potential ally to put pressure on Reagan to end the war. US Congressmen, church leaders, trade unionists, and individual US citizens were encouraged to visit the country. When the US closed the Nicaraguan consulates in June 1983, to try to make it more difficult for US citizens to obtain the visas they needed to visit Nicaragua, the Nicaraguan government simply abolished the visa requirement for US citizens.

The Nicaraguan government insisted that it was interested in pursuing friendly relations with the United States, but only on certain terms. Miguel D'Escoto put it like this.

> We have stressed – and we do so here once again – that the Nicaraguan government genuinely desires an understanding with the United States that would make it possible substantially to improve the relations between our two states on the basis of mutual respect, non-intervention in internal affairs and, above all, on the basis of sovereign equality, independence and self-determination – principles that constitute the foundation of peace and stability in the world and that are found throughout the [United Nations] Charter.[24]

The Sandinista government repeatedly called for an end to US intervention on the basis of principles of international law as outlined in the Charter of the United Nations. Nicaraguan diplomatic efforts were underpinned by repeated calls for respect for these principles. The revolutionary government called for support for the self-determination of the Nicaraguan people, respect for the territorial integrity of the nation, for non-intervention in the internal affairs of Nicaragua, and for an adherence by the United States to the doctrine which allows for the juridical equality of sovereign states, irrespective of size or power capabilities.

Bendaña rather wryly commented that 'We, the revolutionaries, were making the call to respect law and order, and the conservative Ronald Reagan was the one trying to violate established norms to achieve his extremist goals.'[25]

Active diplomacy in multilateral fora

Efforts to prevent the US from invading Nicaragua and to try to stop the contra war through the use of international law were pursued in various multilateral organisations including the United Nations, the International Court of Justice and the European Community. Nicaragua's policy of active diplomacy backed up by military preparedness was most evident in its approach to the Latin and Central American peace processes. The first of these was led by the Contadora Group which was comprised of Colombia, Mexico, Panama and Venezuela and was formed in 1983 to support the peace process in Central America. The second of these forums was that of the five Central American presidents.

In March 1982, after the *Washington Post* had made public that the contras were receiving $19 million in US assistance, and after a series of contra attacks and bombings, Daniel Ortega presented Nicaragua's case at a special session of the UN Security Council. He denounced the escalating US-sponsored aggression and presented a nine-point plan for peace, re-iterating his government's hopes for improved relations with the United States government. In October 1982, Nicaragua gained greater and more visible access to multilateral diplomatic forums when it was elected as a non-permanent member of the Security Council. Despite the fact that the United States had lobbied against Nicaragua, and on behalf of the Dominican Republic, Nicaragua won the seat in the second ballot with the support of 104 countries. Nicaragua's election victory was widely interpreted as a defeat for the US.[26]

The UN again acted as an important forum for Nicaragua's diplomacy in July 1986. Nicaragua's president Daniel Ortega spoke at the Security Council of the United Nations to try to elicit support for the recent ruling from the International Court of Justice which had found the United States in breach of international law because of its interference in Nica-ragua's internal affairs. When it came to the vote the United States were deserted by all their allies. Of the fifteen members of the Security Council, eleven voted for Nicaragua's proposed resolution. Britain, France, and Thailand abstained, and the United States had to use its veto to stop the proposal from being approved. President Ortega reiterated Nicaragua's willingness to enter into bilateral talks with the United States, and called for the United States to alter its policy towards Nicaragua, emphasising the legitimacy of the Sandinistas' case according to international law.

> We do not seek confrontation, nor have we come to the Security Council to hurl insults against the US government, but rather to seek peace and respect for international law; to seek a peaceful and honorable solution to our dif-ferences, to offer the government of the United States another opportunity to reconsider and adjust its conduct to the principles and norms of inter-national law.[27]

Nicaragua had first taken its case to the International Court of Justice (ICJ) at the Hague in April 1984 and on 10 May that body unanimously had ordered the United States to stop mining Nicaragua's ports. The final judgement of the International Court of Justice was reached on 27 June 1986. It stated, among other things, that the United States was in breach of international law because of its support for the contras and its military and economic intervention against Nicaragua.[28]

US credibility was not enhanced by the November 1986 announcement by US Attorney General Ed Meese that the National Security Council had been diverting money from secret arms sales to Iran to clandestine support for the contras. US policy towards Central America, which had been judged illegal according to international law, was now exposed as possibly illegal within the United States. US public debate concentrated on the circumvention of Congress, but some commentators also stressed the alleged violation of the Boland Amendment which was passed into law by the US Congress in December 1982, and had prohibited the US government from using government funds 'for the purpose of overthrowing the government of Nicaragua or provoking a military exchange between Nicaragua and Honduras'.[29]

From 1984, the member states of the European Community engaged in an institutionalised political dialogue with Central America and the Contadora countries, in order to support the regional peace efforts. What united the differing political forces of the Western European governments was their antipathy to the US strategy of reliance on the military option to deal with the Nicaraguan revolution. All West European governments considered that the Central American conflict of the 1980s had at its root socio-economic causation, not Soviet expansionism. Western European governments argued that the best way to avoid Nicaragua becoming a Soviet satellite was to support the regional economies, and to pursue political changes within Nicaragua by offering economic support rather than military challenges. Western Europe, despite US pressure from both the Reagan and Bush administrations to exclude Nicaragua, continued to be an important trade and aid partner for Nicaragua.[30]

One of the first international organisations to voice support for the Contadora initiative was the Non-Aligned Movement, at the meeting of the Coordinating Bureau held in Managua in January 1983, which had been specifically convened to discuss Latin American issues. The links with the Non-Aligned Movement brought both tangible and intangible rewards as material aid and diplomatic support was obtained from a wide range of Third World countries, including India, Algeria, Iran and Libya.[31]

In September 1983 the Latin American Economic System (SELA), gave its support to the Contadora process, and set up varying committees of action, including the Committee of Action and Support for Economic and Social Development in Central America. The Organisation of American States (OAS) made clear its support for the Contadora initiatives in 1986 when OAS Secretary-General Joao Baena Soares, along with UN Secretary-General, Javier Perez de Cuellar, launched a joint initiative, designed to put both international organisations at the disposal of the peace process. Nicaraguan diplomacy took particular care to foster these Latin American initiatives which it eventually saw as the core of its efforts to end the war.

Regional diplomacy and Latin American initiatives
In the immediate post-1979 period, relations between revolutionary Nicaragua and her immediate neighbours appeared friendly. In March 1980 the region's foreign ministers met in San José, Costa Rica, and expressed

> their interest in peaceful coexistence, based upon respect for national sover-
> eignty, territorial integrity and political independence, as well as respect for
> different political systems and nonintervention in the internal affairs of each
> country.[32]

As the war escalated, and the US intervened to organise and arm the contras, the majority of which were based in Honduras, the minority in Costa Rica, so did inter-regional relations deteriorate. In May 1981, at Nicaragua's invitation, the Heads of State of Nicaragua and Honduras met and issued a statement which referred to the necessity of solving bilateral problems through a process of dialogue. By 1982 relations with Honduras had become more problematic, and more belligerent. Honduras consistently refused to participate in serious bilateral negotiations and at least up until the implementation of the peace accords of the mid-1980s, to be a partner in any joint border commissions with the Nicaraguans. Honduran/Nicaraguan relations frequently threatened to degenerate into military conflict or even war. Relations with Costa Rica, although often strained, were more harmonious, allowing for some positive results for Nicaraguan diplomacy including the setting up of a joint Costa Rican/ Nicaraguan border commission in 1982.[33]

In August 1982, as border clashes between Nicaragua and Honduras escalated, the Nicaraguan government invited the Chief of the Honduran armed forces and the Honduran President to talks aimed at reducing tensions. Honduras, backed by the United States, refused to take part in discussions. The Presidents of Venezuela and Mexico, concerned that these armed border skirmishes were the prelude to 'a conflict that could extend to the whole region', wrote to the Presidents of Nicaragua, Honduras, and the United States, calling for peace talks to establish a 'global agreement that may provide true peace between Nicaragua and Honduras, and which will bear a positive result in a framework of world tensions and confrontations'.[34]

Again Honduras and the United States refused to enter into talks, although Nicaragua agreed to participate. Instead the United States sponsored the short-lived 'Forum for Peace', a meeting of the Central American governments, excluding Nicaragua, held in San José.

Venezuela and Mexico pursued their peace efforts, and convened a meeting for 8–9 January 1983 of Central America's four neighbouring states – Colombia, Mexico, Panama and Venezuela – held on the Panamanian island of Contadora. The group discussed how the Central American conflict could be resolved by pacific means, preferably by way of a negotiated, mutually agreed peace treaty.

The Contadora Group issued its first set of proposals in July 1983. It proposed the withdrawal of all foreign military advisers from Central America, the end of all aid to irregular forces, and the cessation of tension generating military manoeuvres in the border regions. In September 1983 the Contadora Group produced a draft 21-point peace treaty which was drawn up after consultation with the Central American countries. This 'Document of Objectives' was primarily concerned with security issues, although the treaty included some references to internal issues such as promoting national reconciliation, the establishment of 'democratic, representative and pluralistic systems', and respect for human rights.[35]

These peace proposals were accompanied by intense regional diplomatic activity. The Contadora Group met eleven times in 1983. The Central American foreign ministers met six times as part of the Contadora process. The technical commission, composed of representatives from all the Central American countries met four times.

In July 1983 the Nicaraguan government issued a six-point peace proposal incorporating the July Contadora proposals, and calling again for the immediate signing of a non-aggression pact between Honduras and Nicaragua. In December 1983, Nicaragua submitted eight draft peace treaties to the Contadora Group, calling for peace agreements to be negotiated within Central America and with the United States. In January 1984 the Contadora Group and the Central American nations attempted to strengthen the process by creating three joint committees, to deal with security, political, and social and economic issues.[36]

In June 1984 Contadora presented its 'Draft Act on Peace and Cooperation'. After amendments from all five republics were incorporated into a September revised act, Guatemala and Costa Rica both agreed to sign. Of the five governments, Nicaragua had been one of the most critical of the revised act, 'disliking the Act's proposal for international monitoring of internal political processes and openly unhappy at the prospect of establishing regionally-defined force limits while direct US military pressures and the war with the "Contra" rebels continued.'[37]

Yet on 21 September 1984, it was the Nicaraguan government which became the first of the five to sign the Act. The US reacted to this entirely unexpected decision by persuading Honduras to convene a meeting of the Central American countries, again excluding Nicaragua. In October 1984 Honduras, El Salvador and Costa Rica produced the 'Tegucigalpa document' which contained a series of amendments to the Contadora Act designed to weaken its impact and legitimise a continuing US military presence in the region. The US had objected to those parts of the Act which prohibited international military exercises and foreign military bases and which called for the immediate cessation of arms acquisitions. The Tegucigalpa document proposed to 'regulate' military exercises as opposed to ending them. It also would have allowed for a continuation of foreign military bases in the region. A leaked US National Security Council Document discussed how, through intensive US regional diplomacy, 'We have effectively blocked efforts made by the Contadora Group to impose their second version of the Contadora Act.'[38]

The Contadora Group carried on meeting throughout 1985, although it faced continued intransigence from the United States, which initiated more massive military exercises in Honduras in February 1985. In April 1985, the United States attempted to transfer the peace process from within the framework of the Contadora process to the OAS. The only support for this proposal came from Honduras, El Salvador, Costa Rica and the now pro-US Grenada.

In June and July 1985, vice-president Sergio Ramirez embarked on a tour of Latin America in an effort to retake the diplomatic initiative and revive active support for the peace process. As a result of this visit, Argentina, Brazil, Peru and Uruguay agreed to create a support group for the Contadora process, the 'Lima Group'. Collectively the Contadora and Lima Groups became known as the 'Group of 8'. Attempts by the United States to enlarge the group to include the more pro-US Ecuador and the Dominican Republic were unsuccessful.[39]

The formation of the Lima Group gave an impetus to the search for peace, at more or less the same time that the United States Congress approved a massive $100 million of contra aid. The Contadora and Lima Groups continued to meet through 1985, presenting yet another draft of the Contadora Act in the September. This time the draft was unacceptable to Nicaragua, as it allowed for the continuation of US military exercises, and gave no guarantees as to the cessation of US funding for the contras. However, in December 1985 the Nicaraguan government made another proposal for peace to the Contadora Group. The proposal called for a dialogue with the United States based on equality and mutual respect. It also called for a general treaty to be negotiated for all the Central American countries, to be signed at a meeting of the Central American presidents in May 1986.

The most important step in the next stage of the peace process was taken at Caraballeda, Venezuela, with the issuing of a statement from the Contadora and Lima Groups in January 1986. The Caraballeda Declaration called on the United States to resume talks with Nicaragua, to suspend aid to the contras, and to withdraw its troops from the region. The Central American presidents supported this declaration, as did representatives from all the major political parties of both the left and right in Western Europe. The United States refused to comply. On 11 February 1986, Secretary of State George Shultz told a visiting delegation of foreign ministers of the Contadora and Lima Groups who had come to Washington to discuss the Caraballeda Declaration, that the United States would not hold talks with the Nicaraguans until the Nicaraguan government talked to the contras. President Reagan had refused to receive the Latin American foreign ministers, although in the same week of their visit he had found time to meet representatives of the contras.

The US military and naval exercises on Nicaragua's borders, illegal US military reconnaissance flights in Nicaragua's airspace, and a request by President Reagan to Congress for yet another $100 million of contra aid, sharpened tensions but also increased the determination of the Latin American nations to continue with an active diplomatic policy to search for peace. After the abortive meeting with Shultz the Group of 8 met in Punta del Este, Uruguay, to reiterate the necessity for the US to stop funding the contras and for a negotiated solution to the conflicts. The Contadora Group met several times during 1986, in Managua, Panama and Colombia.

By 1986 even President Reagan's staunchest allies in Central America were looking for ways to stop the militarisation of the region so as to be able to concentrate efforts on domestic affairs, in particular the economic crisis facing all five republics. This incipient common interest in reaching some form of regional settlement provided the backdrop to the first of the meetings of the Central American Presidents, held at the suggestion of the Nicaraguans, and held in Esquipulas, Guatemala, in May 1986. The discussions centred around economic issues, as the newly elected President Arias had been reluctant to concede democratic legitimacy to

President Ortega. The meeting produced little of substance, save a commitment that the Central American presidents would continue to meet, and an agreement to create a Central American parliament.[40]

Inter-regional tensions still persisted. In November 1986 serious border incidents occurred between Honduras and Nicaragua. On 7 December, the Honduran air force bombed the Nicaraguan town of Wiwili and a military base at Congojas Valley. Two children and ten Sandinista soldiers were killed. The US moved its troops in Honduras to within 40 kilometres of the Nicaraguan border. Both the Soviet Union and a representative of the Pope warned the US against an invasion of Nicaragua, the latter stating that such an intervention would be 'an act of madness'.[41]

Nicaragua reacted by reinvigorating the military underpinnings of its diplomatic strategy. The army was mobilised and in late December 1986 military exercises were carried out just ten kilometres from the Honduran border. The exercises were designed to be a dry run in the event of a foreign invasion from Honduras, and were defended by the Guatemalan government, among others, as being part of Nicaragua's 'sovereign right' to hold exercises within national territory. At the same time that Nicaragua was indicating its willingness to defend itself if necessary by force of arms, the government also attempted to find a resolution to the conflict via diplomatic means. The Nicaraguan government suggested to the Honduran government a joint demobilisation plan for the contras, which would be supplemented by United Nations assistance in helping to repatriate Nicaraguan refugees from Honduras. Nicaragua also invited the UN, the OAS, the Contadora Group and the Lima Group to send an inspection committee to the troubled border zone to investigate the various incidents. At the end of 1986 the Contadora Group proposed to move forward with this idea, proposing the establishment of a peace commission comprising the foreign ministers of the Group of 8, and the General Secretaries of the UN and the OAS.

Nicaraguan diplomacy also benefited from political changes which were taking place in Central America which were to facilitate a move towards peace, and which promoted a certain independence of action from the United States by its allies in the region.

In January 1986, a civilian president, Cerezo, assumed office in Guatemala with a commitment to restoring democracy and working for peace, while a new president took office in Costa Rica in May 1986, Dr Oscar Arias Sánchez. Even before taking office, President Arias had committed his future government to an active foreign policy as a 'promoter of peace and democracy', and had stated that he would not allow the contras to operate from Costa Rica. President Azcona of Honduras had also committed his government to ridding the country of the contras, and President Duarte of Salvador, who was facing domestic attacks from both left and right, was searching for a foreign policy success, partly to shore up his own political credibility.

In the first half of 1987 President Arias of Costa Rica put together the first version of his proposed plan for peace. This version was rejected by the Guatemalans as discriminating against Nicaragua. After modification by President Cerezo, the revised plan called for the withdrawal of all foreign military advisers from the region, a complete cease-fire, and the holding of free and pluralist elections in all the countries of Central America. Despite President Reagan's personal disapproval of the new peace plan, and a last-minute intervention by President Reagan supported by senior Democrat Jim Wright on the eve of the Central American Summit, the Central American presidents ratified their own proposals for peace. On 7 August 1987 the five presidents signed the 'Procedure for the Establishment of a Strong and Lasting Peace in Central America', more commonly known as the 'Esquipulas II' peace agreement.[42]

The Esquipulas agreement recognised that the root causes of the conflict in the region were due to social and economic factors. It also asserted the necessity for representative and participatory democracy, and called for national independence. The Central American nations were committed by the accord to move forward in a process of national reconciliation, to take measures to bring about cease-fires, to declare amnesty for political prisoners, to end any states of emergency or states of siege, to hold free and pluralistic elections, to stop all aid to irregular forces in the region, not to allow their territory to be used by these irregular forces, and to set up National Reconciliation Commissions. The accords were to be overseen by an International Verification and Follow-up Commission (CIVS). This international commission would be composed of foreign ministers of the Group of 8, the foreign ministers of the Central American countries, and the Secretary-Generals of the UN and OAS. In addition the accord set up a timetable for compliance with these commitments.

The Esquipulas accords received widespread international support. The accords were supported by among others, the Group of 8, the UN and OAS Secretary-Generals, the European Community, by Canada, and by the Socialist bloc countries. In recognition of the world-wide approbation for the peace agreement, President Arias was awarded the 1987 Nobel Peace Prize. The accords also received support from important political sectors within the United States.

The Nicaraguan government responded within the framework of its by now well-established diplomatic/military strategy. It continued to defend the country against the still widespread contra attacks and began to implement the decisions reached at Esquipulas, at the same time as calling for international political and economic support to ensure that the agreements would not be subverted by the United States. Nicaragua declared a unilateral cease-fire in three of the northern war zones, declared its intention to implement domestic changes including the re-opening of La Prensa and Radio Catolica, and appointed as head of the Nicaraguan National Reconciliation Commission one of the Sandinista's sternest critics, Cardinal Obando y Bravo.[43]

These concessions did not go far enough for President Reagan. On 23 September Congress approved another $3.2 million for the contras. On the eve of the scheduled 8 October OAS meeting President Ortega announced further attempts at domestic conciliations. The Nicaraguan government would release from prison 1,000 ex-National Guard members. It would lift the state of emergency and offer a general amnesty once the United States had stopped all aid to the contras. More unexpectedly, President Ortega announced that the Nicaraguan government would enter into cease-fire negotiations with the contras, through a mediator who would be Cardinal Obando y Bravo.

Ortega visited Washington to try to solicit support for the peace plan. Senior Democrat Jim Wright who had abandoned the 'Reagan-Wright' plan, adopted a policy of active backing for the Esquipulas accords. President Reagan's call for $270 million of contra aid accompanied by demands for further unilateral concessions by the Sandinista government provoked a public denunciation by Wright. He called Reagan's proposals 'ridiculous', and stated publicly that Presidential advisers seemed to be trying to topple the peace process.[44]

The Reagan administration's policies towards Nicaragua had collapsed. The attempts to isolate Nicaragua had failed. Instead Nicaragua, backed by the Latin American peace efforts had isolated the Reagan administration. Alejandro Bendaña summed up the political implications of the changes that had come about because of the Peace process as follows.

> Diplomacy has enabled . . . other Central American countries, the prime US allies, to recognise, as they did in Esquipulas, the legitimacy of the Nicaraguan revolution, to recognise the Nicaraguan government as a legitimate government. This is something the United States fought tooth and nail against.[45]

In January 1988 the International Verification and Follow-up Commission (CIVS) reported back to the third Central American Presidential

Summit (Esquipulas III) that steps had been made towards implementation of the accords. The Commission spoke positively about the Nicaraguan efforts to implement democratic reforms, 'despite the grave harassment of war that the country is facing'. After commenting on Nicaragua's compliance with the amnesty requirements, the Commission compared this with other unnamed countries where 'it was standard practice to physically eliminate captured members of irregular groups or insurrectional forces, who might have been eligible to benefit under the recent decrees.'[46]

The Commission condemned the United States for its continued aid to the contras. They stated that 'Definitive cessation of such assistance continues to be a prerequisite for success of the peace efforts and of the Guatemala procedure as a whole.'[47]

Such actual and implied criticisms of the United States and its allies were not well received in some quarters. Presidents Duarte and Azcona seemed particularly determined to allow the summit to end without issuing an agreed position. On the second day of the summit President Ortega again took the diplomatic initiative. He announced that Nicaragua would unilaterally take four major steps in order to advance the peace process. The state of emergency would be immediately lifted, without waiting for the US administration to stop funding the contras. The amnesty would also be unilaterally implemented. Municipal and Central American parliament elections would take place. And in the most unexpected announcement of all, the President announced that the Nicaraguan government would talk directly to the contras. These talks would not be political discussions, but would cover the terms and conditions of a negotiated cease-fire. The Nicaraguan President also renewed his call for bilateral talks with the United States, commenting that the US administration had frequently stated that it would talk to the Nicaraguan government if the Sandinistas would talk to the contras.

The Nicaraguan initiative gave the space for an agreed communiqué to be formulated by the Summit. This communiqué reiterated the major points made by the CIVS, that all funding to irregular forces should cease. Despite protests, Nicaragua was obliged to concede the abolition of the CIVS, and its replacement by a monitoring team composed of the Central American presidents. As one observer commented, from the Nicaraguan point of view, this was like letting the fox keep guard over the chicken house.

Despite continued efforts by the outgoing Reagan administration to block the accords in 1988, the peace process continued. The Esquipulas accords retained their international support as evidenced by, *inter alia*, the recommendations of the OAS in November 1988 to continue to back the process. The peace process lost some of its momentum in 1988, however, as many of the region's political forces waited to see who would be the next President of the United States, preparing for a possible change of policy.

The February 1989 Summit took place therefore at a particular hiatus in the peace process, and before the new US President George Bush appeared to have formulated any clear policies for the region. Again the Nicaraguans took the initiative, insisting on external verification of human rights in Central America, to be undertaken by such respected bodies as Americas Watch or Amnesty International. El Salvador and Guatemala opposed such outside verification, and refused to agree. Again the second day of the summit brought a surprising development. All five Central American presidents, at the request of President Azcona of Honduras, agreed a plan which would disarm and demobilise the contras within ninety days of the summit. President Cerezo commented after the Summit that

> The truth is that events are imposing peace on us. To do the contrary, to continue violence, is to go against development and the solution to the region's economic and social problems ... We reached the Esquipulas 2 agreement that frankly set the bases for a new phase in international policy. Now we talk about negotiation, and the mechanism of confrontation and war is rejected.[48]

The Central American peace accords and Nicaraguan diplomatic initiatives did not achieve peace. Between 1 January and 10 April 1989, 42 civilians and soldiers were killed, as were 193 contras. In the same period there were 403 contra attacks within Nicaragua. There were 60 illegal US military reconnaissance flights in Nicaraguan airspace.[49]

Despite the fact that all the peace agreements had called for a cessation of contra aid as an indispensable factor in bringing about peace, in April 1989 the US Congressional Republicans and Democrats approved a 'bi-partisan accord' which allowed $50 million in 'humanitarian aid' to the contras. The Bush administration also, unsuccessfully, pressurised its European allies to desist in providing economic aid to Nicaragua.[50]

The war (but not the political violence) ceased in 1990 after the FSLN lost the February elections of that year and the US stopped funding the contras. Revolutionary Nicaragua's importance for US foreign policy also changed towards the late 1980s as Gorbachev's *perestroika* policies allowed for the collapse of Soviet-oriented regimes in Eastern Europe and a wholesale change in the international balance of power. In addition, by the late 1980s the onset of a global recession meant that the US would have to reconsider its huge defence expenditure. International systemic changes, therefore, combined with political changes within Nicaragua to ensure that for US policy makers, Nicaragua's importance diminished dramatically in the early 1990s. Communism appeared to be more or less defeated world-wide and the FSLN, which the US had always considered a communist party, was also defeated at the polls. For the FSLN, shocked by its electoral defeat, foreign policy was no longer of any importance. Its priority became to try to maintain its now demoralised party as an effective political force within Nicaragua.

International solidarity

During the Sandinista years in government, in line with the strategy developed before the revolutionary victory, the FSLN sought to build alliance with sectors of society in various countries, particularly within the US. By 1989, it was estimated that some 2,500 solidarity organisations existed world-wide. These organisations provided material aid and political support, and one of the objectives of the solidarity campaigns was to prevent Nicaraguan international isolation. Ligia Vigil from the Managua-based 'Nicaragua Must Survive' campaign commented that 'one of the objectives of United States imperialism is to isolate Nicaragua . . . Solidarity is a means for us to fight against disinformation'.[51]

In the US, churches, sister-city links, and information networks lobbied Congress, kept up the flow of information about Nicaragua, and provided substantial material aid. The sister city or twinning movements are particularly active in the US and Western Europe. In 1988 there were over 77 such links with communities in the United States, and over 200 with Western Europe. Their aims were to provide political support, technical assistance and economic co-operation. This development of municipal foreign policy had direct political implications. In the United States some state governors have refused to allow state National Guard units to participate in military exercises in Central America, causing the US Congress to pass new legislation to take away the state governors' power of veto.[52]

Nicaragua further encouraged the development of this 'people-to-people' diplomacy and thousands of individuals from the US, Western Europe and elsewhere converged on Nicaragua during the Sandinista years. Alejandro Bendaña's view of the US citizens visiting Nicaragua was that we are absolutely sure that in the vast majority of cases they might not become outright supporters of the Sandinistas, far from it, but they will be able to see through some of the lies of their government, that this is not the 'totalitarian dungeon' that is portrayed in the Reagan administration's speeches . . . The flow of ideas, the flow of images cannot be contained, and this has been tremendously important. Because there has been no single nationality that has visited Nicaragua more than that of Americans. And each of these people go back . . . and they become our little ambassadors. They might not necessarily agree with everything that is happening . . . but they do agree . . . that one has to be willing to respect self determination.[53]

Reviewing the record

The FSLN came to power committed to following a policy of non-alignment in foreign policy. Non-alignment provided a broad framework through which foreign policy makers sought to operate, but the main thrust of revolutionary foreign policy was not taken up with abstract ideals but instead with trying to ensure the physical survival of the revolution and, from 1982, ending the US-sponsored war. The principles that revolutionary Nicaragua increasingly rested its case on in the international arena were those enshrined in classical international law. These included sovereignty and non-intervention. Global ideals were not forgotten although when enunciated these were often linked to the specific context in which revolutionary Nicaragua was situated. Bendaña for instance argued that the Nicaraguans had fought 'for a set of ideals that are not the patrimony of Nicaraguans but of humanity as a whole'.[54]

To a certain extent FSLN policy had been successful. The US did not achieve its aim of isolating and demonising the Sandinista government. The Sandinistas retained considerable public sympathy in the US even while the US government was engaged in a proxy war against them. This should be compared to the more successful attempts by US foreign policy makers to diabolise Kim Il Sung in north Korea, Colonel Ghadaffi in Libya, Saddam Hussein in Iraq and to a certain extent Castro in Cuba. The legitimacy of intervention in these countries is more or less unquestioned because of the perceived illegitimacy of their governments. Throughout the entire Reagan period, the US presidency could never achieve a majority in the opinion polls or in Congress for intervention in Nicaragua. This was one of the reasons for US foreign policy towards Nicaragua being forced (literally) underground into the illegal gunrunning operations led by Ollie North from the White House basement.

The FSLN also managed to achieve the second of its important foreign policy objectives which was to mobilise support for Latin and Central American peace initiatives, and the third objective, to isolate the US diplomatically and to delegitimate US policy, was also achieved.

The United States was also successful in that the FSLN was removed from office in 1990, thus achieving a key goal of the Reagan administration. It was perhaps less successful in destroying the constitutional and social changes brought about by the revolution, although this is a debate still to be settled.[55]

An assessment as to how far it was Sandinista strategy and tactics which contributed to the achievement of foreign policy objectives, and how far credit should be given to other factors, is almost impossible to make, given the multi-variate nature of foreign policy making and implementation. What can tentatively be concluded, however, is that the active diplomatic pursuit of a very broad range of international alliances did not hinder, and arguably was of considerable importance for, the achievement of those objectives.

Two important further points should be made about Sandinista diplomacy. First of all it was backed up by a clear commitment to military superiority over the enemy. Secondly, the diplomatic offensive was based on what Bendaña rightly termed some very 'conservative principles': those of sovereignty, non-intervention and the rule of law.[56]

Explaining Nicaraguan and US policy

At first sight it would appear that revolutionary Nicaragua's foreign policy can best be explained by theories drawn from within the Political Realist framework. In summary this framework considers the state as the most important actor within a system characterised by anarchy, that is no common government. The primary foreign policy instrument is the use of military force and to a lesser extent diplomacy. The state's role is to pursue power in the national interest through policies of self-help, and the overriding normative concern is of preserving and sustaining order. The goal of foreign policy makers is a rational policy based on prudential self-interest and the making of foreign policy is considered a separate enterprise from domestic decision making. In classical political theory these ideas have an ancient history and can be most famously identified in the works of Thucydides and Machiavelli.[57] The articulation and transformation of these ancient ideas into a more or less coherent intellectual framework was accomplished by a number of scholars, the most well known of which are E. H. Carr and Hans Morgenthau in *The Twenty Years Crisis, 1919–1939* and *Politics Among Nations* respectively.

Contemporary scholars, working within the framework of Political Realism, have sought to elaborate and refine some of the theories developed by Carr, Morgenthau and others. In the 1970s and 1980s two fairly distinct 'neo-realist' approaches could be detected in the literature. One approach, developed by the US theorist Kenneth Waltz sought to explain world politics by reiterating the importance of states, at the same time as importing a new important variable into the Realist framework. This was the idea of 'structure' where structure was a fairly static concept which merely referred to the way that states were positioned in relationship to each others' respective power capabilities. It was, importantly, power capabilities, essentially military power capabilities, which counted in world politics. According to Waltz, states and structure combined produced different types of international system, some more conducive to stability than others. For Waltz a stable bipolar system, such as the post-war US/USSR balance, provided for a more satisfactory management of international order than that offered by multipolar systems.[58]

Hedley Bull, who more or less accepted classical Realist tenets, particularly the centrality of the sovereign state in the modern international system, is distinct in that although he argued that the world indeed could be characterised as anarchical it could not be considered, as the most pessimistic Realists might have it, as in a Hobbesian state of nature and therefore of war. This was because the condition of anarchy was mitigated by elements of society or community. These were in particular the institutions of balance of power, international law, diplomacy, war and Great Power management. What distinguished Bull's view was not his agreement that states were the supreme authorities in world politics but rather his insistence that in the *anarchical society* states also were the bearers of rights and duties and these rights and duties were accepted on the basis of reciprocity by all states. This contributed to the maintenance of order in the system. Thus international law for Bull was more than simply a system of codified morality, if much less than something akin to a municipal legal system. International law provided a framework which, along with the balance of power, constrained conflict and was accepted as necessary and useful by all states in the system.[59] Bull argued as follows.

> The first function of international law has been to identify, as the supreme normative principle of the political organisation of mankind, the idea of a society of sovereign states . . . Order in the great society of all mankind has been attained, during the present phase of the modern states system, through

general acceptance of the principle that men and territory are divided into states, each with its own proper sphere of authority, but linked together by a common set of rules. International law, by stating and elaborating this principle and by excluding alternative principles – such as the Hobbesian notion that international politics is an arena in which there are no rules restricting states in their relations with one another, or the notion that mankind is properly organised as a universal state based on cosmopolitan rights, or as a universal empire founded on the supremacy of a particular nation or race – establishes this particular realm of ideas as the determining one . . . , and so precludes the opening of questions without end and the eruption of conflicts without limit.[60]

Revolutionary Nicaragua's foreign policy seems to be quite well explained by classical Political Realism. Foreign policy decisions received little discussion domestically and the political or foreign policy sphere remained autonomous of domestic welfare and economic concerns. Indeed Sandinista supporters were often baffled by and hostile to the leadership's foreign policy decisions particularly from the mid-1980s onwards when massive changes in policy appeared to take place on very many occasions. The Foreign Ministry along with the Ministry of Defence and the Presidency presented a consistently united appearance to the world in foreign policy making and implementation. Here the revolutionary state could quite properly be understood as a rational, unitary, purposeful actor.[61] Military force provided the backbone of an active diplomatic offensive. Most of all the *state* of Nicaragua was defended as the bearer of sovereign rights in the international anarchic system where no other state had the *right* to intervene in Nicaragua's domestic affairs.

FSLN foreign policy makers, however, appeared to take a view of international law similar to that of Hedley Bull. They gauged, like Bull, that international law though weak, applied some protection for small states and shaped their foreign policy accordingly. This did not mean that the FSLN adopted an Idealist position with overreliance on international organisations and the sheer force of international law. The Sandinistas maintained the instruments of military power to back up their diplomatic calls for respect for international law.

United States foreign policy, by contrast, appears better explained by the Waltzian approach. The global balance of power was understood as the defining context for foreign policy. It seemed enough to rely on military force as the primary instrument of foreign policy and on the supremacy of US power. Foreign policy was conducted in the context of an understanding of the world which emphasised the war of all against all, the Hobbesian/Waltzian view. There is little evidence that US foreign policy makers were governed by the alternative Grotian/Bullian conception of world politics as being partially shaped by common institutions and rules.

Two of these institutions were Great Power management of world politics and the conduct of diplomacy. Although Bull accepted that in most circumstances major powers could and would impose their will on smaller states he also argued that they could only do so in certain circumstances. The most important condition was that such Great Power management must be 'accepted clearly enough by a large enough proportion of the society of states to command legitimacy.'[62]

By the mid-1980s US policy towards Nicaragua clearly did not command legitimacy within the international community.[63] Additionally the United States seemed, in its emphasis on the 'pure force' model of international politics, to have neglected the practice of diplomacy, an important aspect of foreign policy making, not just for Grotian influenced theorists like Bull, but also for classical realists like Morgenthau. It was Morgenthau who had warned that

> Of all the factors that make for the power of a nation, the most important, however unstable, is the quality of diplomacy . . . The conduct of a nation's foreign affairs by its diplomats is for national power in peace what military strategy and tactics by its military leaders are for national power in war. It is the art of bringing the different elements of the national power to bear with maximum effect upon those points in the international situation which concern the national interest most directly.[64]

By contrast it seemed that it was revolutionary policy makers that seemed to have developed a diplomatic strategy which benefited from an appreciation (consciously or unconsciously) of these classical Realist insights.

Yet somehow none of these Realist explanations quite fit FSLN foreign policy making. Bull's theory offers one understanding of how Nicaraguan foreign policy makers attempted to manipulate the international environment in their favour. Yet it cannot fully explain how a small, poor state with a population of just three million managed to conduct an internationally successful campaign to delegitimise and isolate the most powerful state in the world. A satisfactory explanation would have to take into account how non-state actors mobilised to support the Sandinista revolution. Revolutionary foreign policy was underpinned by an international strategy which relied on the loosely directed mobilisation of social forces covering the global political spectrum from liberal through to communist opinion. How these social forces were mobilised and how their views affected the international political climate has been little documented and certainly untheorised.

Current explanations are inadequate.[65] The Realist framework does not give non-state actors significance as explanatory variables in world politics. Pluralist explanations are inadequate here as these mainly concern themselves with the role of elites and governmental institutions in the making of foreign policy. We might expect more satisfactory explanations from the underutilised theory-building resources of structuralism. However, for a whole number of both intellectual and sociological reasons, structuralist and/or Marxist analysis of foreign policy making and implementation is almost non-existent.[66] What developed theory building there is within the structuralist paradigm focuses, in some ways similarly to Realist writers, on a system level as opposed to unit level explanations of international politics.

The conclusion must be that there is scope for much more intensive study of the foreign policies of small revolutionary states. Sandinista Nicaragua's foreign policy can be partially explained by recourse to Bull but there are still too many gaps. Why could the US not impose its will on Nicaragua, a small state in its own 'backyard', for so long? How did the FSLN mobilise international public opinion in its support? These questions matter because it is conceivable that the world may face another 'wave' of revolutions as it has so frequently in the past.[67] In that case both revolutionary and *status quo* states would benefit from a more sophisticated understanding of revolutionary foreign policy than that which is available to us now.

Notes

1   For an overview of Nicaraguan history from the colonial period through to the 1990s, including a discussion of the 1990 elections, see Hazel Smith, *Nicaragua: Self-determination and Survival* (London: Pluto, 1993).

2   FSLN, Historic Program, in Bruce Marcus (ed.), *Sandinistas Speak* (New York: Pathfinder, 1982), pp. 13–22.

3   Hedley Bull, *The Anarchical Society: A Study of Order in World Politics* (London: Macmillan, 1985).

4   Kenneth Waltz, *Theory of International Politics* (New York: Random House, 1979).

5   FSLN, Historic Program, in Marcus, *Sandinistas Speak*, p. 20.

6   Smith, *Nicaragua*, pp. 61–100.

7   There is a massive amount of literature on US policy towards Central

America. Two of the most useful are Jenny Pearce, *Under the Eagle: U.S. Intervention in Central America and the Caribbean* (London: Latin American Bureau, 1981) for a good historical overview and Edward Best, *US Policy and Regional Security in Central America*, (Aldershot: IISS/Gower, 1987) for a discussion which concentrates on the Reagan years.

8   For Sandino's proposals for Latin American unity see 'Plan for the Realization of Bolivar's Ultimate Dream, March 20, 1929', in Karl Bermann (ed.), *Sandino without Frontiers* (Hampton, VA: Compita, 1988), pp. 61–74.

9   Humberto Ortega, 'Nicaragua-The Strategy of Victory', in Marcus, *Sandinistas Speak*, pp. 79–80.

10   Ortega, 'Nicaragua-The Strategy of Victory'.

11   For a critique of Idealism in foreign policy see E. H. Carr, *The Twenty Years Crisis, 1919–1939* (London: Macmillan, 1981).

12   Daniel Ortega, 'Nothing will hold back our struggle for Liberation', in Marcus, *Sandinistas Speak*, p. 45.

13   Miguel D'Escoto, speech to 37th General Assembly of the United Nations, 15 October 1982, excerpt in *Nicaragua: Situation Report Number 4*, Embassy of Nicaragua, January 1983.

14   *Ibid.*

15   Interview with Alejandro Bendaña, 'Nicaragua's Foreign Policy: Ten Years of Principles and Practice', in *Envio*, Vol. 8, No. 87, August 1989, p. 26.

16   Alejandro Bendaña, author's interview. Managua, September 1988.

17   William Hupper, mimeoed speech, Transnational Institute, Amsterdam, 14 May 1983, p. 13.

18   Alejandro Bendaña, 'The Foreign Policy of the Nicaraguan Revolution', in Thomas W. Walker (ed.), *Nicaragua in Revolution*, (New York: Praeger, 1982), p. 326.

19   John Lamperti, *What Are We Afraid Of?* (Boston: South End Press, 1988), pp. 43–4.

20   William M. Leogrande, 'The United States and Nicaragua', in Thomas W. Walker (ed.), *Nicaragua: The First Five Years* (London: Praeger, 1985), pp. 425–46.

21   *Nicaragua's Peace Initiatives*, mimeo, Nicaraguan Embassy, London, 1985.

22   President Portillo, speech in Managua, February 1982, reprinted in English in Robert S. Leiken and Barry Rubin (eds), *The Central American Crisis Reader* (New York: Summit Books, 1987), pp. 631–4.

23   Best, *US Policy and Regional Security in Central America*, pp. 80–5.

24   Miguel D'Escoto, speech to the 37th General Assembly of the United Nations, in *Nicaragua: Situation Report Number 4*, Nicaraguan Embassy, January 1983.

25   Bendaña, interview, in *Envio*, Vol. 8, No. 27, August 1989, p. 26.

26   Walter Queiser Morales and Harry E. Vanden, 'Relations with the Non-aligned Movement', in Walker, *Nicaragua*, p. 476.

27   *Envio*, August 1986, p. 14.

28 International Court of Justice, *Nicaragua versus the United States* (The Hague: ICJ, 1986).

29 See Peter Kornbluh, *Nicaragua: The Price of Intervention* (Washington, DC: Institute For Policy Studies, 1987), pp. 54–7.

30 For details of Western European aid and trade with Nicaragua see Solon Barraclough *et al.*, *Aid that Counts: the Western European Contribution to Development and Survival in Nicaragua* (Amsterdam: TNI/CRIES, 1988. For an account and analysis of the Western European relationship to the Central American peace process see Hazel Smith, 'European Community Works Toward Political and Economic Cooperation in Central America', in *Council for Human Rights in Latin America Newsletter*, Oregon, Spring 1989.

31 For detail see Theodore Schwab and Harold Sims, 'Relations with the Communist States' and Walter Queiser Morales and Harry E. Vanden, 'Relations with the Nonaligned Movement', both in Walker, *Nicaragua*.

32 *Nicaragua's Peace Initiatives*, mimeo, Nicaraguan Embassy, London, 1985.

33 In May 1984 Contadora representatives were added to the Commission, which became the Commission of Supervision and Control.

34 Luis Herrera Campíns and José López Portillo, 'Letter to President Reagan, September 1982', in Robert S. Leiken and Barry Rubin (eds), *The Central American Crisis Reader* (New York: Summit Books, 1987), pp. 635–6.

35 For the Contadora 'Document of Objectives' in English see Leiken and Rubin, *The Central American Crisis Reader*, pp. 638–40.

36 For detail on the various peace initiatives see Isabel Rodriguez, 'Contadora: after three years of existence, peace continues to be the challenge', in *ANN Bulletin*, 20 January 1986, pp. 9–12; the chronology in the appendix to *Nicaragua's Peace Initiatives*, Nicaraguan Embassy, London: 'Chronologie des efforts de négociation en Amérique Centrale (1979–1987)', in Pierre Harrisson, *Etats-Unis Contra Nicaragua* (Geneva: CETIM, 1988), pp. 213–33; Michael Stuhrenberg and Eric Venturini, *Amérique Centrale: la cinquième frontière?* (Paris: La Decouverte, 1986), pp. 225–6; 'Selected Chronology of Events', in Bruce Marcus (ed.), *Nicaragua: the Sandinista People's Revolution* (London: Pathfinder, 1985), pp. xiii–xviii.

37 Best, *US Policy and Regional Security in Central America*, p. 81.

38 Harrisson, *Etats-Unis Contra Nicaragua*, p. 215.

39 The Group of 8 evolved into an institutionalised mechanism of Latin American co-operation, naming itself the 'Rio' Group, in 1986. The group held its first presidential summit in Acapulco in November 1987. Its agenda prioritised resolving the debt crisis.

40 On President Arias' attitude to President Ortega at this meeting see Central American Historical Institute, *Update*, Washington, DC, 9 May 1988.

41 For detail on these border incidents and the reaction to them see *Envio*, January 1987, pp. 3–12.

42 For detail on US efforts to prevent the signing of this agreement see Harrisson, *Etats-Unis Contra Nicaragua*, pp. 218–22.

43 For comments on the implementation of the Esquipulas accords from different perspectives see 'The Arias Plan', in *Spotlight: International MNR Bulletin*, Mexico, Sept.–Nov. 1987; and Liisa North and Tim Draimin, *The Central American Peace Process: An Overview* (Toronto: Canada-Caribbean-Central America Policy Alternatives, February 1988).

44 Harrisson, *Etats-Unis Contra Nicaragua*, p. 227.

45 Bendaña, author's interview, Managua, September 1988.

46 CIVS, 'Comments, Observations, and Conclusions of the International Commission on Verification and Follow-Up', in *Progress Report on Implementation of the Accords of the Procedure for the Establishment of a Firm and Lasting Peace in Central America*, mimeo, unofficial translation, 14 January 1988, pp. 59–65.

47 CIVS Report, unofficial translation, p. 62.

48 BBC Summary of World Broadcasts, ME/0387 D/1, 17 February 1989.

49 *Envio*, June 1989, p. 24.

50 Paul Bedard, 'Bush asking European leaders to Halt Nicaraguan Aid', *Washington Times*, 10 May 1989.

51 Ligia Vigil, author's interview, Managua, September 1988.

52 See Hazel Smith *et al.*, *Local Authorities and Nicaragua* (London: London Borough of Lambeth, 1986); and Liz Chilsen and Sheldon Rampton, *Friends In Deed: The Story of US-Nicaragua Sister Cities* (The Wisconsin Coordinating Council on Nicaragua, 1988).

53 Bendaña, author's interview, Managua, September 1988.

54 *Ibid.*

55 See Smith, *Nicaragua*, for a discussion of this issue.

56 Bendaña, author's interview, Managua, September 1988.

57 Thucydides, *History of the Peloponnesian War*, translated by Rex Warner (Harmondsworth: Penguin, 1972); Niccolò Machiavelli, *The Prince*, translated by Harvey C. Mansfield Jr (London: University of Chicago Press, 1985).

58 Waltz, *Theory of International Politics*.

59 Bull, *The Anarchical Society*.

60 Bull, *The Anarchical Society*, p. 140.

61 Graham Allison argues that the Realist or classical model is based on an understanding of the state as a rational, unitary, purposeful actor. See Graham T. Allison, *Essence of Decision: Explaining the Cuban Missile Crisis* (Boston: Little, Brown and Company, 1971).

62 Bull, *The Anarchical Society*, p. 228.

63 For a discussion of West Europe's doubts in respect of US policy see Hazel Smith, *European Community Intervention in Central America* (London: Macmillan, forthcoming 1994).

64 Hans Morgenthau, *Politics Among Nations* (New York: Knopf, 1967), p. 158.

65 In this paragraph I utilise Michael Banks' well-known categorisation of intellectual frameworks in the modern study of international relations. See Banks, 'The Inter-paradigm Debate', in Margot Light and A. J. R. Groom (eds),

International Relations: A Handbook of Current Theory (London: Pinter, 1985), pp. 7–26. The major omission here is of course the post-positivist input into the discipline, but on the grounds that it is too early to assess their contribution to the field I will stay with the more conventional approaches.

66 See Hazel Smith, 'Marxism and International Relations', in Light and Groom, *Contemporary International Relation Theory*, second edition (London: Pinter, forthcoming 1994).

67 Fred Halliday discusses three waves of Third World revolutions in the post-1945 period in *The Making of the Second Cold War*, second edition (London: Verso, 1986).

Two African states (Angola and Ethiopia) and the motifs of revolution

This chapter has a point of departure in 1974, a year of two revolutions. One was in Europe, in Portugal, and the result of that was the birth of not only (though briefly) a European revolutionary state, but four African ones as well: Angola, Mozambique, Cape Verde and Guinea-Bissau. The second revolution occurred in Ethiopia, with the overthrow of Emperor Haile Selassie. All these states declared socialist policies. Two of the African states, however, forged international military alliances with the Soviet Union that facilitated not only large arms shipments to them, but the arrival of Cuban combat troops. Cuban armed forces played an important role in Angola from 1975; they began arriving in Ethiopia in 1977 and were fielded against the Somali army in 1978. When, in 1979, Soviet troops invaded Afghanistan, it was not simply this one invasion that alarmed the West and ended *détente*, but that it seemed to culminate a series of Soviet or Soviet-proxy military interventions around the world. Ethiopia, Angola and Mozambique all adopted forms of party and governmental apparatus that sufficiently emulated the Moscow Leninist model, so that many saw the expansion of communism – not just in terms of ideology, but in terms of state system – into Africa. These states came to be regarded as Marxist and revolutionary, but their foreign policies could not always be so neatly described. This chapter examines Ethiopia and Angola, in particular, since their foreign policies brought a highly visible and active Soviet support, not to mention Cuban military personnel, and, in broad readings of the military map in the climate of the late 1970s, Soviet interests in these countries seemed poised to threaten Western interests in the Horn of Africa and the Cape of Good Hope.

Revolution as indigenous

It would be wrong, however, to view the revolutions in Ethiopia and Angola, and the foreign policies of these two revolutionary states, as having emanated from Moscow. In the case of both countries, long histories of civilisation and senses of independence were at work. In the Horn of Africa, superpower interests certainly intruded and sought to use the politics of the region, but did not animate the politics of the region. Woodward points out how competition for scarce resources fuelled the local conflicts of the Horn.[1] In Angola, superpower intervention – as opposed to support – came only after years of local resistance to Portuguese colonialism. By 1974, there had built up a substantial politics of resistance and liberation. The organising vocabulary, if not ideology, of this resistance took a Marxist base; however, as with the writings of Amilcar Cabral in Guinea-Bissau and Cape Verde, there was a firmly conceived African variation of the European Marxist norm, and a distinct African application.[2] Moscow, in addition, could be a most clumsy and, indeed, alienating patron. In 1973, Moscow suspended support for the Neto faction of the MPLA in Angola, and threw its weight behind the Chipenda faction. What was a coup attempt within the MPLA failed, and it was Neto who later came to power. This section of this chapter seeks to examine further some of the older indigenous bases for revolution in Angola and Ethiopia.

In Angola, the archetypes for revolution and rebellion are mixed. The indigenous adaptation of Christianity for political purposes began in the highly sophisticated Kongo kingdom in the late fifteenth and sixteenth centuries. There followed the development of a creole or Afro-European elite and culture and, importantly, a literate governmental culture that carried out an epistolary diplomacy at least with European governments and the Vatican. Kongo regarded itself as a sovereign state in the European sense, and retained something of this until the late nineteenth century and the arrival of conquering Portuguese forces (anxious, in the European 'scramble for Africa', to secure territory in advance of, or in accordance with, the Berlin map of 1884–85 – a prototype, perhaps, of the late twentieth-century Bosnian tragedy and the Vance/Owen map). The Kongo archives were destroyed in the fighting. Despite this loss, however, it is clear from oral histories, scattered African records and European accounts, that various cultures of resistance were growing in different Angolan kingdoms. The most developed of these, in the seventeenth century, was also the one with the most sophisticated foreign policy. Queen Nzinga resisted Habsburg conquistadores, fought the great merchant houses of Brazil, formed an alliance with the Dutch West India Company in her war against Portugal, bought weapons and mercenaries from Europe, invited Franciscan missionaries to educate and Westernise her court, became a Catholic and thus gained access to church diplomacy and conflict mediation, and broke the power of the ethnic provinces in favour of an overarching state identity. As David Birmingham put it, she was a 'nationalist in the modern sense of the work and the precursor of the state builders of the twentieth century . . . Her legacy of armed freedom stood the test of time for nigh on two centuries.'[3] For centuries before our own, therefore, there existed in Angola a purposeful blend of local and international culture, which established a tradition of defending local interests. This was initiated by revolution in Kongo, and was an instrument of resistance, nationalism and revolutionary change under Queen Nzinga. To consider that history disappeared entirely under Portuguese rule, so that Angola was simply a blank slate for Marxism, would be excluding Eurocentrism.

In Ethiopia, a continuously recorded history, the legacy of literate societies, stretches back even further. A kingdom existed at Axum in 100 BC, and the Axumite empire embraced Christianity in the fourth century AD. In the several hundred years that followed, with shifts of power from region to region, the Coptic Church remained a unifying force. When Ras Teferi became regent in 1916, therefore, and led Ethiopia into the League of Nations, he was leading a discordant civil society, with an unresolved nationalities problem, but one whose complexities had been charted, and its conflicts mediated by its own ancient church. It was as Emperor Haile Selassie that Ras Teferi entered the Western consciousness, pleading at the League of Nations in 1936, unsuccessfully, for help against the Italian invasion.

Mussolini's armies took Addis Ababa later that year but, in 1941, the allies, spearheaded by South African soldiers, retook Addis for the Emperor and his army to enter it in the manner of De Gaulle and the Free French later in Paris. Haile Selassie concentrated a great many of his energies on establishing Ethiopia in the community of states. His foreign policy led to the headquartering of the Organisation for African Unity, and the UN Economic Commission for Africa, in Addis. When he fell to the coup of September 1974, Ethiopia had a recorded history as extensive as many in the West, and a twentieth-century diplomacy and foreign policy that had impinged upon the West.[4]

Exogenous influences on revolution

Revolutionary states are seldom unitary actors. The Soviet support for Chipenda was one indication of factions within the Angolan MPLA. Although Neto, after assuming power, was said to have joked about being a Marxist out of pragmatism, and not out of ideological commitment, or even ideological understanding, there was certainly a powerful pro-Moscow faction within the MPLA and, in its ranks, ideological commitment was not wanting. In Ethiopia, the Dergue or military junta that grew out of the overthrow of Haile Selassie not only contained various ideological strands, it co-operated with other political parties. Such co-operation was almost always uneasy; however, the Trotskyite Ethiopian People's Revolutionary Party (EPRP), and the All-Ethiopian Socialist Movement (MEISON), were, for the first two years of the Ethiopian revolution, important political actors. Only in February 1977, when Mengistu seized power in a coup, were the EPRP and MEISON banned (and most of their leaders executed). Even then, the Mengistu Dergue was unable to solve the nationalities problem and, although national groups such as the Eritreans waged war against the Dergue rather than seeking to work with or within it, it cannot be said that Mengistu depended on an unforced unanimity within the Dergue. Ongoing ruthless suppression of dissent meant that dissent was still in existence. Having said that, it should also be said that what was being debated in the early days of the revolution were variants of socialism. Haile Selassie was overthrown in September 1974; by December, Ethiopia had been declared a socialist state; in 1975, before Mengistu's coup, a wave of industrial and rural land nationalisations took place. It was not as though the EPRP or MEISON were dissenting from revolutionary change. In 1979, with the EPRP and MEISON proscribed, Mengistu continued such change with a highly successful national literacy campaign. These social measures, though often accompanied by force and resettlement programmes, nevertheless accomplished sufficient benefit for the revolution to be painted, outside Ethiopia, in less than bloody hues; some Western academics were, in fact, quite impressed by what was happening.[5]

What tended to consolidate factions in both the MPLA and the Dergue, however, was not revolutionary development, but external threat. In Angola, there had been not only Soviet support for the MPLA, but a history of Western support for the FNLA (National Front for the Liberation of Angola), and a combination of western and Chinese support for UNITA. The Portuguese, after their own revolution, anxious to be rid of troublesome colonies, engineered the Alvor Agreement between all three, which was meant to lead to power-sharing and, eventually, elections. This agreement lasted a very short time indeed, and full-scale hostilities among the three Angolan groups were in earnest throughout 1975. Although the West expressed its anxiety that the Soviets were arming the

MPLA and giving it a military advantage over its rivals, it would appear that an arms race was in fact in progress: the MPLA advantage derived from the fact that its Soviet arms were latest-generation, whereas the US supplied Korean war surplus arms to the FNLA. The major controversy of 1975, however, was the arrival of the Cubans. This remains the stuff of debate, and it is clear there was a small Cuban contingent in Angola by early 1975. It would seem that full-scale Cuban military contingents arrived later, as a response to the incursion of South African troops. Rather than deterring or overthrowing a 'Marxist' MPLA, the South African action resulted in the Organisation for African Unity closing ranks behind the MPLA, so that in Africa at least the Cubans were seen as anti-racist allies of the MPLA state – and there they stayed until the end of the 1980s.

In Ethiopia, diplomatic ties were maintained with the West, including the USA, from the fall of Haile Selassie in 1974 until early 1977. Diplomatic ties with the US were then broken, partly because of US complaints of human rights abuses, and partly because of the US refusal to supply arms to Ethiopia. The rupture was partly to do with Mengistu's coming to power, and the bloodshed that involved, but partly also to do with storm clouds gathering over the Ogaden region of Ethiopia, along the border of which Somali forces were massing. In March 1977, one month after Mengistu's coup, the Somali army crossed the border. There followed one of the abrupt, if not cynical, switches of the late twentieth century, when the Soviets, who had hitherto supported the Somalis, turned this support to the Ethiopians. The socialist government of the first Dergue had given way to the more avowedly pro-Moscow 'Marxist' second Dergue of Mengistu, and the Ethiopian position in the Horn of Africa commanded greater advantages for Soviet interests than what was available in Somalia. The arms Ethiopia was unable to secure from the USA came now from the USSR. In February 1978, equipped with Soviet weaponry and ranged alongside 16,000 Cuban troops, the Ethiopians counter-attacked in the Ogaden. The Somali army withdrew in March, though Somali partisans continued an irregular war for some time afterwards.

By 1975 and 1978 respectively, Angola and Ethiopia were committed to foreign policies that embraced substantial Soviet support and a protective armed Cuban presence. War with South Africa, rather than MPLA revolutionary fervour, meant the retention of Soviet and Cuban assistance in Angola. Tension with Somalia, together with the growing resort to armed struggle on the part of Eritrea and Tigray, meant the continuation of Soviet and Cuban military assistance to Ethiopia. In Angola, there were contradictions within a pro-Soviet foreign policy. MPLA soldiers guarded US Gulf Oil installations against US Government-supported UNITA incursions. In Ethiopia also, contradictions emerged. In 1984, the year of most sustained attempt to create a government structure along Marxist-Leninist lines, a huge interest in Ethiopia developed among Western governments and donor groups alarmed by the ferocity of the regional drought and the resultant famine; and the Ethiopian Leninist government, though it sought to do so conditionally, had no choice but to accept and seek Western assistance. The foundations for these contradictions are explored in what follows.

A vast literature has grown up around both countries. The war waged by southern Africa against its neighbours, including the use of its own army in Angola for more than eight years, has been well documented.[6] The developments in Ethiopia, involving traditions of long independence, resistance to European powers in the mid-twentieth century, and the appropriation of at least forms of Leninist revolutionary apparatus in the later twentieth century, have also been widely studied. Two recent works, by Keller[7] and Clapham,[8] are major investigations, and the aim here is not to repeat or summarise what these have said. Rather, the aim, in studying the contradictions noted above, is to put forward the hypothesis that, for these two revolutionary governments, foreign policy had to become quite quickly less revolutionary than ideology or even military alliances would have suggested.

Contradictory influences

For Ethiopia, a Leninist model seemed appropriate for two major reasons. Firstly, it seemed 'scientific', and therefore capable of modernising both the means of production and the apparatus of the state – till that time feudal, and based to a significant extent on personal relationship and patronage. Secondly, precisely because Ethiopia had been feudal, the organisational device of an elite vanguard party meant the transition of power from a highly centralised monarchical source to a highly centralised party source. The transfer of power, therefore, meant little change in the style by which people were governed. The revolution did not enfranchise the masses but, the proscription of other parties notwithstanding, did not unduly disrupt them either – that is if the masses were urban dwellers. Although parallels have been drawn between the Ethiopian revolution and those other revolutions that overthrew monarchies – in

France, Russia, to an extent China – suggesting precedents for the nar-
rowness of vanguard party power that followed, the revolution in Ethiopia faced a problem that had not affected the others. That problem was a
lack of resource base capable of sustaining a revolution, led centrally by a
small elite in cities. Here, the oft-diagnosed situation of a dual economy
comes into play. The supporters of the party and government – in the
case of Ethiopia including a growing civil service and a burgeoning military – need to be sustained in their city locations. It is not so much that
production systems in the countryside are altered (although many development economists would think this is sin enough), but that the system
of exchange is biased. Food produced in the countryside is bought by a
central authority to feed its organised supporters in the cities, and other
city-dwellers because they are amenable – in concentrated areas – to
organisation; people need to be rewarded and bought off. This means
a great expense for the central authority concerned and, since it is a monopoly purchaser, it seeks to drive down the cost involved. Because of poor
prices and the lack of alternative purchasers, peasant producers have no
incentives to produce. If, on top of that, there are resettlement problems
or reluctance to resettle, the fear of violence because of the growing
militarisation of the nationalities issue, and famine to boot, then the supportive indigenous base of the revolution is squeezed immeasurably. If
the governing elite is to survive, it must look to exogenous sources. If,
in the case of Ethiopia, the Eastern bloc already has heavy commitments
to military support, only the West can provide disaster relief and support
for the lives of millions of citizens.

In Ethiopia, as suggested above, there were also internal party factions.
In part, these consisted of a tension between the military on the one hand,
and the party on the other, both existing as instruments of centralised
authority. To an extent, that tension was allayed by the incorporation of
military figures into the ruling councils of the party. Nevertheless, the
military remained distinct from the party, if only because it was fighting
wars, first against the Somalis, then against the Eritreans and Tigrayans.
Under the stress of combat, military purges for political reasons could not
enhance the morale of the military, nor endear the party to it. When, in
the famine of 1984, certain Western donor countries and agencies insisted
on food reaching exactly the Eritrean and Tigrayan opponents of the
Ethiopian military, what was being undermined was not only military
strategy but confidence in party policy and authority.

By the time of the final battles of the war against the Eritreans (led now
by the EPLF), the Ethiopian army was a hollow force, easily outflanked

by a textbook feint on the approach routes to Asmara. In May 1991, the EPLF (Eritrean People's Liberation Front), under Isaias Afewerki, marched without firing a shot into Asmara. In the same month, the rebel forces of Meles Zenawi took Addis Ababa. Both new governments (a provisional government in Eritrea until a referendum approved independence in April 1993) had revolutionary credentials, but the doors of both capitols have been thrown open to international capital and an amazing amount of international diplomatic, educational and commercial traffic – much of it opportunistic and not all of it longlasting or even briefly beneficial. Notwithstanding the lack of a contemporary alternative to the West, and bearing in mind that the former alternative had supported Mengistu's efforts to suppress the rebels and secessionists who had now come to power, the openness of foreign policy from Asmara and Addis would still have been surprising, had it not been for the fact that the case for an open, non-ideologically-directed foreign policy had been building for many years. Dependence at first on the US for arms, then the Soviet Union and Cuba in place of the US, then the West for famine relief, and a continuing dependence on the Soviet Union for military training, strategic direction and arms – until the Soviet Union itself was about to fall – suggested that no one exogenous source could provide all the support which the Ethiopian revolution of 1974 to 1991 needed. The successor states have understood this.

In Angola, from the beginning, foreign policy had to take into account many actors. Although Cuban troops in 1975 had held and shaken South African units on the approach routes to Luanda, it was not Cuban military prowess alone that caused the withdrawal of South African forces. A refusal by the US Congress to entertain the prospect of US involvement in foreign wars, except under conditions agreed by Congress itself, had meant the withdrawal of US support for the South African incursion. Later, the future of Angola was linked with the future of Namibia, with the withdrawal of Cuban and South African forces respectively being advanced as quid pro quos for each other. The Western Contact Group that sought to broker such an arrangement meant that Angola could scarcely avoid diplomatic involvement with the West, notwithstanding the lack of recognition from the US of the MPLA government. The Western Contact Group was, among other things, a point of contact with the US.[9] During the Reagan years, South Africa was seen as a focus of US diplomacy. Whatever may be said of 'constructive engagement', it certainly was taken by the South Africans as a permission to destabilise 'Marxist' regimes such as Angola. The UNITA leader, Jonas Savimbi, assiduously cultivated his links with the US, and did so with some success. Although it is possible to demonise Savimbi, particularly in view of his refusal to abide by the 1992 election results, he was, as Bridgeland pointed out in some detail, a complex and sophisticated man.[10] The MPLA government of Angola, therefore, always had to keep a counter-diplomacy in play, to minimise the Savimbi-effect in the US. This was pursued in part under the cover of regional diplomacy, so that the 1984 Lusaka accord, to which both Angola and South Africa were signatories, seemed in keeping with Kenneth Kaunda's regional policy of mediation. Both it and the 1984 Nkomati accord between South Africa and Mozambique, however, depended in no small measure on US pressures and covert diplomatic initiatives. Although Angola continued its heavy dependence on Cuban and Soviet military support, non-public and unofficial diplomacy with the US and other Western powers continued. Much of this, from time to time but particularly towards the end of the 1980s, was channelled through Lisbon. Venancio has detailed this relationship from Portugal's point of view for southern Africa as a whole,[11] for Mozambique,[12] and for Angola.[13] This coincided with the regional diplomacy of Zaire, Zambia and, particularly, Zimbabwe,[14] so that Angolan foreign policy was multi-faceted and, essentially, pragmatic – given its military situation; it was reliant on the East for military support, but this did not diminish its search for diplomatic support elsewhere.

The operational nature of this dualism was spectacularly demonstrated by the battle of Cuito Cuanavale in 1988. In so far as anybody 'won' this battle (and it was probably more a series of outflanking manoeuvres backed up by displays of strength in reserve), it was the Soviet-orchestrated, Cuban-officered, MPLA military alliance – if only because its strength in reserve, Soviet-supplied at considerable expense, was greater and, in air power particularly, capable of causing more losses and greater costs than the South African strength. But, after this 'victory', accomplished by Angola's allies from the East, it was the US Assistant Secretary of State, Chester Crocker, who involved the Angolans in diplomatic negotiations. Although Crocker paints a fine picture of himself in this process,[15] and the chronology of negotiation suggests a purely Western exercise (none of the ten formal negotiating rounds was held in an Eastern bloc city),[16] this should not exclude the role played by Cuban negotiators at those talks. They impressed their US counterparts.[17] There was, therefore, some overlap of military and diplomatic support from the Cubans; having said that, the bulk of the aftermath of Cuito Cuanavale was indeed taken up by the West – and Angola, as it had been to a great many Western diplomatic movements in the years before, was amenable to this. In this context, the guarding of Gulf Oil installations by MPLA soldiers seems less surprising that it might at first glance.

Foundations for revolution

All this is to say that a revolutionary state's foreign policy need not be determined by its ideology or, more importantly in the case of much existing scholarship, by the class structure of its revolution. There has been a tendency among Africanists to adopt a two-pronged, but largely separable, analysis. The first is to propose a distribution of power in the international political economy; to make the clear and supportable point that the movement of international capital originates largely from, and is largely controlled by the West; that developing countries, including African countries, are dependent on the West for capital flows, and for the benefits of development which require capital investment. This part of the analysis then proceeds to make two important claims. One is that the 'West' should not be seen as an amorphous entity, but that it has its own class relationships, and the control of capital is associated with the emergence of a certain class within a class structure. The dependency of the non-Western world is located upon this class. The other claim has two sub-divisions of its own. The West, in its colonial enterprise, purposely created, if not an equivalent class structure in its former colonies, a sympathetic elite ruling class. The ruling classes collaborate on the movement of capital. However, the developing countries are dependent on the Western ruling class for the flow of capital only because their own local elites transferred capital to the West in the first place. This transfer was forced in colonial times and is accomplished by class collaboration today. The Western ruling class has a monopoly over capital flows only because it has first accumulated that capital from elsewhere. The mechanism of accumulation from elsewhere depends on the local elite's satisfaction with the benefits of collaboration, and the Western ruling class seeks to assure this.

The second prong of this analysis proposes that class formation is occurring in developing societies. An elite capitalist class has obviously formed, or been formed, first. The remainder of the local class structure may differ from jurisdiction to jurisdiction, or may even be enigmatic, but there will be something resembling a proletariat which can be identified because it is poor. The suggestion is that its poverty results from its having been immiserated. The elite, by contrast, is not poor because of its international collaborationism, and this process of collaboration is an active immiserating cornerstone of the developing class structure.

In the case of Ethiopia, though it was never colonised in the 'scramble for Africa', and was under Italian rule for only a brief period of five years, 1936–41, analysis of this sort suggests that, even without colonisation, Ethiopia was nevertheless 'created', 'invented', or largely shaped as a dependent state by the same capitalist forces that used colonialism as an instrument upon her neighbours. Ibssa and Holcomb have most recently made an analysis of this sort.[18] In southern Africa, the 'non-revolutionary' states, such as Zambia, have long been subjected to such analysis,[19] whereas Angola, as a 'revolutionary' state has been self-evidently at war with the forces and agents of international capital, assisted in this struggle by the forces of imperfect but actually-existing socialism.

The present author, in the case of Zambia, has put forward a list of conceptual, empirical and procedural objections to such analysis.[20] In addition, however, there are two overarching objections to the analysis in general. The first is that it elevates structure over human agency, to the extent that it fetishises structure and, except in conditions of armed liberation struggle or revolution, i.e. in conditions of extreme response, treats agency lightly. To a significant degree, history has been determined from above, rather than created from below. The second overarching objection is that this analysis proposes a starting-point for history consonant with the 'peripheralisation' of the developing world into the capital structures of the West. This is a history therefore in terms of Western impingement upon the non-West – whereas, as the beginning of this chapter suggested, history and culture in Ethiopia and Angola predate 'peripheralisation' in quite complex and recorded forms and that, in Angola, the early stages of contact with Western capitalism did not result at all in a one-way traffic.

That there are determining agents from below, drawn from cultural dynamics, either of the past or reinvented from the past, seems an important point – one made for England in the 'cultural Marxism' of Thompson and Williams, and made for southern Africa in a host of recent, field-based studies.[21] That it is possible to combine cultural foundations with political economy, to produce a more complex, human, and less determining structure – which nevertheless plays a part in a sophisticated and modern critical theory of the world – is not within the present author's doubt. It does mean, however, three comments relevant to the current chapter. The first two are quick observations.

In the Ibssa and Holcomb study of Ethiopia, the West sought the collaboration, not of a national class, but of an Ethiopian nationality, the Abyssinians, in order to gain control over other nationalities. This thesis is contentious but, if persuasive, is persuasive against the idea of an international class collaboration – and bespeaks an imperialism far more opportunistic and pragmatic in its alliances than the neatness of class theory suggests. Secondly, in Angola, the very revolutionaries were also those most likely to have been class collaborationists. They were the products of the Portuguese assimilation policy, but used their elite status instead to inspire and lead resistance to colonialism. Birmingham has noted how, in Luanda at least, all discourse, including political discourse, continues to be conducted in Portuguese. It is the language of the revolution.[22] The MPLA hierarchy is more 'assimilated' than the Portuguese authorities could ever have hoped or dreamed. The instruments for inducing collaboration are not invariably successful. There is nothing easy about securing, over a very short period, the formation and determination of a single, small class.

Thirdly, and importantly, if elite class formation is not evident or not easy, it is much more difficult to achieve an indigenous mass class base for revolution. Some scholars have certainly begun to address this problem. Gebre-Medhin has sought to uncover a peasant base to Eritrean nationalism at least, and to ascribe this to the EPLF's revolutionary credentials.[23] The new Ethiopian government of Meles Zenawi has quite purposefully posed as a government drawn not from the cities and their elites, but from the peasants and farmers. If, however, all this – from the points of view of both Asmara and Addis – is to stand in contradistinction to the 'revolutionary base' of the Dergue and Mengistu, then a 'true' revolution never took place in 1974 or 1977. Similarly, in Angola, there has never been any great doubt over Savimbi and UNITA's foundation support, not in an Angolan class but within an ethnic group. As with Ibssa and Holcomb's depiction of Western use of the Abyssinian nationality, the West here has sought a non-class-based collaboration. It is the MPLA that has been the party of the cities during the war against UNITA and South Africa, that has spoken the language of the colonisers, and which, in the Gulf Oil example, has protected the interests of Western capital. Here also, if ever there was any revolutionary base, it was not sustained in the years after 1975. What made both Angola and Ethiopia 'revolutionary' was not an indigenous basis for revolution so much as an exogenous linkage with the Soviet Union and Cuba. Rather than being the foreign policy of revolutionary states, this was the foreign policy of states with perhaps revolutionary aspirations but, as yet, no true revolutionary foundations. Even then, as noted above, foreign policy soon took in a great number of dealings with the West. US recognition of the MPLA government of Angola in May 1993, after Savimbi had refused to accept the results of the West-urged and UN-supervised elections of 1992, was a triumph for Angolan foreign policy.

The motifs of revolution

In both Ethiopia and Angola, such revolution as there was may well have aspired to a freedom from Western domination of capital flows – the rhetoric suggests so – but owed also to histories of resistance, attempts (in Ethiopia) not so much of peasant mobilisation as peasant resettlement, and elite leadership (the armed forces and, at first, intellectuals in Ethiopia, and the Lusophonic elite in Angola). Both Angola and Ethiopia attempted to create a Leninist party and governmental structure. This may be seen not as a proof of revolution, but as a motif of a declared (though not conclusively actual) revolution. Such motifs were fielded, perhaps out of elite ideological belief in them, but as much to secure continued assistance from other 'revolutionary' states. In time, each confirms the other: the party structure attracts assistance; the assistance strengthens the party structure – a revolving confirmation and, in its literal mechanistic sense, revolutionary.

Notes

1 Peter Woodward, *War-or-Peace in North-East Africa?*, London, Conflict Studies No. 219, 1989.

2 See Strike Mkandla, 'The Thought of Amilcar Lopes Cabral of Guinea-Bissau', unpublished Ph.D. thesis, University of Kent, 1983.

3 David Birmingham, *Frontline Nationalism in Angola & Mozambique*, London, James Currey, 1992, pp. 9–10.

4 See e.g. Christopher Clapham, *Haile Selassie's Government*, New York, Praeger, 1969.

5 E.g. Fred Halliday and Maxine Molyneux, *The Ethiopian Revolution*, London, Verso, 1981. For a technical consideration, see A. P. Wood, 'Rural Development and National Integration in Ethiopia', *African Affairs*, 82, No. 328, 1983. Wood has taken his study of Ethiopian development through all the stages of the revolution: 'Aid and Politics in Ethiopia', *Land-Use Policy*, 3, No. 4, 1986; 'Natural Resource Conflicts in South-west Ethiopia: State, Communities, and the Role of

the National Conservation Strategy in the Search for Sustainable Development', *Scandinavian Journal of African Studies*, forthcoming 1993; *inter alia*.

6   See e.g. Paul L. Moorcraft, *African Nemesis*, London, Brassey's, 1990; Phyllis Johnson and David Martin (eds) *Destructive Engagement*, Harare, Zimbabwe Publishing House, 1986; Kenneth W. Grundy, *The Militarization of South African Politics*, Oxford, Oxford University Press, 1988; Victoria Brittain, *Hidden Lives, Hidden Deaths*, London, Faber and Faber, 1988; Stephen Chan, *Exporting Apartheid*, London, Macmillan, 1990.

7   Edmond J. Keller, *Revolutionary Ethiopia: From Empire to People's Republic*, Bloomington, Indiana University Press, 1988.

8   Christopher Clapham, *Transformation and Continuity in Revolutionary Ethiopia*, Cambridge, Cambridge University Press, 1988.

9   See Vivienne Jabri, *Mediating Conflict: Decision-making and Western Intervention in Namibia*, Manchester, Manchester University Press, 1990.

10   Fred Bridgeland, *Jonas Savimbi*, Edinburgh, Mainstream, 1986.

11   Moises Venancio, *Portugal, Africa and the European Community, 1974–1992*, unpublished M.Phil thesis, University of Cambridge, 1992.

12   Moises Venancio, 'Mediation by the Roman Catholic Church in Mozambique 1988–1991', in Stephen Chan and Vivienne Jabri (eds), *Mediation in Southern Africa*, London, Macmillan, 1993.

13   Moises Venancio with Carla McMillan, 'Portugese Mediation of the Angolan Conflict in 1990–91', in Chan and Jabri, *Mediation in Southern Africa*.

14   See Hasu H. Patel, 'Zimbabwe's Mediation in Mozambique and Angola 1989–1991', in Chan and Jabri, *Mediation in Southern Africa*.

15   Chester Crocker, *High Noon in Southern Africa*, New York, Norton, 1993.

16   For a chronology of negotiation, see Geoff Berridge, 'Diplomacy and the Angola/Namibia Accords', *International Affairs*, 65, No. 3, 1989.

17   Jorge I. Dominguez, 'Pipsqueak Power: The Centrality and Anomaly of Cuba', in Thomas G. Weiss and James G. Blight (eds), *The Suffering Grass*, Boulder, Westview, 1992.

18   Sisai Ibssa and Bonnie Holcomb, *The Invention of Ethiopia*, Trenton, NJ, Red Sea Press, 1990.

19   See e.g. Timothy M. Shaw, *Dependence and Underdevelopment: The Development and Foreign Policies of Zambia*, Athens, Ohio, Ohio University Centre for International Studies, 1976.

20   Stephen Chan, *Kaunda and Southern Africa: Image and Reality in Foreign Policy*, London, I. B. Tauris, 1992, pp. 117–27.

21   E. P. Thompson, *The Making of the English Working Class*, London, Gollancz, 1963; Raymond Williams, *Problems in Materialism and Culture*, London, Verso, 1980; Leroy Vail (ed.), *The Creation of Tribalism in Southern Africa*, London, James Currey, 1989; Preben Kaarsholm (ed.), *Cultural Struggle and Development in Southern Africa*, London, James Currey, 1991; Terrence Ranger, *Peasant Consciousness and Guerilla War in Zimbabwe*, London, James Currey, 1985,

cf. David Lan, *Guns & Rain: Guerillas and Spirit Mediums in Zimbabwe*, London, James Currey, 1985.

22   David Birmingham, 'Angola Revisited', *Journal of Southern African Studies*, 15, No. 1, 1988, pp. 43.

23   Jordan Gebre-Medhin, *Peasants and Nationalism in Eritrea*, Trenton, NJ, Red Sea Press, 1989.

The determinants of Iraqi foreign policy behaviour in the 1980s

The determinants of foreign policy behaviour are extremely varied and very complex. They are usually divided into internal and external components, and their impact on behaviour differs from one state to another and, more importantly, from one issue-area to another. In this chapter, it will be suggested that domestic tangible and non-tangible variables have had a considerable role in shaping, processing and producing Iraqi foreign policy behaviour, especially in the last two decades. Therefore, in an attempt to understand Iraq's foreign behaviour, significant inputs such as the evolution of its political structure, the idiosyncratic characteristics of its elite members, Iraq's social stratification and finally, its geopolitical attributes will be analysed. Much of the focus of the chapter will be on Iraq's foreign policy behaviour during the presidency of Saddam Hussein from 1979 onwards.

The evolution of Iraqi domestic political structure

The present-day Iraq, once part of the Ottoman empire, turned into a state in 1920. In the absence of commonly-accepted indigenous elite groups, Faisal, a Sharifian prince, was placed in power by the British Mandatory authorities to lead a constitutional parliamentary system under a hereditary monarchy. The first order of business for the new king was to legitimise his rule and bring stability to the political process in Iraq. But it did not take too long for Faisal to experience what other rulers of Iraq of later periods and regimes were to experience: that consensus-building was almost impossible in a country where diverse communities with opposing interests and incessant antagonisms lived together.

The heterogeneity of religious, economic, sectarian and political groups only fostered suspicion and hostility between them. From the beginning,

Prince Faisal was caught between satisfying domestic groups and the demands of the British Mandate authorities. Faisal depended heavily on the British to remain in power, so he could not afford to alienate them. On the other hand, he naturally had to engage in a process of building support among the various internal groups. The interests of the British did not quite fit the interests of the domestic communities destined for self-assertion and some degree of autonomy, and suspicious of 'national cohesiveness'.[1]

It therefore was no surprise that survival rested on ruthless political manoeuvring and all-encompassing military force. These two political traditions have continued to be applied with ever greater violence into the latter decades of the twentieth century of Iraqi domestic politics. Political and ideological diversity in Iraqi politics have persistently delayed and also hindered its state-formation from a classical point of view. Faisal's successor, his son Ghazi, was also unable to establish a cohesive state. Ghazi's death and the rise of Prince Abd al Allah and Nuri as Said exacerbated the divisions and antagonisms among political and ethnic groupings, and his government's non-conciliatory approach towards the opposition led these groups to go underground and to adopt revolutionary behaviour. The political spectrum was divided among the minority who ruled with force and external support, and the isolated majority which was excluded from the political process and decision making by coercion.[2]

The Hashemite monarchy was overthrown on 14 July 1958. Abd al Karim Qasim became the next ruler to manoeuvre between the Sunnis and the Shias, the Arabs and the Kurds, the Shaikhs and the urban middle class, and the communists and the nationalists. On the domestic front, Qasim, like his predecessors, aligned himself with one set of groups against the others but had to worry constantly about coups, uprisings and opposing coalitions. Externally, he fomented an atmosphere of tension by claiming Khuzestan, a province in south-western Iran, and the newly independent state of Kuwait, both adjacent to Iraqi territory.

During Qasim's monopolised rule, the diversity among groups turned to violence and the traditional tribal social and political structure in Iraq was disturbed to a point where no group trusted any other community and any potential basis for nationhood was jeopardised. In this hopeless context, the Baathists and Nasserites orchestrated a coup against Qasim and the foundations of a new regime were created in Iraqi modern politics. However, from February 1963 to July 1968, four military coups with diverse orientations were undertaken but, finally, power was regained by the Baathists. Given the social disintegration and political chaos that prevailed at the time, it was not too inept when the Baath coup leaders declared in 1968 that their ideology was grounded upon socialism, freedom and unity, indicating a suitable melange of Arab nationalism, social equality and political decisiveness.[3]

But as later events demonstrated, political tranquillity is an unknown expression in the Iraqi political vocabulary. As the inexperienced Baathists learned how to remain in power and expand their domain of dominance, they proved unable to bring stability, calmness, orderly succession and a civil mentality to the process of decision making both for the domestic process of government as well as for foreign policy. Like all governments in the past, the Iraqi leadership under the Baath portrayed deep insecurity in its active and reactive behaviour and also dissatisfaction in dealing with other governments, especially in the Middle Eastern region.

The Baath party and the evolution of Iraqi politics

The Baathists came to power determined to stay and develop a national and, more ambitiously, a regional pan-Arabists agenda and action plan. The Baath party (or 'renaissance') was established in Syria in the early 1940s, the founders being Michel Aflaq, a Christian, and Salah al Din al Bitar, a Sunni Muslim. The Iraqi branch of Baath, unlike its core establishment in Damascus, was small – an ephemeral organisation, numbering fewer than 300 members in 1955.[4]

Ahmad Hassan al Bakr led one of the camps within the party and by the mid-1960s his camp had gained the dominant power base in the Baath party. His right-hand man, a 'fixer' and a person who would solve all bureaucratic and organisational problems, was Saddam Hussein.[5] With the 1967 Arab-Israeli war, Nasser's influence in Iraq diminished and on 17 July 1968 the Baathists regained control of power in Iraq. The party then began a series of organisational restructurings to expand its functions and presence throughout the rural and urban areas of Iraq. Non-Baathists were eliminated or given ambassadorial posts abroad, and in this process of Baathist consolidation in Iraq after 1968, Saddam Hussein played a key role.[6]

Government policies after 1968 were the first attempts in Iraq's modern politics to establish centralisation and central control. This forced centralisation of the state, the people and the national agenda around an ideology called Baathism, brought about an era within which certain foreign policy traits can be discerned. Iraqi post-independence politics, after a long period of discontinuity, uncertainty and disintegration, now became a scene by which the political and ideological directives of two men – Ahmad Hassan al Bakr and Saddam Hussein – shaped its directions, outlook and decisions; a period which Hussein called 'an era of trial and error'.

The Baath and Iraqi foreign policy

Iraqi territorial conflicts with its neighbours, an aspiring assertive role in the Arab world and a strategic desire for a visible presence in the Persian Gulf were all foreign policy issues before the Baath era. But after 1968, these same issues were expressed and portrayed with greater vigour, seriousness and decisiveness.

Regardless of the orientation and type of government in Iraq, any group of rulers in Baghdad potentially face certain stable issues or problems in that country. These issues or problems are:

(a) Iraq's relative landlockedness which provokes territorial conflicts with neighbouring countries;
(b) Iraq's strategic desire for a larger and accountable visibility and presence in the Persian Gulf;
(c) Iraqi inclination to assertiveness in Arab politics;
(d) the Kurdish problem in northern Iraq;
(e) Iraq's heterogeneous ethnic and political groupings which become bargaining as well as threatening elements in dealing with neighbouring states.

Hypothetically, various elite groups would approach these issues differently. Among their approaches we could number confrontation, conciliation, adventurism, gradual resolution, evolutionary integration, acceptance of the *status quo* and perhaps depoliticised economic development both at the domestic and regional levels. What has been the direction of Iraq's behaviour given the aforementioned set of national constancies? The Iraqi leadership under the Baath and especially during Saddam Hussein's rule, has shown an attitude of complete dissatisfaction with Iraq's political and geo-political boundaries. If one were to apply A. F. K. Organski's classification of states,[7] Iraq under the Baath would be a powerful but dissatisfied state at the Middle Eastern regional level.

The political traditions in Iraq's domestic evolution since 1920, namely military force as the mechanism for statecraft, the deprivation of ethnic expression, the imposition of a state's will on the public, radical ideological shifts and the use of military means for conflict resolution have more or less been extended to its external behaviour. In many ways, one can substantiate a major axiom in foreign policy analysis with regard to the Iraqi case, that, 'foreign policy is a continuation and extension of domestic politics'. The peculiar characteristics involved in the evolution of Iraqi domestic politics are unequivocally transformed into its external outlook, behaviour and pursuits. Furthermore, the militarily-oriented political traditions coupled with the idiosyncratic characteristics of Iraqi statesmen have collectively led to a confrontational and adventurist foreign policy under the Baath. As a result, Baathist foreign policy, especially under Saddam Hussein, has been consistent with Iraqi internal structure and orientations.

There are basically two events in the Iraqi foreign policy of the Saddam Hussein era that can be looked at as case studies to explore the peculiarities of Baath foreign policy. These events are the Iran-Iraq war and Iraq's temporary annexation of Kuwait and the subsequent Persian Gulf war. The input and output processes of both cases reflect the insecure nature of the Iraqi state, the idiosyncratic characteristics of its elite, its bellicose approach towards conflict resolution, its dissatisfaction with Iraqi geopolitics, and unimaginable levels of political manoeuvring and short-term political idealism.

But the most important input of all are the idiosyncratic variables, for it is key individuals who make decisions, who interpret data, who draw inferences, who perceive and misperceive and who are victims of certain cognitive processes. In this context, understanding Saddam Hussein's role is paramount in tracing Iraq's domestic and external politics in the last two decades. It was his interpretations, conclusions and needs that shaped the turbulent foreign policy of Iraq in the 1980s.

Similar to the role of all revolutionary leaders in national crisis, Saddam Hussein's personality, outlook and ideals have had a profound influence upon Iraqi foreign behaviour during the aforementioned conflicts. How has Iraq behaved within the context of Iraqi domestic and geo-political deficiencies? In the following paragraphs, it will be argued that, to a large degree, Iraqi foreign policy behaviour has emanated from Saddam Hussein's idiosyncratic traits.[8]

In the earlier days of Baathist consolidation, Hussein's 'organizational and operational skills proved indispensable for the party's survivability'.[9] He had moved from a regular member of the party to the second most influential person in the country:

Despite his youthfulness, Hussein adjusted ably and quickly. He was realistic enough to know that holding on to his position, let alone moving forward to the presidential palace would be a precarious and tortuous process. Yet he also was confident that he possessed the necessary qualities for this hazardous journey: great caution, endless patience, intense calculation and utter ruthlessness.[10]

Hussein as a believer in pragmatism and grandeur, and a somewhat visionary person has consistently demonstrated himself to be an ambitious, assertive, self-regarding and a self-congratulatory individual.

In the mid-1970s, Hassan al Bakr was beset by illness, and unofficially turned over statecraft and national decision making to Saddam Hussein. Iraqi claims over Iran's share of the Shatt al Arab river and the Iranian south-western province of Khuzestan, its revolutionary rhetoric directed against the Persian Gulf states, its support of South Yemen's communist government and especially its territorial claims on Kuwait had created an atmosphere of political discomfort, the perpetuation of frictions and antagonistic foreign policy behaviour in the region. In such a context, Iraq had alienated both Iran and the Arab countries, reducing trust and neighbourly relations to a minimum. A statement of the Baath party in the 1970s displays the degree of self-regarding and protective behaviour of Iraq towards the region: '. . . Iraq, as the most important and advanced Arab country in the area, and the one with the largest potential, must bear the heaviest burdens in protecting it against dangers and encroachment.'[11]

In 1975, Saddam Hussein, the main architect of Iraqi foreign policy, feeling overwhelmed by the profits of petroleum price increases, initiated a series of improvements of relations with its neighbours. In 1974, Baghdad tried to assassinate the leader of the Kurdish Democratic Party (KDP) Barzani. But by signing a treaty of friendship and co-operation with Moscow and reaching an agreement with the Iraqi Communist Party (ICP), Saddam Hussein succeeded in terminating Soviet and ICP support for the KDP.[12]

However, another enemy of the Baath, the Shah of Iran, upgraded Iran's support for the Kurdish movement fighting against the Iraqi regime, in order to intimidate Iraq and also to further its territorial claims. Using Iranian anti-tank missiles and artillery as well as military aid from Syria and Israel, the KDP inflicted heavy losses on the Baath forces and Hussein had no choice but to reach a rapprochement with Iran. In the 1975 Algiers agreement, Saddam Hussein unwillingly but pragmatically dropped all Iraqi claims on Iranian territory and recognised the thalweg as the boundary in the Shatt al Arab between Iran and Iraq. In return, the Shah of Iran ceased supporting the KDP in northern Iraq. Furthermore, Iraq ameliorated its relations with Saudi Arabia, the smaller sheikhdoms of the Persian Gulf and ended its support for South Yemen's communist regime. In addition to this improving mood in the region, the signing of the Camp David Accords provided an opportunity for an Iraqi political, economic and ideological assertiveness in the Arab world.[13]

During the 1975–79 period, Iraq displayed a co-operative attitude toward its neighbours, and this was a time when pragmatism with a long-term view was at its peak. But the Shah's downfall in Iran created serious problems of domestic insecurity and illegitimacy for the Baath leadership. The religious content of the Iranian revolution provided an occasion for the Iraqi Shia population, which made up the majority underprivileged class in the country, to undermine Baath domination:

> The discomfort felt by the Iraqi government in the wake of the revolution was palpable and manifested itself in the anxious and cautious policies subsequently adopted by Iraq. Initially, the Iraqi government congratulated its Iranian counterpart on the success of the struggle. Moreover, the regime was reluctant to criticize Iran's revolutionary leader, Ayatollah Khomeini, 'for fear of the impact of the movement in Iraq'. It rapidly became clear from the Iraqi perspective, however, that adopting such a conciliatory policy would not prevent the revolution from having such an impact. By 1980, the Iraqi view was that, 'if Ayatollah Khomeini's Shia Islamic republic consolidates itself, it is bound to cover southern Iraq, home of the country's large Shia population and of the Shia holy cities of Najat and Kerbala.[14]

Iraq decided to deter Iran's revolutionary appeal and on 22 September 1980 began a war that ended as a long and protracted confrontation between the two states for a period of eight years. In pushing the war forward, Saddam Hussein acted very pragmatically with the West, the Arab world and the USSR. Despite years of rhetoric against the US, Hussein improved relations with Washington. He also developed a close military relationship with France, the USSR, China and Egypt. In order to finance the war, Saddam Hussein received more than $60 billion from the Arab countries.

The Iran-Iraq war had no clear victors, and Iraq did not gain a foothold in the Persian Gulf or an opening for its landlockedness. For the duration of the war, the Kurdish problem and the domestic heterogeneity problem were put aside, but Iraq was not able to defeat the Iranian revolution and cause its internal disintegration as had been planned by its war effort. In fact, the war actually helped the consolidation of the Iranian revolution. The only, but significant, gain of the war for Saddam Hussein was the devastation of the Iranian economy and the deterrence of a perceived Iranian threat to Iraqi legitimacy and its regime structure. Once again, Saddam Hussein, a master of surviving in politics, maintained the *status quo* in Iraq, and most important of all, preserved his power base in the country.[15]

Although Saddam Hussein orchestrated the political, financial and military dimensions of a protracted war rather well and in a context where his interests converged with the interests of many regional and international powers, it should be pointed out that he was so preoccupied with his interpretations, inferences and outlook that like most revolutionary leaders, he was caught between idealism and pragmatism, between dogmatism and political manoeuvring, and between subjectivity and objectivity; ingredients of a political strategy that has not so far endured in any one country. For Saddam Hussein, the Iran-Iraq war was an intermarriage between grandeur and self-preservation.

The Iraqi annexation of Kuwait on 2 August 1990 was another test of Saddam Hussein's self-centredness. Upon the termination of the Iran-Iraq war, Hussein engaged in a series of symbolic gestures and posturing to portray himself as 'the living embodiment of Iraqi history, from Babylonian to Hashemite rule'.[16]

> The most extravagant demonstration of the alleged Iraqi victory was the imposing 'arc de troimphe' which appeared in central Baghdad in the immediate wake of the war . . . In 1989, Hussein held official burial ceremonies for the remains of the Babylonian Kings and built new tombs on their graves . . . A $1.5 million prize was promised to the architect who would re-erect the Hanging Gardens of Babylon, one of the Seven Wonders of the Ancient World . . . A new Palace envisaged by Hussein [was to be built] as the 'new wonder of the world that would overshadow the Pyramids'.[17]

Serious economic difficulties, however, compounded social and political problems at home. Baghdad also confronted financial hardships immediately after the end of the war with Iran. In a period of tensions with Kuwait and Persian Gulf sheikhdoms, Saddam Hussein made his demands clear: sharp decreases of 'excessive' Kuwaiti oil production, a complete moratorium on war loans and substantial grants for the purposes of reconstruction. The neighbouring Arab countries reacted negatively and resisted widespread Iraqi pressures and threats.

A number of assassination attempts, the alleged espionage of Behzad Bazoft – a journalist working for the London *Observer* – investigating an explosion in an Iraqi military complex (later to be executed), the seizure of forty electronic capacitators to be used as nuclear triggers at London Heathrow Airport on board an Iraqi airplane and fears of an Israeli attack on Iraqi military and strategic centres, all contributed to Saddam Hussein's increasing suspicions, paranoia and obsessions about conspiracies against him. He needed another crisis for personal and regime survival as well as a scapegoat to redirect the mounting domestic discontent.

At the regional level, Hussein felt that Iraq possessed the only military capability able to deter Israel and to achieve political superiority in the region. Furthermore, mixed signals from Washington and the stance that, 'the U.S. government has no opinion on inter-Arab rivalries', led Saddam Hussein to a grave miscalculation of American interests and intentions. Hussein perhaps felt assured of American neutrality, the support of the Arab masses and, confident of his military superiority, he annexed the state of Kuwait.[18] Once again, Saddam Hussein, in order to accomplish regional hegemony for the purposes of materialising his dreams,[19] and finding a military and belligerent formula to delay problems of insecurity and illegitimacy at home, had brought his country to a devastated, isolated and demoralised state.[20]

Conclusion

Although Iraq as a political unit has serious and stable national deficiencies to prevent its move in the direction of a cohesive nationstate and naturally experiences the complex processes of state-formation, the way in which its intricate internal difficulties and geo-political inferiority are resolved largely depends, and has depended in the past, on leadership perceptiveness, qualities and legitimacy. The lack of such qualities and legitimacy among Iraqi statesmen in the past have led this country into chaos, unresolvable crises and personalised politics.

Iraqi foreign policy, especially in the last two decades, has been subject to this chaotic internal situation. In this context, the idiosyncrasies of Iraqi leaders have placed profound influences on Baghdad's foreign policy decisions. Saddam Hussein's peculiar mentality and in a way revolutionary approach, one of intertwining idealism and pragmatism, has particularly dominated Iraq's foreign policy behaviour.[21] As one writer has pointed out. 'This wide gap between dreams of grandeur and the grim realities of weakness has generated a political legacy of frustration and insecurity . . . In the permanently beleaguered mind of Saddam Hussein, politics is a ceaseless struggle for survival.'[22]

From a theoretical standpoint, Iraqi foreign policy is one of intransigent adaptation with regard to its environment. This is one type of foreign policy behaviour among others – acquiescent, promotive and preservative – as delineated by James Rosenau.[23] According to Rosenau, intransigent foreign policy adaptation is the readiness of a political unit to alter its environment and to make it consistent with the demands inherent in at least one of its attributes. The foreign policy behaviour of such a state is formulated in such a way as to make the environment accommodate to its domestic attributes.[24] Iraqi foreign policy under the Baath and Saddam Hussein has been based on internal and personal needs and desires. In this decision making framework, the environment of the Iraqi political unit has been a testing ground for realising those needs and desires.

Notes

1   David Pool, 'From Elite to Class: Transformation of Iraqi Political Leadership', in Abbas Kelidar (ed.), *The Integration of Modern Iraq*, (New York: St Martin's Press, 1979), pp. 73–5.

2   Helen Chapin Metz (ed.), *Iraq: A Country Study* (Washington, DC: US Government Printing Office, 1990), pp. 45–8.

3   *Ibid.*, pp. 52–4.

4   Efraim Karsh and Inari Rautsi, *Saddam Hussein: A Political Biography* (New York: The Free Press, 1991), p. 13.

5   *Ibid.*, p. 26.

6   Christine Moss Helms, *Iraq: Eastern Flank of the Arab World* (Washington, DC: Brookings Institution, 1984), p. 73.

7   A. F. K. Organski, *World Politics* (New York: Knopf, 1968), pp. 294, 361.

8   For a discussion of idiosyncratic variables in foreign policy analysis, see Robert Jervis, *Perception and Misperception in International Politics* (Princeton: Princeton University Press, 1976), pp. 117–54 and James Rosenau, *The Scientific Study of Foreign Policy* (London: Frances Pinter, 1980), pp. 128–35.

9   Karsh and Rautsi, *Saddam Hussein*, p. 32.

10   *Ibid.*, pp. 35–6.

11   *The 1968 Revolution in Iraq: Experience and Prospects*, The Political Report of the 8th Congress of the Arab Ba'th Socialist Party in Iraq, January 1974 (London: Ithaca Press, 1979), p. 133.

12   Metz, *Iraq*, pp. 61–2.

13   Samir al-Khalil, *Republic of Fear* (New York: Pantheon Books, 1989), pp. 268–9 and Metz, *Iraq*, pp. 61–3.

14   Philip Robins, 'Iraq: Revolutionary Threats and Regime Responses', in John Esposito (ed.), *The Iranian Revolution and Its Global Impact* (Miami: Florida International University Press, 1990), pp. 83–4.

15 On Iran-Iraq war, see Gerd Nonneman, *Iraq, the Gulf States and the War* (London: Ithaca Press, 1986); E. Karsh (ed.), *The Iran-Iraq War: Impact and Implications* (London: Macmillan, 1989); R. King, *The Iran-Iraq War: The Political Implication*, Adelphi Papers, No. 219 (London: The International Institute for Strategic Studies, 1987) and Shahram Chubin and Charles Tripp, *Iran and Iraq at War* (London: I. B. Tauris, 1988).

16 Karsh and Rautsi, *Saddam Hussein*, p. 196.

17 *Ibid.*, pp. 195–6.

18 *Ibid.*, pp. 214–16.

19 Once Saddam Hussein proclaimed to an audience that, 'Iraq is as great as China, as great as the Soviet Union and as great as the United States'. *Ibid.*, p. 136.

20 See *Newsweek*, 22 July 1991, pp. 27–9.

21 For an analysis of Arab culture, see Halim Barakat, 'Beyond the Always and the Never: A Critique of Social Psychological Interpretations of Arab Society and Culture', in Hisham Sharabi (ed.), *Theory, Politics and the Arab World* (New York: Routledge, 1990), pp. 132–59.

22 Karsh and Rautsi, *Saddam Hussein*, pp. 2–3.

23 James Rosenau, *The Study of Political Adaptation* (London: Frances Pinter, 1981), p. 66.

24 *Ibid.*

Part IV
Conclusion

11   *Stephen Chan and Andrew Williams*
Sympathy for the Devil

When Mick Jagger sang 'Sympathy for the Devil', it was with his usual mock heroics, but he also introduced to rock music an underlying sense of an 'other' working in contemporary history to undermine Western values. Popular culture very often appreciates, at least intuitively, what academic culture may take paradigmatic generations to explicate and accept. In taking this time it mirrors certain fears of political society. William Connolly, in his most recent book, discusses what he calls the 'Augustinian imperative', in which the West converts living signs that threaten its ontological self-confidence into modes of otherness to be condemned and punished.[1] In time, this otherness may be itself converted, at least partially, and at least into academic discourse, and this epistemological project helps to restore ontological self-confidence.

This book hardly does that. It has sought to take its place at the very beginnings of a discourse on how revolutionary states might be, if not appreciated, then not fully misunderstood in International Relations. It is to do with the widening of a discipline, rather than the full explication of the other, let alone its conversion. Even so, in its brief parade, it has indicated how certain revolutionary states might be best viewed, or viewed afresh, by taking into account *their* epistemologies and ontologies, looking at their cultures and ideologies dispassionately, if not sympathetically. Despite this, other studies in this book show how some states can be better understood by using current methodologies with more care. The variety and number of revolutionary states make a general theory, at this early stage of their appreciation by International Relations, impossible – so what this book is *not* is an attempt to advance a general theory. It does, however, contain a number of preliminary theoretical insights.

To summarise the approach of the book's authors, Andrew Williams seeks to expound upon the seminal qualities of the French and Russian revolutions. Not all of these seminal qualities should be taken for granted. Stephen Chan's very conscious decision to present a cultural animation for the Chinese revolution suggests the possibility of entirely other sources and inspirations. By contrast, Hazel Smith deliberately minimises the invention and reinvention of history that has taken place in the Democratic People's Republic of Korea, and gives a reading of foreign policy informed by rational realism, albeit with different qualities over two periods of time. She applies the test of political realism to her study of Nicaragua as well. The mixture of political realism and cultural animation can be seen in Philip Philip's study of Iran. Even so, there emerges a foreign policy with quite specific if ambitious ends and short-term goals to do with Iran's position as a 'middle power'. Mahmood Sariolghalam applies the test of Western theory to Iraq. Drawing from Rosenau, he sees Iraq as an 'intransigent foreign policy adapter', seeking to alter its environment to make it consistent with its own internal attributes. This process may have entirely rational characteristics to do with versions of political realism. Finally, Stephen Chan studies two African states which were revolutionary for different reasons, which had differing mixtures of cultural animation.

There seems to emerge a tripartite methodology for future work: firstly, to do with the influence of metropolitan ideologies, particularly as transmuted by local needs and objectives; secondly, to do with the appreciation of these needs and objectives in their regional settings and the political realism and rationality that local conditions demand; thirdly, to do with the cultural, religious and ideological histories of the revolutionary state, which can perhaps help determine how revolutionary it feels in its own eyes. There are, therefore, different levels of analysis, and a holistic (if not universal) International Relations might begin to consider how to work with all three. This is to say that what is required is, if not a sympathy for revolutionary states, a refusal by scholars to adopt enquiries that reflect only Western concerns and worries about them.

Paul Rich, in his chronology of the generations of writers on revolutionary states, and the Introduction to this book, both suggest that only recently have revolutionary states been treated as an object of enquiry in International Relations, one requiring a special problematique. Previously analysed in terms of their domestic structures and dynamics, they had largely been represented as ready-made objects for the scholar of International Relations. Yet the phenomenon of intense centralisation of state power, as tends to occur in moments of revolution, and the effect this can have on foreign policy formulation, cannot be ignored. All the contributors to this volume have variously sought to argue this. Secondly, as the world enters an as yet primitive form of international civil society, those outside the rough bounds of such citizenship and civility can only be properly appreciated if the animation of their international behaviour is sought in their endogenous bases, as well as in the influence of, and alliances with, others.

What is distinctive about revolutionary states is that they encompass a plurality of foundations. Omitting one or several in favour of those comfortable to Western methodologies of enquiry can only contrive to produce incomplete or false analyses. In terms of cultural, religious or ideological foundation, some of this can be obscure and require, for International Relations, the assistance of other disciplines – area studies, religious studies, philosophy, history and social anthropology. Only by so doing can reasonably-based discussion on normative issues take place. The simple question, 'whose normality?', begs greater questions as to how some norms are supposed to be universal and more universally binding than others.

Stephen Chan has elsewhere sought to suggest reasons for the assumption of universal normativity, and it is not proposed to repeat them here.[2] An essential summary, however, of his enquiries may be stated as follows:

1. Differently in different states, and at different times, culture has been affiliated to nationalism, and nationalism to state, to give a differentiated identity to the rest of the world.
2. This is a dynamic and continuing process and occurs in various locations at the present moment.
3. Each process of identity and differentiation creates its own 'other'.
4. Epistemological processes reinforce the rational base of identity and differentiation and, either directly or by extension, call into question the 'truthfulness' of the 'other'.
5. In various situations, this critique of the 'other', combined with a vindication of self, is represented by complex eschatological and soteriological systems.
6. Popular rhetoric of damnation and reward is founded on complex thought systems.
7. There is no such thing as a simple or 'fundamental' theological state, and no reduction possible that constructs a simple model of a revolutionary state.
8. All such states, however, are socialised to one degree or another into the international system.

9. They may consent to this for reasons of practical association, but not always or necessarily for purposive association.

10. In this process of socialisation, the question proposed by Western scholars has consistently been lopsided: 'How much of ours has been adapted by them?' rather than 'How much of theirs has been adopted by us?' The imbalance in global socialisation has been mistaken as an acceptable normative foundation in International Relations.

What this book has sought to do has not been to investigate fully such issues. Certainly it has been happy to raise them. It has sought to present such issues, and the questions they raise, alongside a set of case studies that represent the complexity of such enquiry. If this complexity is better appreciated by scholars of International Relations, then the editors and authors will feel happy.

Notes

1   William E. Connolly, *The Augustinian Imperative: A Reflection on the Politics of Morality*, Newbury Park, Sage, 1993.

2   Most recently in: 'Small Revolutions and the Study of International Relations: The Problematique of Affiliation', *Political Science*, Vol. 43, No. 2, 1991; 'Cultural and Linguistic Reductionisms and a New Historical Sociology for International Relations', *Millenium*, Vol. 22, No. 3, 1993; 'Culture and Absent Epistemologies in International Relations', *Theoria*, Nos 81/2, 1993; 'International Relations outside the North-West: Six Eastern Examples', in Margot Light and A. J. R. Groom (eds), *Contemporary International Relations: A Handbook of Current Theory*, London, Pinter, 1994.

List of contributors

Stephen Chan is a Senior Lecturer in International Relations at the University of Kent at Canterbury and Director of the University of Kent's London Centre of International Relations. His previous books include: *Exporting Apartheid: Foreign Policies in Southern Africa, 1978–1988* (1990), *Kaunda and Southern Africa: Image and Reality in Foreign Policy* (1992) and (edited with Vivienne Jabri) *Mediation in Southern Africa* (1993).

Philip George Philip successfully defended his Ph.D. thesis on the Islamic Republic of Iran and the United Nations at the University of Kent at Canterbury in 1993. He presently lives in Calcutta, India.

Paul Rich is a Reader at the University of Melbourne, Australia. He has also held posts at the Universities of Warwick and Bristol. Among his recent works are: *Hope and Despair* (1993), *The Dynamics of Change in Southern Africa* (1994), and he has recently completed *State Power and Black Politics in South Africa* for Cambridge University Press.

Mahmood Sariolghalam is Professor of Political Science at Shaheed Beheshti (Melli) University in Tehran, Iran. His previous works include: (in Farsi) *Development, the Third World and the International System* (1989), *The Evolution of Method and Research in International Relations* (1992) and *Rationality and Development* (1993).

Hazel Smith is a Lecturer in International Relations at the University of Kent at Canterbury. Recent books include *Nicaragua: Self-Determination and Survival* (1993) and *The European Community and Central America* (1994).

Andrew Williams is a Senior Lecturer in International Relations at the University of Kent at Canterbury. His previous books include: *Labour and Russia: The Attitude of the Labour Party to the Soviet Union, 1924–1934* (1989); *Trading with the Bolsheviks: The Politics of East-West Trade, 1920–1939* (1992) and *Reorganising Eastern Europe: European Institutions and the Refashioning of Europe's Security Architecture* (1994).

Index